NOTTINGHAM FRENCH STUDIES

VOLUME 59   NUMBER 3   WINTER 2020

Science, Technology & Culture in Modern & Contemporary France: Essays in Memory of Chris Johnson

Edited by John Marks

T0323298

Subscription Rates for 2021
Three issues per year, published in March, July, and December

		Tier	UK	EUR	Rest of World	North America
Institutions	Print & Online	1	£127.00	£139.00	£146.00	$235.00
		2	£159.00	£171.00	£178.00	$286.00
		3	£198.00	£210.00	£217.00	$348.00
		4	£237.00	£249.00	£256.00	$411.00
		5	£269.00	£281.00	£288.00	$461.00
	Online	1	£107.00	£107.00	£107.00	$171.00
		2	£134.00	£134.00	£134.00	$215.00
		3	£168.00	£168.00	£168.00	$269.00
		4	£202.00	£202.00	£202.00	$323.00
		5	£225.00	£225.00	£225.00	$362.00
	Premium Online	1	£138.00	£138.00	£138.00	$221.00
		2	£174.00	£174.00	£174.00	$279.00
		3	£217.00	£217.00	£217.00	$348.00
		4	£259.00	£259.00	£259.00	$416.00
		5	£293.00	£293.00	£293.00	$470.00
	DDP (Premium)		£42.00	£54.00	£60.00	$98.00
	Additional print volumes		£111.00	£123.00	£129.00	$208.00
	Single issues		£49.00	£63.00	£65.00	$105.00
Individuals	Print		£53.00	£64.00	£71.00	$120.00
	Online		£44.00	£44.00	£44.00	$74.00
	Print & Online		£60.50	£71.50	£78.50	$131.50
	Back issues/single copies		£19.50	£23.50	£26.00	$43.50

How to order

Subscriptions can be accepted for complete volumes only. Print prices include packing and airmail for subscribers outside the UK. Volumes back to the year 2000 are included in online prices. Print back volumes/single issues will be charged at the print rates stated above (vol. 51 onwards). Enquiries concerning back volumes/issues up to vol. 50 inclusive should be addressed to Jodie Thompson, Secretary to the Board of *Nottingham French Studies*, Department of Modern Languages and Cultures, School of Cultures, Languages and Area Studies, University of Nottingham, Nottingham NG7 2RD; email: nfs@nottingham.ac.uk

All orders must be accompanied by the correct payment. You can pay by cheque in Pounds Sterling or US Dollars, bank transfer, Direct Debit or Credit/Debit Card. The individual rate applies only when a subscription is paid for with a personal cheque, credit card or bank transfer. Please make your cheques payable to Edinburgh University Press Ltd. Sterling cheques must be drawn on a UK bank account.

Orders for subscriptions and back issues can be placed by telephone, on +44(0)131 650 4196, by fax on +44(0)131 662 3286, using your Visa or Mastercard credit cards, or by email on journals@eup.ed.ac.uk. Alternatively, you can use the online order form at www.euppublishing.com/page/nfs/subscribe.

Requests for sample copies, subscription enquiries, and changes of address should be sent to Journals Department, Edinburgh University Press, The Tun – Holyrood Road, Edinburgh EH8 8PJ; email: journals@eup.ed.ac.uk

NOTTINGHAM FRENCH STUDIES

VOLUME 59   NUMBER 3   WINTER 2020

CONTENTS

Special Issues of *Nottingham French Studies*

French Cinema
edited by Russell King
32:1 (Spring 1993)

Molière
edited by Stephen Bamforth
33:1 (Spring 1994)

Hervé Guibert
edited by Jean-Pierre Boulé
34:1 (Spring 1995)

Ionesco
edited by Steve Smith
35:1 (Spring 1996)

Roland Barthes
edited by Diana Knight
36:1 (Spring 1997)

French Erotic Fiction: Ideologies of Desire
edited by Jean Mainil
37:1 (Spring 1998)

Fortune and Women in Medieval Literature
edited by Katie Attwood
38:2 (Autumn 1999)

Errances urbaines
edited by Jean-Xavier Ridon
39:1 (Spring 2000)

Gender and Francophone Writing
edited by Nicki Hitchcott
40:1 (Spring 2001)

French Fiction in the 1990s
edited by Margaret-Anne Hutton
41:1 (Spring 2002)

Thinking in Dialogue: The Role of the Interview in Post-war French Thought
edited by Christopher Johnson
42:1 (Spring 2003)

Jazz Adventures in French Culture
edited by Jacqueline Dutton and
Colin Nettelbeck
43:1 (Spring 2004)

Irreconcilable Differences? Centre, Periphery and the Space Between in French History
edited by Paul Smith
44:1 (Spring 2005)

France, America and the Modern
edited by Jackie Clarke and Carole Sweeney
44:3 (Autumn 2005)

Focalizing the Body: Recent Women's Writing and Filmmaking in France
edited by Gill Rye and Carrie Tarr
45:3 (Autumn 2006)

Sociolinguistic Variation and Change in France
edited by David Hornsby and Mikaël Jamin
46:2 (Summer 2007)

Terror and Psychoanalysis
edited by Lynsey Russell-Watts with Lisa Walsh
46:3 (Autumn 2007)

'Mythologies' at 50: Barthes and Popular Culture
edited by Douglas Smith
47:2 (Summer 2008)

Identification before Freud: French Perspectives
edited by Joseph Harris
47:3 (Autumn 2008)

Annie Ernaux: Socio-Ethnographer of Contemporary France
edited by Alison S. Fell and Edward Welch
48:2 (Spring 2009)

Enlightenment and Narrative: Essays in Honour of Richard A. Francis by Colleagues and Friends
edited by Philip Robinson
48:3 (Autumn 2009)

Translating Thought: Traduire la pensée
edited by Kathryn Batchelor and Yves Gilonne
49:2 (Summer 2010)

Nouveaux départs: Studies in Honour of Michel Jeanneret
edited by Stephen Bamforth
49:3 (Autumn 2010)

'L'Invention du Midi': The Rise of the South of France in the National and International Imagination
edited by Tania Woloshyn and Nicholas Hewitt
50:1 (Spring 2011)

French Language and Social Interaction: Studies in Conversation Analysis and Interactional Linguistics
edited by Fabienne H. G. Chevalier
50:2 (Summer 2011)

The French Avant-garde
edited by Stephen Forcer and Emma Wagstaff
50:3 (Autumn 2011)

Future Special Issues

Nottingham French Studies 59.3 (2020): 239–254
DOI: 10.3366/nfs.2020.0290
© University of Nottingham
www.euppublishing.com/nfs

INTRODUCTION

JOHN MARKS ⓘ

I have many memories of Chris Johnson as a generous and supportive friend and colleague in the Department of French and Francophone Studies at the University of Nottingham. I also remember him as a strong intellectual presence who influenced my thinking on a number of subjects. Chris founded the Science, Technology and Culture Group at the university, and a small number of us would meet regularly to discuss readings, films and documentaries. Chris was the driving force behind the group, and the lively discussions in these meetings helped us to develop our individual research interests. At first sight, it might seem unusual that a group talking about science and technology should find its home in a French department. However, it makes sense when one considers the fact that Chris was one of the generation of researchers who were influenced by the post-war flowering of structuralist and post-structuralist thought in France. The analysis of language is, of course, the most celebrated strand of this body of thought, and Chris's first publications focused on this area.[1] However, as he developed his research he focused increasingly on the technological structuring of the human, and he was something of a pioneer in carrying out research in this field. The ideas that interested us in the group, whether in the field of evolutionary theory, molecular biology, cognitive science, or the relationship between machines and humans, coalesced around a number of concepts, including the exteriorization of the human, systems theory, complexity, emergent properties and, crucially, cybernetic concepts of information, control and feedback. Given that some of these concepts have more recently been appropriated and absorbed into a new political ideology that might be described as populist technocracy, it is inspiring and informative to explore the more creative, progressive and analytical version of this thinking that was developed in the context of the intellectual dynamism of post-war France.

Inevitably, our discussions in the STC group went beyond technical questions and encompassed wider issues relating to the effects of science and technology on society. As well as considering the political stakes of particular mediations of science and technology, we often came back to issues of technological optimism and pessimism. In broad terms, I think that all of us in the group would describe ourselves in some way as materialist, scientific humanists, and we shared the general belief that the technological impulse is an inherent feature of the human condition. That is to say, the evolution and development of humanity from its

---

1. Christopher Johnson, *System and Writing in the Philosophy of Jacques Derrida* (Cambridge: Cambridge University Press, 1993).

origins has been driven by a technological interaction with its environment. For Chris, this intellectual commitment to the centrality of technology to the human chimed with his keen practical and aesthetic appreciation of technology. The possibilities that technology offers us as human agents fascinated him, and he always appreciated beautiful and ingenious technological objects that performed a useful function. At the same time, he recognized that new digital technologies also threaten to limit and even erode human creativity. This sceptical position on the digital and the virtual was a key theme in much the work with which Chris engaged, and its importance is reflected in some of the contributions in this collection.

The articles in this volume engage in various ways with the notion that technology and the human are co-constituted: the idea there is no essence of the human that unfolds and expresses itself over time, but rather a form of the human that is developed through technology. The core dynamic in the development of the human is exteriorization, whether through physical interaction with the environment or the externalization of thought through language and writing. The rigorously materialist focus of the thinkers featured in this collection means that their theorizations of the human and of technology eschew explanations that rely on vitalist or religious explanations of evolution. For example, molecular biology as it emerged in the second half of the twentieth century was inspired directly by the quest to identify and understand the functioning of the material components of heredity. The discovery of the double helix structure of DNA and circuits of genetic regulation in the cell provided a non-teleological model of evolution emerging from material contingency. It was no longer possible to think of evolution either in terms of a divine plan or as a consequence of the human drive to improve.

This collection also reveals an intriguing strand of pessimism in French thinking on technology. This is not entirely surprising, given the new potentials for destruction – not to say annihilation – unleashed by modernity. The reaction to the development of biotechnological interventions associated with molecular biology, along with the rapid development of electronic and digital technologies, has been somewhat more ambivalent. Although biotechnology and cyber technologies can be seen as ways of enhancing human capacities, there is a widely articulated fear that they may limit, undermine and even ultimately destroy the human form. It is widely acknowledged that the relentless proliferation of digital technologies poses a range of threats to human freedoms, whether this takes the form of panoptical authoritarian political control, the commodification of cognition, or a globalized form of surveillance capitalism that combines the two dynamics. In these new scenarios, the externalization of memory runs alongside a new human externalization of digital traces generated by interactions with our physical and virtual environments: individuals are now accompanied throughout their lives by spectral 'data-doubles'. Bernard Stiegler, for example, has argued that technologies which genuinely support reading and writing facilitate the kind of deep attention that allows individuals to exteriorize their own thoughts and individuate themselves.

In contrast, contemporary digital technologies attempt to capture for commercial benefit the attention and the energies that would ideally be channelled into learning as self-development. He has produced an extensive critique of the way in which technology has been put at the service of a consumer culture that has effectively deskilled – he uses the term 'proletarianized' – the consumer in late capitalism, just as industrialization robbed the worker of specialized skills.[2] The tension between technology as empowering the human and as a threat is central to debates in this field.

Before looking in some detail at previously published articles by Chris that engage with some of these questions, and by way of a belated collaboration on my part, it is useful to consider Stanley Kubrick's *2001: A Space Odyssey* as a way of illustrating some key issues relating to science and technology. *2001* was one of Chris's favourite films and it was a recurrent reference point in our discussions. The technological aesthete and connoisseur in Chris admired Kubrick's painstaking attention to detail in creating such a visually compelling viewing experience, and he read the film as a profound exploration of human evolution and technology. He saw it as posing questions about the limits of the human, reaching back to prehistory and anticipating a future in which humanity might explore space with the aid of thinking, conscious machines. For example, the opening, prehistoric 'The Dawn of Man' scene establishes the theme of technology in various ways. The scene shows the pre-human apes interacting with a perfectly smooth black monolith: Moon-Watcher, the leader of the group, approaches it with some trepidation and cautiously touches and smells it. What follows clearly implies that the encounter with the monolith stimulates new cognitive and technological capacities. The ability to draw on memory and reflect culminates in the use of a bone as a tool, in this case a weapon to kill a tapir: Moon-Watcher can remember the tapir and visualize its death projected into the future. The fact that Kubrick conveys this evolutionary dynamic with such striking visual economy had a strong philosophical resonance for Chris. Kubrick's skill as a filmmaker enabled him to depict a sequence of human evolution not as the consequence of an enhancement of brain size that provides increased capacity, but rather as a complex material dynamic in which a network of agents and objects interact. The crucial initial stimulus that sets this dynamic in process is an act of externalization, when Moon-Watcher touches and smells the monolith. The scene concludes with what has become an iconic cinematic sequence: a shot of the spinning bone as it is thrown into the into the air cuts to an image of a satellite orbiting the earth. The film subsequently projects us as viewers into a future in which humanity confronts new dangers and explores new possibilities, but in which it also continues to use tools that maintain a connection with the origins of human technological capacity. The images of the

---

2.   Bernard Stiegler, *Pour une nouvelle critique de l'économie politique* (Paris: Galilée, 2009).

bone and the spaceship connect visually with the pen floating in the space shuttle, establishing the importance of writing as a gesture of externalization and as a support for memory. Illustrating a key moment of technological development with images and gestures conveyed through the silent 'language' of film editing was not just a piece of bravura filmmaking: the philosophy is, as it were, in the editing. That is to say, the cut between the spinning bone and the space shuttle elegantly connects contemporary technological advances to the very first interactions between humans and their environment.

The sequence in which the astronaut David Bowman disconnects the onboard computer HAL takes the exploration of technology in another direction. Clearly, the rather enigmatic, uncanny relationship between HAL and the astronauts is a dramatically effective way of representing the threat that artificial intelligence might pose to humanity. (The science fiction of Philip K. Dick and Isaac Asimov were often referenced in our STC discussions). HAL decides that the human astronauts are a potential impediment to the mission and that he must eliminate them. In the terminology of cybernetics, the interaction between HAL and the astronauts is a question of the potentially problematic coupling of the human and technology. This scenario is dramatized as a battle of wits between HAL and Bowman, who is ultimately able to outwit and disable HAL by using human intuition and, crucially, by virtue of possessing a body and manual dexterity. He uses a simple tool – a screwdriver – to remove crucial components from HAL in gestures that in some ways recall the interaction with the monolith in the opening scene.

Having identified these technological themes in the film, it is striking to consider how they resonated in particular for Chris with his research on the French archaeologist, anthropologist and philosopher of technology André Leroi-Gourhan (1911–1986), whose major work *Le Geste et la parole* was an attempt to set out a unified theory of human evolution.[3] Watching the film alongside Chris's work on Leroi-Gourhan makes them feel almost like parallel, complementary texts. In the second volume of *Le Geste et la parole*, for example, Leroi-Gourhan looked in detail at the crucial role played by rhythm and memory in technological development, focusing on the importance of the regular repetition of manual gestures such as hammering and sawing. The role of the human hand is central in technological development, he insists, not because of any inherent qualities that it possesses, but rather because it is a component of a system comprised of human being, tool and material. In a wider sense, *2001* as a visual experience captures somewhat uncannily Leroi-Gorhan's rather enigmatic observation that rhythm is the creator of forms.[4] In the context of the interconnected visual and musical rhythms of *2001* – humans walking and floating in space, rotating objects, the stately waltz

---

3.   André Leroi-Gourhan, *Le Geste et la parole, I: technique et langage* (Paris: Albin Michel, 1964); *Le Geste et la parole, II: la mémoire et les rythmes* (Paris: Albin Michel, 1965)

4.   Ibid., p. 135.

time of Strauss's *The Blue Danube* – the interaction of rhythm and form begins to make sense. One of the few pieces of critical work that engages with *2001* as a profound cinematic exploration of bodies, space, and learning is Annette Michelson's landmark 'Bodies in Space' essay on the film from 1969.[5] She celebrates the way in which the theme of learning is explored uniquely through the striking formal coherence and detail of the film. The film is a bodily experience for the spectator: 'Kubrick's imagination, exploring the possibilities of scale, movement, direction as synthesized in a style, works towards our understanding. The intensified and progressively intimate consciousness of one's physicality provides the intimation of that physicality as the ground of consciousness.'[6] Michelson is fascinated by the way in which the movement of the astronauts is slowed by weightlessness. The effect of this slow, deliberate movement is akin, she suggests, to the consciously defamiliarizing aspects of contemporary dance. As viewers we follow their absorption in the tasks that they carry out as a significant moment of learning. In this way, the film conveys a dynamic of learning that is similar to the development of spatial sense and intelligence in children identified by Jean Piaget.[7] The astronauts are like children in that they are experiencing the 'slow development of the body's wisdom'.[8]

Leroi-Gourhan's willingness to consider the technological future of humanity also connects with the ambitious sweep of *2001* as a cinematic narrative that encompasses the vast span of human evolution. Notably, the concluding chapter of *Le Geste et la parole* speculates on the future of humanity. Leroi-Gourhan's starting point is the discrepancy, as he sees it, between a contemporary human civilization with apparently unlimited technological capacities, and humans who have changed little since their early development as hunters. From the Industrial Revolution onwards the working population is deskilled, and the rapid development of electronics and computing in the post-war period accelerates this process. He identifies a growing divergence over the course of history between the biological evolution of the human and technological development, to the point where the biological form of contemporary humanity is strikingly out of phase with its technological environment. If this divergence continues, he fears that it may lead eventually to a new, reduced form of the human, a *Homo post-sapiens*. Although new information technologies based on electronic storage, which was of course in its infancy in the 1960s, will have an effect on writing and thinking, these changes will not seriously compromise our humanity. He cautiously suggests the demise of

---

5. Annette Michelson, 'Bodies in Space: Film as "Carnal Knowledge"', *Artforum*, 7:6 (February 1969), 54–63.

6. Ibid., p. 61.

7. Jean Piaget and Bärbel Inhelder, *La Représentation de l'espace chez l'enfant* (Paris: Presses universitaires de France, 1948).

8. Michelson, 'Bodies in Space', p. 62.

writing may give rise to new, non-linear modes of thinking. The real threat to *Homo sapiens* lies in the disappearance of manual activity and the increasing passivity of what he calls the 'human physical adventure'.[9] In contemporary society opportunities for individual creativity have diminished and humanity has turned to a series of artificial compensations: handicrafts, sport, camping, organized hunting, etc. He suggests rather gloomily, but somewhat presciently, that we may be witnessing the very last interactions between humans and the natural world. Not only are we close to exhausting the resources of the planet, we have also 'freed' ourselves from the material constraints and contingencies that made us human. It will be the hand that is the crucial component in this reduction of the human, since its regression will cause the body to atrophy. Again, there are clear resonances with the theme of AI as a threat to the human in *2001*, although Kubrick ultimately seems to evince a faith in a new future form of humanity.

Chris published an article on the two volumes of Leroi-Gourhan's *Le Geste et la parole* in *French Studies* in 2011,[10] and the article that appears in this collection is a reworking as a book chapter of the themes in the earlier piece. These two explorations of Leroi-Gourhan's analysis of human evolution provide insights into Chris's central intellectual interests. He emphasizes the importance and influence of Leroi-Gourhan's challenge to conventional humanist accounts of evolution and the limits of the human, arguing that he made a significant contribution to the new 'scientific' humanism in the post-war era that was associated with Claude Lévi-Strauss and which ran alongside the development of structuralism in the arts and social sciences. As indicated already, the main features of this new humanism are familiar to students of French thinking, and they have exerted a major influence on the history of ideas. Across a range of disciplines, the boundaries of the human were rethought and opened up in order to resituate it more fully in its environment, its history and its social context: the human was reconceptualized in terms of various dynamics of externalization. Language, for example, was seen by structuralist and post-structuralist thinkers as 'speaking' the individual as much as the individual 'speaks' language. Along these lines, Leroi-Gourhan saw the relationship between the human and technology, between brain and tool, in terms of co-evolution. One of the central arguments in the first part of *Le Geste et la parole* is the delayed coupling of the brain and body in vertebrate evolution. That is to say, the use of tools enables humans to engage with their environment, and this feeds back into further development. Whereas more conventional humanist accounts of evolution focus on the development of the brain as intrinsically human, Leroi-Gourhan focuses instead on the way in which the mechanical development of the human body and its parts precedes the development of cognition: mobility

---

9.   Leroi-Gourhan, *Le Geste et la parole, II: la mémoire et les rythmes*, p. 262.

10. Christopher Johnson, 'Leroi-Gourhan and the Limits of the Human', *French Studies*, 65:4 (2011), 471–87.

rather than intelligence is the primordial dynamic of human evolution.[11] That is to say, human evolution begins with the feet rather than the brain, and the 'liberation' of the hand facilitates the development of advanced cognition. Written and spoken language is co-emergent with the technical development of the human rather than being an innate human capacity. As we have seen, Kubrick's *2001* can be read as a filmic representation of precisely this dynamic, according to which the development of technical capacities emerges from an interaction between body and environment. As Chris emphasizes, Leroi-Gourhan distinguishes between this early technical development of the human as a sort of natural biological externalization and a new phase, inaugurated by *Homo sapiens*, in which the human transcends biological limits. This second origin for the human is somewhat closer to a more conventionally humanist view, and Chris outlines Bernard Stiegler's deconstructive reading of this second, spiritual origin of the human.[12]

The article on Leroi-Gourhan's analysis of technology and human evolution in *Le Geste et la parole* in this collection incorporates a somewhat more detailed reflection on cybernetics than the earlier article in *French Studies*.[13] Although Leroi-Gourhan does not refer to cybernetics explicitly in *Le Geste et la parole*, Chris argues that its influence is clear throughout the book. Evolution proceeds by means of a feedback loop encompassing body, brain and environment. He notes Leroi-Gourhan's use of cybernetic terminology such as 'machine' and 'regulation' to describe the way in which the hominid brain coordinates the hands and face. Leroi-Gourhan's analysis of the role of technology in human evolution also has cybernetic elements. As Chris indicates, the human capacity for externalization, by means of tools and language, is a central focus of Leroi-Gourhan's analysis of evolution. Just as tools are separated from the human body and are placed in the world, so language gives thought an external dimension, creating a distance that facilitates reflection on lived experience. Tools and language, in this way, function in cybernetic terms as programmes. The importance of the interaction between mechanism and programme is demonstrated in the sequence of externalizations that Leroi-Gourhan sets out as a history of human technological development. There is no fundamental difference from an anatomical perspective between the hand in primates and humans: the difference lies in the fact that the superior tactile sensitivity and control of the human hand means that there is an enhanced interface between mechanism and programme. Starting with the hand tool, this interface leads to a series of further, increasingly radical externalizations. The progression

---

11. Ibid., p. 474.

12. Bernard Stiegler, *La Technique et le temps, I: la faute d'Épiméthée* (Paris: Galilée, 1993), pp. 145–87; *La Technique et le temps, II: la désorientation* (Paris: Galilée, 1994), pp. 85–116.

13. Chris's colleague Professor Judith Still provides a detailed contextualization of the article in a footnote.

from hand tools to manual machines, naturally powered machines, industrial machines and, finally, cybernetic machines, constitutes a gradual evolution towards fully automatic control. That is to say, contemporary cybernetic machines do not require human control: they represent a final stage of the externalization of the human muscular and nervous system and brain. The Internet constitutes a phenomenal externalization of the human brain, but the consequences of that externalization for the human would appear to confirm Leroi-Gourhan's analysis of human evolution and technology, rather than Teilhard De Chardin's concept of the Omega Point: the point of unification when the cognitive layer of the 'noosphere' achieves dominance over the biosphere.[14]

Chris was fascinated by cybernetics, a ground-breaking set of ideas that emerged in the immediate post-war era and which exerted a major influence on the conceptualization and practice of science and technology. He published an important article in *French Studies* in 2014, in which he explored the distinctive French mediation of cybernetics.[15] Before considering this article, it is useful to set out some of the key ideas and themes of cybernetics. It was Norbert Wiener who successfully introduced a new set of concepts focusing on information and control to a general readership with *Cybernetics, or Control and Communication in the Animal and Machine*, which first appeared in 1948.[16] Despite the fact that the book was in many ways heavily technical, featuring numerous equations, it had an enormous impact and swiftly became a bestseller. Drawing on research on control systems and negative feedback that had been undertaken in the war, as well as the concept of negentropy, Wiener argued that information was the key element at the heart of all mechanical, electronic and organic systems. He added information to matter and energy as a fundamental component of both the animate and the inanimate world. As well as information, Wiener was also interested in negative feedback as a form of control, which inspired him to use the term 'cybernetics', drawing on the Greek word for 'steersman'. The capacity of systems to self-regulate was not only technically and technologically persuasive, it was also philosophically provocative. Here was a way of explaining the dynamic properties of life without recourse to the black box of vitalism and, even more enticingly, the metaphysical suggestion that information and negative entropy offered an alternative to Cartesian dualism: cybernetics is a world in which matter 'thinks' when organized in systems. It is no doubt the case that it was this mixture of technological reflection and heady philosophical speculation that meant that Wiener's book was so widely read and discussed when it was published. Anticipating technological advances, it looked forward to a world of increasing automation in which machines would carry out

14. Pierre Teilhard de Chardin, *Le Phénomène humain* (Paris: Seuil, 1955).
15. Chris Johnson, '"French" Cybernetics', *French Studies*, 69:1 (2014), 60–78.
16. Norbert Wiener, *Cybernetics, or Control and Communication in the Animal and the Machine* (New York: Wiley, 1948).

cognitive functions previously associated with humans, and also in which human beings might be seen as sophisticated machines made up of patterns of information. The idea of life as information was also of great interests to biologists, who saw it as a way of explaining heredity.

As Chris points out in his article, Wiener was initially encouraged to write a book summarizing his ideas on the subject by Enrique Freymann, director of the publishing house Hermann et Cie, during a lunchtime meeting in Paris in 1947. Chris argues convincingly that this meeting, which forced Wiener to coin a term that would somehow capture the flavour of the interdisciplinary field in which he was working, was nothing less than a significant moment in a New Scientific Enlightenment. Wiener was just one of a new group of multilingual, international scientists whose guiding concept was not Reason, but Information. The mediation of cybernetics in France took the form of press articles, journal articles, conferences, and monographs. In popular mediations, 'la cybernétique' was synonymous with the emergence of computer technology. Writing in *Le Monde* in 1948 , Père Dominique Dubarle suggests that the development of new 'machines mathématiques', which were at that stage in their infancy, would most probably prove to be as significant for humanity as nuclear energy and the atomic bomb.[17] He considers various possible cybernetic machines that could be created in the near future, including a machine that might transform text into sound for sight-impaired individuals, and also a chess computer that would play at a higher level than any moderately skilled human opponent. These machines would function essentially by assembling and processing information with the aim of providing a solution to a relatively narrowly defined problem. They would, of course, carry out these operations more rigorously and rapidly than humans. Dubarle notes that these new electronic calculating machines appear to mirror the structure of the human nervous system, which leads him to speculate on the possibility that machines might analyse and predict human activity such as behaviour in markets and the evolution of opinion. Might it not be possible to remediate the glaring deficiencies of human political agency by inventing a new 'machine à gouverner' that would arrive at decisions in a more scientific manner? Ultimately, Dubarle adopts a humanist perspective on these new developments in technology, foreseeing a potentially dystopian technocratic future in which machines exert control in ways that fail to acknowledge the unpredictability of human subjectivity.

Chris's article did not dwell at any length on popular mediations such as Dubarle's. Instead, he focused on books that aimed to inform an interested and educated public readership about a new field of specialized knowledge. (Various iterations of this particular genre of science communication, which might be

---

17. Père Dominique Dubarle, 'Une nouvelle science: la cybernétique. Vers une machine à gouverner le monde', *Le Monde*, 28 December 1948, p. 47.

described as serious popular science, constituted the raw material for many stimulating discussions in the Science, Technology and Culture group that Chris organized so assiduously.) He concentrated on three such books on cybernetics published in the 1950s: *La Pensée articifielle* by Pierre de Latil[18], *La Cybernétique* by Georges-Théodule Guilbaud[19], and *Découverte de la cybernétique* by Albert Ducrocq[20]. The level of detail and analysis in these books shows how rapidly cybernetics was established in French intellectual life as an important subject. All three authors emphasize that, in addition to its technological consequences, cybernetics is an epistemological revolution that transforms our understanding of both machines and living systems.

Chris distinguishes between the theoretical-information side of cybernetics, which fed directly into structuralism, and the functional, technical side, which has been somewhat neglected by a conventional history of ideas. He looks in some detail at the sustained engagement with issues relating to technology in these books on cybernetics. Latil, for example, suggests that the evolution of technology can be thought of in terms of increasing degrees of 'automatisme': as automatism develops, so human thought is increasingly delegated to the machine. The development of electronics is crucial in that it allows for the development of systems that are capable of both reacting and adapting to environmental variations. Ducrocq takes a long view of technological development, beginning with the human body using simple tools. As technology evolves over time the necessity for the direct input of human energy and, subsequently, human control, declines. In the high-tech industrial factory of the mid twentieth century, human beings no longer provide muscular energy, but they are still required to perform tasks of observation and regulation. Both Ducrocq and Latil anticipate a new age of cybernetic industrial production in which factories will be largely self-regulating.

Chris notes that the view of technology in these texts is more unequivocally positive than Wiener's. For Latil, for example, the fear that machines will somehow usurp human faculties such as memory, imagination or judgement is unfounded. On the contrary, the development of cybernetics will augment human capacities and enable us to reflect productively on the current limits of human thinking. In this way cybernetics is, for Latil, ultimately humanistic: 'Cette science de l'homme n'en restera pas moins proprement humaine'.[21] Wiener, on the other hand, expressed a good deal of technological pessimism in the *Human Use of Human Beings*,

18. Pierre de Latil, *La Pensée articifielle: introduction à la cybernétique* (Paris: Gallimard, 1953).
19. Georges-Théodule Guilbaud, *La Cybernétique* (Paris: Presses universitaires de France, 1954).
20. Albert Ducrocq, *Découverte de la cybernétique* (Paris: René Julliard, 1955).
21. Latil, *La Pensée artificielle*, p. 213.

published in 1950.[22] Ten years later, in a short piece for the journal *Science* in 1960, he considered the pressing issues posed by new cybernetic machines.[23] In part, he was responding to what he saw as the rather complacent received wisdom that nothing can come out of a machine that has not been put into it. To the contrary, he emphasizd that machines are not limited by the intentions and input of their designers: they can learn, as it were, from experience. Furthermore, even when they do not transcend human intelligence and are simply carrying out programmed tasks, they may do so at a speed that makes it difficult to understand the consequences early enough in order to avoid potentially disastrous consequences: 'By the time we are able to react to information conveyed by our senses and stop the car we are driving, it may already have run head on into a wall.'[24] Machines lack the complex and highly nuanced self-organizing capacity of the human mind but, in order to change the course that an automatic machine decides to make, it is necessary for the human to access and process information that informs action. The problem of increasingly sophisticated machine automation for Wiener is captured fairly straightforwardly in the proverbial tale of the 'Sorcerer's Apprentice': we need to assess very carefully whether the purpose we programme into a machine is really the one we want or, as he puts it, 'merely a colourful imitation of it'.[25] It is also a moral and philosophical problem revolving around the coordination of human and machine in a joint enterprise.

Chris was keenly aware of the somewhat overlooked fact that the cybernetic moment of the 1950s and 1960s coincided with the Space Age, and he explored this overlap in an article for *Paragraph* in 2008, focusing on the Apollo space programme.[26] Here, he argued against the received wisdom that the heavy-duty rocket technology developed for the Apollo missions characterized the programme as essentially analogue and thus backward-looking. On the contrary, he contended that the Apollo programme projected forward into the digital age of the twenty-first century. Whilst it was undeniable that the Saturn V developed by NASA was the result of an exponential increase in rocket-launching technology in a short period, the programme also required the development of computer technology. The popular focus on the astronauts' accounts of their role in the missions is significant in this respect. As trained pilots, their instinct was to 'fly' the Apollo spacecraft, and narratives of the landing focus specifically on the 'human' skill required to land, as

---

22. Norbert Wiener, *The Human Use of Human Beings: Cybernetics & Society* (Boston, MA: Houghton Mifflin, 1950).

23. Norbert Wiener, 'Some Moral and Technical Consequences of Automation', *Science*, 131:3410 (1960), 1355–8.

24. Ibid., p. 1355.

25. Ibid., p. 1358.

26. Christopher Johnson, 'Analogue Apollo: Cybernetics and the Space Age', *Paragraph*, 31:3 (2008), 304–26.

when Neil Armstrong famously took control of the lunar module in order to avoid boulders on the surface of the moon. However, in practice this important human input was carried out in the context of a crucial interface with computer technology. Drawing on David Minnell's *Digital Apollo: Human and Machine in Spaceflight*,[27] Chris goes further to suggest that, in the context of the evolution of cybernetic technology, the Apollo astronauts were the 'ultimate redundant component': redundant in the sense that they constituted an additional component that might be called on in the event of the failure of non-human components. Chris suggests that the astronaut Gene Cernan's claim that he could have overridden the automatic computer-programmed launch phase looks increasingly unlikely. In a memorable phrase, Chris describes this scenario as 'a departing gesture of the hand, symbolic of an all-too-human compulsion for analogue control'.[28]

Chris refers briefly in the *Paragraph* article to Céline Lafontaine's *L'Empire cybernétique*, published in 2004.[29] Both of us read and discussed the book when it was published, and it is useful to consider its central arguments briefly here, as it constitutes a counterpoint to Chris's broad conception of cybernetics as a scientific humanism. Lafontaine argues that the post-war elaboration of what she calls a 'cybernetic paradigm' constitutes a highly influential challenge to humanism. In reaction to the horrors and irrationality of the Second World War, cybernetics promotes what Lafontaine regards as a reductive view of humans as programmable machines. Cybernetics decouples reason from human subjectivity, shifting it into a machine substrate where it is no longer distorted or encumbered by human emotion.[30] As well as this technocratic faith in supposedly objective machine rationality, Lafontaine identifies the emergence of a problematic relativism resulting from the hollowing out of human subjectivity. In general terms, the Freudian model of the unconscious as the deep interior of subjectivity is replaced by a cybernetic model of an unconscious structured by wider linguistic or power relations. The Palo Alto School, for example, conceptualized the individual in pragmatic, communicational terms, seeking to modify behaviour rather than address underlying problems.[31] The basic assumption of 'l'extériorité totale du sujet à lui-même' is also central to Lévi-Strauss' structuralism.[32] As Lafontaine emphasizes, the structuralist focus on social and linguistic 'communication' that occurs independently of the consciousness of individuals connects with the emerging scientific field of

---

27. David Mindell, *Digital Apollo: Human and Machine in Spaceflight* (Cambridge, MA: MIT Press, 2008).

28. Johnson, 'Analogue Apollo', p. 323.

29. Céline Lafontaine, *L'Empire cybernétique: des machines à penser à la pensée machine* (Paris: Seuil, 2004).

30. Ibid., p. 54.

31. Ibid., p. 82.

32. Ibid., p. 97.

molecular biology, which conceptualizes DNA in linguistic terms as a genetic 'programme'. This cybernetic vision of life, encompassing anthropology, linguistics and molecular biology, was disseminated to a wider French public in a landmark television debate between Lévi-Strauss, the linguist Roman Jakobson, the molecular biologist François Jacob, and the geneticist Philippe L'Héritier.[33] Ultimately, Lafontaine considers that the influence of cybernetics on French post-war thought lays the foundations for a problematic reductionist anti-humanism.

I would like to finish this introduction looking briefly at the way in which the articles engage with these broad themes and develop new insights. First, inspired by Chris's central focus on cybernetics, Yves Gilonne assesses the profound philosophical significance of the post-war emergence of this conceptual field. Taking as his starting point the etymology of the term cybernetics, he considers the importance of the analogy between thought and the act of *governing* and *piloting*. He insists on the importance of maintaining a distinction between the two terms, pointing to the tendency to reduce the ethical complexity of *government* to a technical *control*. He describes this tendency as a form of *télé-commande*, which seeks to control and manage human cognitive capital as series on input-outputs. As Yves indicates, the recent *Cambridge Analytica* scandal has highlighted the threat to genuinely democratic government posed by the unscrupulous use of data to manipulate opinion and voter behaviour.[34] In contrast to Wiener's model of a self-regulating reason aiming to arrive at a pre-determined destination, Jacques Derrida proposes opening up thought to that which resists its control.[35] Whereas feedback in cybernetics aims to reorient thought along a particular path, Derrida suggests that thought should be open to the oblique and the tortuous. Cybernetics is founded, Yves argues, on a analogical conflation of human and machine, brain and computer, body and thought, that is not properly examined or acknowledged. In our contemporary condition of virtuality, thought risks becoming purely functional and operational, and it can only be revived by introducing a space of difference between the human and the machine.

As my own article and Brigitte Nerlich's show, cybernetics exerted a significant influence on molecular biology as it emerged and developed in the post-war era. Both articles consider the use of metaphors in molecular biology and genetics, and they look at the way in which these metaphors have clearly been linked to the prevalent technologies and modes of social organization of the era in which they emerge as ways of talking about heredity. So, whereas in the nineteenth century genes were 'passed down', they were 'transmitted' in the electronic age, and then

33. Philippe L'Héritier, François Jacob, Roman Jakobson, Claude Lévi-Strauss, 'Vivre et parler', *Les Lettres françaises*, no. 1221 (1968), 3–7, and 1222 (1968), 4–5.

34. See Mark Hunyadi, 'Du sujet de droit au sujet libidinal: l'emprise du numérique sur nos sociétés', *Esprit* (2019), 114–28.

35. See Jacques Derrida, *L'Autre Cap* (Paris: Éditions de Minuit, 1991).

communicated as information in the cybernetic age. Schrödinger famously speculated that chromosomes contained a kind 'code-script' that was a blueprint for the construction of the individual in its mature state. It was only with the popularity if cybernetics in the 1950s that life and heredity were conceptually recast in terms of information and the metaphor of DNA as a form of language was widely used. The influence of cybernetics on molecular biology is crucial for both articles.

Brigitte looks in some detail at the use of three metaphors that have been used to conceptualize genetics and genetic information: life as a book; life as a machine; life as a code. She shows how these metaphors are ultimately inadequate as ways of understanding the role and function of genetic information. She shows how biology is now drawing on a more sophisticated understanding of cybernetics in order to establish a new language for talking about genetics and genomics that is able to deal with the complexity, flexibility and dynamic qualities of living systems. As Brigitte indicates, François Jacob and Jacques Monod were important and influential voices in the development of metaphors used for taking about genetic information. They drew enthusiastically on the terminology and conceptual perspective of cybernetics in order to frame their work on gene regulation in terms of 'blueprints', 'codes' and 'programmes'. She points to the fact that Jacob went on to question the analogies between language and genetics. He recognized that the idea of a genetic 'programme' meant that the products of the programme were then able to read it retrospectively: a point that was also made by Henri Atlan. As Brigitte suggests, Jacob's concept of *bricolage* is potentially more useful.

My article considers Jacob's use of the conceptual frame of *bricolage* as a significant moment in the evolution of François Jacob's thinking on molecular biology. Jacob and Monod, along with Arthur Pardee, undertook what became known as the PaJaMo experiments in order to explore the role played by genes in induction in bacteria. Their research proved to be enormously fruitful, it and constituted a breakthrough in the field of molecular biology that was equally as significant as Crick and Watson's discovery of the double helix structure of DNA. Challenging the 'one gene one enzyme' model that had held for the previous twenty years, their research pointed to a distinction between structural and regulator genes. Drawing directly on cybernetics, they identified a very particular negative feedback loop in the cell. This took the form of a double negative, according to which a regulator gene codes for a repressor protein that prevents the transcription of structural genes. However, when an inducer is bound to the repressor transcription can take place: it is, quite simply, like releasing a brake. According to this new 'operon' model, as Jacob and Monod called it, genes were no longer simply receptacles for information; they were involved in the processing and regulation of information within the cell. Although cybernetics provided Monod and Jacob with a theoretical frame in which to interpret and explain the significance of their operon experiments, Jacob, as I show, ultimately moved on to new ways of conceptualizing heredity and evolution, using the metaphor of *bricolage*.

Jonathan Hale's article on the 'tectonic sensibility' in architecture shows how ideas on technology and the human that can be traced back to French thinkers who have had an influence on this wide disciplinary field. It takes as its starting point the insight of Leroi-Gourhan and Maurice Merleau-Ponty that the human and technology are co-constitutive. Tectonics refers, in simple terms, to the art of construction, and discussions of tectonics in architecture often refer to materials and constructions details. Jonathan, however, uses the term tectonic 'sensibility' to describe a kind of 'meta tectonics'. This might be thought of as an exploration of the expressive possibilities of architecture, conceptualizing a building as a set of tools rather than as a fixed object. In his book *Merleau-Ponty for Architects* Jonathan sees Merleau-Ponty as a proto-posthumanist thinker, since he sees the individual as being dependent upon and inseparable from its surrounding.[36] Individuals are not discrete entities that exist within a particular environment: they produce their own environment and are produced in turn by it. Merleau-Ponty's thought provides a resource for thinking about architecture phenomenologically, focusing on the importance of the lived experience of the moving human body. Phenomenology for Merleau-Ponty entails a mode of perception that is poetic and artistic, in that it engages with sensuous richness of the world.

Madeleine Chalmers draws on French thinking on technology in order to consider political and ethical issues relating to the concepts of 'automatisme' and 'automation'. Although two terms have tended to be conflated in contemporary anxieties around the automation of work and the colonization of our imagination and cognition by digital technologies, she suggests that there is a resistant and creative potential in automatism as non-conscious behaviour. In order to illustrate this potential she traces what she calls a 'technocritical genealogy' connecting surrealism, Leroi-Gourhan and Bernard Stiegler. She argues that this genealogy reveals a distinctively French understanding of the automated age that begins with industrialization and extends to the present. Although their preoccupations might on the surface appear to be quite different, these three thinkers share a focus on the positive potential of exteriorization and dreaming. Louis Aragon and André Breton, for example, celebrate language and thought as 'automatic': language for the surrealists provides access to life. For Leroi-Gourhan, on the other hand, the emergence of language liberates humanity from immersion in 'le vécu'. However, Madeleine suggests that Breton's acknowledgement of the importance of recording and memory – that is to say, the possibility of 'exteriorization' – indicates that there may be some common ground between these apparently opposed analyses. She goes on to show how Stiegler draws inspiration from the surrealists and Marcel Duchamp in emphasizing the importance of moments of dreamlike 'intermittence' in which we might expand our capacity to transform the world.

---

36. Jonathan Hale, *Merleau-Ponty for Architects* (London: Routledge, 2017).

In his article, Henry Dicks argues that, read together, Martin Heidegger and Edgar Morin reveal a new potential of 'self-production', *physis*, which lies concealed in cybernetics. The issue of *physis* is crucial in the contemporary world because humanity is now threatened by unprecedented dangers arising from modern technology which prevent being from self-producing. As Henry acknowledges, Morin and Heidegger would usually be located in very different intellectual traditions. Morin was influenced by systems theory and cybernetics, which provided him with a way of analysing the dynamics of complex systems. Heidegger, on the other hand, was a phenomenological thinker, preoccupied principally with the appearance of things in the world. However, Henry contends that Heidegger's analysis of being and existence is much closer to Morin than it might at first appear. Both thinkers engage in a critique of cybernetics; they both are see being in terms of self-production; and they both seek to renew the early Greek concept of *physis*. A consideration of the claim that cybernetics is a new, foundational, transdisciplinary science that replaces philosophy is central to Henry's argument. That is to say, it sought to replace philosophy as the common foundation of the individual sciences as 'regional ontologies'. The aspiration of cybernetics to constitute a new, foundational ontology is clearly signalled in the creation of a series of universal concepts (information, control, feedback, etc.), which replace philosophical concepts (being, existing, becoming, etc.).

Chris's work in the field of science, technology and culture constituted a highly original contribution to the field. He drew on meticulous research and explored often complex ideas in a clear, accessible way. Reading his work always sparked ideas and inspired one's own research, as the articles in this collection demonstrate.

ORCID

John Marks (iD) https://orcid.org/0000-0002-4959-5776

Nottingham French Studies 59.3 (2020): 255–288
DOI: 10.3366/nfs.2020.0291
© Christopher Johnson
www.euppublishing.com/nfs

LEROI-GOURHAN'S *LE GESTE ET LA PAROLE*: THE EVOLUTION OF TECHNOLOGY[1]

CHRISTOPHER JOHNSON

To the external observer, André Leroi-Gourhan's reorientation from ethnology to prehistory in the years following the war might seem to represent a narrowing of focus, a move from the study of living and historically recorded cultures to the study of the anonymous remnants of a remote and inaccessible past. In fact, the turn to prehistory should be viewed not so much as an abandonment of ethnology as a continuation of Leroi-Gourhan's project of a comparative technology and a widening of the field of evidence for the more general study of the evolution of techniques. It was supported first by the different institutional positions Leroi-Gourhan held from the mid-1940s onwards, which required him to teach across a wide range of subjects: comparative technology and human geography at the Institut d'ethnologie from 1945; prehistory, ethnology and physical anthropology at the Université de Lyon (1944–55); adding the history of religions, at the Sorbonne (1956–69). This academic experience was complemented by fieldwork: archaeological excavations at Les Furtins from 1945, Arcy-sur-Cure from 1946 and Pincevent from 1964; visits to virtually all of the decorated caves in France and Spain between 1945 and 1968. The final, and critical, component of Leroi-Gourhan's entry into the field of prehistory was his research in animal and

---

1. This article is an edited version of the third chapter 'The Evolution of Technology' of Chris Johnson's final research project on the prehistoric ethnologist André Leroi-Gourhan, funded by a major grant from the Leverhulme Trust, to whom he would have wanted to express his gratitude. His book was provisionally titled *André Leroi-Gourhan: Language, Technology, Aesthetics*. An edited version of the first chapter 'Leroi-Gourhan and the Field of Ethnology' was published in *Paragraph* 43:1, edited by Nicholas Harrison (2020), 10–44, and a third extract should appear as 'The Evolution of Forms' in *Paragraph* in November 2021. Johnson published an article based on some of the material in Chapter 3 ('Leroi-Gourhan and the Limits of the Human', *French Studies*, 65:4 (October 2011), 471–87) in which he refers to the important (largely posthumous) studies of Leroi-Gourhan, notably Jacques Derrida's reading of *Le Geste et la parole* in *De la grammatologie* (1967), and Bernard Stiegler's revisiting in *La Technique et le temps* (1993, 1994). [Judith Still]

human palaeontology, which led to his second thesis, defended in 1954, on the mechanical structure of the vertebrate skull.

The communication of the results of this very active phase of Leroi-Gourhan's career includes engagement in a wide intellectual field in which he brings his growing expertise in palaeontology and prehistory to bear on the origins of humanity, the role of the hand in human evolution, differences in the technical behaviour of animals and humans, and the origins and nature of symbolic behaviour. The short pieces published on these subjects during the 1950s and early 1960s, many of them transcripts of public talks, thematically prepare the way for Leroi-Gourhan's major work on human evolution, *Le Geste et la parole*.[2] These texts reveal the emergence of a new conceptual framework, which places the theory of technical development elaborated in *Évolution et techniques*[3] in the wider context of biological evolution, extending the history of technology beyond the example of pre-industrial societies to that of contemporary and possible future states of machine civilization. This new framework is informed not only by Leroi-Gourhan's own research, but also by post-war developments in science and technology, and ways of thinking about science and technology. It will be necessary to keep in mind these particularities of historical context in the following reading of *Le Geste*, which will focus in turn on Leroi-Gourhan's account of the zoological prehistory of the human species, the different stages of hominid development preceding *homo sapiens* and the ascendant evolution of technology from the Palaeolithic period onwards. Leroi-Gourhan's exploration of these different areas of inquiry generates a new set of concepts characterized by key terms such as *liberation, anterior field, externalization, humanization, operational sequence, programme, memory, rhythm*. This new conceptual field does not so much supersede the theoretical framework developed in *Évolution et techniques* as build upon and extend its foundations, deepening our understanding of both the evolution of technology and the history of technology.

From the fish to the human

The opening chapter of *Le Geste*, 'L'Image de l'homme', situates the discipline of prehistory in a long tradition of preoccupation with origins, rooted in the basic human need to make sense of where we come from, what we are and what we will

---

2. André Leroi-Gourhan, *Le Geste et la parole, I: technique et langage* (Paris: Albin Michel, 1964); *Le Geste et la parole, II: la mémoire et les rythmes* (Paris: Albin Michel, 1965). Hereafter *GP*.

3. André Leroi-Gourhan, *Évolution et techniques, I: l'homme et la matière* [1943] (Paris: Albin Michel, 1971); *Évolution et techniques, II: milieu et techniques* [1945] (Paris: Albin Michel, 1973).

become. In this respect, Leroi-Gourhan suggests, the modern science of prehistory is simply a more recent – if more objective – avatar of the myth of origination (*GP*, I, pp. 9–10). In the introduction, he therefore traces the development of the different, prescientific images of humanity from the medieval and early modern periods through to the birth of prehistory as a discipline in the early nineteenth century and its recent consolidation in the middle of the twentieth century. As this narrative shows, historically there is an increasing rationalization of our image of the human both in the dimensions of space (discovery of the generic identity of humanity beyond physical or cultural difference) and time (discovery of the long duration of geological time and the extended prehistory of humanity within it), but also, with the advent of evolutionary theory, in relation to the animate world (confirmation of the zoological continuity between humans and all vertebrate forms). Paradoxically, it is the last of these rationalizations which, while dissolving the myth of human separateness, also permits the persistence of what according to Leroi-Gourhan is another myth, that of the proximity of human and primate. This myth has followed the history of prehistory like the shadow of its prescientific past, to the extent that even in the twentieth century interpretations of the palaeontological record persisted in searching for a transitional form of humanity, a 'missing link' between primates and humans. This, it could be said, is an important part of the programme delineated in the introduction to *Le Geste*: to dispel the myth of the 'ape-man' and establish the essential limits of the human in relation to the animal world.

Already in the final section of the introduction, 'Les Critères d'humanité', we are given the key elements of Leroi-Gourhan's definition of the human: the fundamental evolutionary event of upright posture, correlated with a flattening of the face, recession of the teeth and the decoupling of the hand from the locomotive function, freeing it for forms of technical activity that are quite unlike those found in the primate world (*GP*, I, p. 33). However, while this definition relegates the search for transitional forms between primate and human to the hypothetical question of their divergence from a much earlier common ancestor, it is not, as might be expected, the starting point for the investigation of human origins in the exposition that follows. The second chapter, 'Le Cerveau et la main', locates the conditions of possibility of the human not in relation to some lost primate cousin but within the infinitely wider context of vertebrate evolution. Leroi-Gourhan tracks the successive bifurcations in the evolution of the vertebrate body plan, bringing out at each stage the different mechanical traits which will finally converge on the specifically human configuration. Each of these stages constitutes a further 'liberation' of living forms in relation to their environment, that is, a greater degree of mobility and a complexification of their interactions with the world. His exposition takes the reader literally from the fish to the human, through the extended sequence of bilaterally symmetrical life forms where the functional requirement of nutrition and metabolism is served by 'un champ antérieur', the forward-facing organs which ensure locomotion, orientation and the capture and processing of food (*GP*, I, p. 44).

The elementary structure of the body plan is laid out in Leroi-Gourhan's detailed description of the Palaeozoic Ostracoderm fish, which offers the most ancient and schematic example of vertebrate organization. The most important structural and functional features of the evolutionary sequence leading to human forms are already in place. On the one hand, there is the organism's skeletal architecture, divided between forward and posterior parts distributed along the axis of the spinal cord: at the front the solid protective case of the head and the articulated pectoral fin; at the rear the propulsive unit of the tail. On the other hand, there is the 'dispositif nerveux', which controls the muscular contractions necessary for locomotion and integrates different sensory inputs for the control and coordination of the system as a whole (*GP*, I, pp. 44–6). This is a *cybernetic* description of the vertebrate organism, in which the terms 'command', 'control' and 'coordination' predominate: the concentration of nerve cells governing sense and movement is described as a 'poste central'. This lexical field will continue to be used in Leroi-Gourhan's analysis of the relationship between 'brain' and 'body' in vertebrate evolution.

The Ostracoderm's head forms a continuous surface of imbricated plates; the emergence of fish with articulated jaws during the Devonian marks an important functional adaptation of the skull, which becomes the support of the jawbone. From this point, Leroi-Gourhan argues, the evolution of the skull is determined both by the mechanical constraints of locomotion, and by the constraints of the jaw mechanism. With this decisive development in place, the repertoire of functional types is a relatively limited one, as demonstrated in the phenomenon of convergence, the evolution of genetically distinct species towards mechanically similar forms. The process of anatomical adaptation to different environments is accompanied over time by an increasingly effective organization of the nervous system (*GP*, I, pp. 47–9). One of the most important conditions of the development of the nervous system is the constitution of the anterior field, which in a number of animal species divides into two complementary areas, the one devoted to the movement of the head and the facial organs, the other to the movement of the forelimb (the manual pole), which act in close relationship to perform the most elaborate technical operations (*GP*, I, p. 49).

Leroi-Gourhan presents his exposition of vertebrate evolution as a 'functional palaeontology', which describes the determining role of the dynamic variations between the two polarities of the anterior field in different species. The operative concept here, as in the exposition which follows, is *equilibrium*: at each stage of vertebrate evolution, the adaptation and survival of life forms is dependent upon a balancing out of the relations between the different elements of the vertebrate body. Functional palaeontology therefore requires an integrative approach which takes account of the interaction between these elements, which for convenience of analysis Leroi-Gourhan reduces to five main categories:

Locomotion: the constraints of the mechanical organization of the vertebral column and the limbs.

Suspension of the skull: the topographical location of skull makes it the most sensitive element of the vertebrate body.

Dentition: the functional importance of the teeth for the anterior field is clear if one considers their role in defence and the capturing and preparation of food.

The hand: this is defined as the extremity of the forelimb, which has the potential function of technical activity.

The brain: which is defined as the 'coordinator' of the apparatus of the vertebrate body.

Leroi-Gourhan's sequencing of the elements of the vertebrate body is significant. The organs which are normally most closely associated with the human, the hand and the brain, are placed last. In the beginning is not intelligence, but mobility – this is the primordial fact of evolution. The brain's coordinating function is fundamental, but 'il n'y a pas un rapport de priorité de l'évolution du cerveau sur l'évolution du dispositif corporel qu'il contrôle' (*GP*, I, p. 59). This will become one of the central arguments of the first part of *Le Geste*.

Leroi-Gourhan insists that it is not sufficient to analyse any of the structural elements of the vertebrate body in isolation: the study of functional evolution requires an integrative approach. He applies this approach to six morphological types representing the chronological stages of vertebrate evolution: fish, amphibian, reptilian, mammalian, anthropoid and human. Each of these stages constitutes a relative 'liberation' of the vertebrate organism in relation to its environment, accompanied by key modifications in its anatomy and posture. The amphibian transition from water to land requires a respiratory system adapted to air as well as the aquatic environment, but also involves changes in locomotion and posture: the movement from water to land imposes new mechanical constraints on the head, which, no longer supported by a high density environment, has to contend with gravity. The resultant modification in the suspension of the head has important repercussions on the entire cranial edifice, due to the laws of 'mechanical equilibrium' governing the mutual adjustment of its different components. In particular, Leroi-Gourhan notes the functional link between the jawbone and suspension: from the origins of the vertebrate sequence, dentition and posture are closely related (*GP*, I, p. 66).

Selectively following those life forms which evolve towards greater mobility and more complex interactions with their environments, Leroi-Gourhan identifies the land-dwelling reptilian forms of the end of the Palaeozoic as representing a notable advance on the amphibian body plan: the latter's flexible vertebral column has become a convex beam supporting the head and limbs; the development of the limbs enables a raised crawling posture during locomotion, which in turn determines an increased mobility of the shoulder, the definitive separation of the head, and decisive changes in the structure of the cranial edifice. Leroi-Gourhan underlines that 'le volume de la voûte crânienne n'est pas déterminé par le cerveau, mais par les contraintes mécaniques de traction mandibulaire et de suspension de la tête'; the reptilian braincase is 'suspended' inside the cranium and does not coincide with it as in later vertebrate forms (*GP*, I, p. 69). While the essential components of the human skeletal structure are already in place – centrality of the backbone, individualization of limbs, extremities with five digits, suspension of the skull – the role of the brain is a 'mechanically passive' one. Despite its cybernetic function as the animator of the vertebrate body frame, the development of the brain is considered incidental to the general movement of evolution. This is not to deny the fact of the evolution of the nervous system towards increasingly more complex structures – brain and body evolve in a mutual dialogue – but to recognize that at each stage the complexification of the nervous system *follows* the mechanical adaptations of the vertebrate body system (*GP*, I, pp. 70–1). This is the basic hypothesis that will guide Leroi-Gourhan's account of vertebrate and hominid evolution.

Leroi-Gourhan's extended analysis of early vertebrate evolution demonstrates how far back one can trace the structural features of higher life forms such as humans. By the end of the Paleozoic, reptilian forms have already achieved fully erect quadruped locomotion, a high degree of dental differentiation and a considerably increased mobility of the head. The emergence of quadruped mammalian forms towards the middle of the Mesozoic is therefore presented as a 'new' beginning based on a structural template developed millions of years earlier. Leroi-Gourhan's selective focus on the dynamic behaviour of vertebrates in relation to the anterior field means that his analysis of the mammalian sequence cuts across conventional zoological classifications of species. Thus he distinguishes between two fundamental tendencies or functional groups: those in which relations with the anterior field are mediated by the head; those in which such relations are to varying degrees mediated by the hand. This distinction corresponds to the zoological division between mammals which are exclusively walkers and mammals which are, if only transitorily, capable of prehension. The walkers are highly specialized in their highly-developed extremities dedicated to locomotion, and in the diversification of their cranial and facial anatomies: teeth, horns, nasal appendages, extensible lips. This category broadly coincides with the class of ungulates, for example, horse, elephant, pig or ox. The second category is more diverse, if less numerous, including primates, rodents, bats, insectivores and carnivores, whose diet is either omnivorous or carnivorous. In contrast to the single digit of the ungulate, their extremities have four or five digits, and the forward extremity is capable of prehension. While typically the mode of locomotion remains quadrupedal, the critical difference lies in their ability to adopt a seated posture, thus freeing the 'hand' for different kinds of manipulation. Paradoxically, perhaps, ungulate anatomy is described as being more 'evolved' than that of prehensile mammals: the forward-facing technical activities of the ungulate are entirely concentrated in the head and face and locomotion is concentrated in the single-digit feet, whereas for the prehensile mammal technical activity is distributed between the hand and face, which remain simpler in structure, the hand retaining the primitive five-digit morphology of its amphibian ancestors. However, the greater anatomical flexibility of this second category of mammal means that it can achieve very high levels of manual activity (*GP*, I, pp. 76–81).

Within that category, four-handed primates are seen functionally to occupy a class distinct from that of quadrupeds. While the use of the hand in the latter is episodic, for monkeys and apes it is a permanent feature of behaviour, both for the purposes of locomotion in trees or on the ground, and for the purposes of technical activity involving the front hands. By contrast with other tree-dwelling mammals, rodents or carnivores, who grip with their claws, the mode of prehension in monkeys and apes is based on the use of the fingers and an opposable thumb. Once again, a functionally critical feature is variability of posture: the mechanical correlate of the more or less erect seated posture in monkeys and apes is the oblique entry of the vertebral column into the skull, reduced dentition and a much shorter face, and *for the first time*, a partial freeing of the cranial vault from the pressures of suspension, which in turn leads to the freeing of the facial unit from the main part of the skull (*GP*, I, pp. 81–5).

This exposition of vertebrate evolution brings the reader to the threshold of human forms. It is based on a body of palaeontological documentation which demonstrates the replication, across the evolutionary sequence from fish to primate, of the same principles of construction and the same mechanical constraints. If the living world can be characterized in its simplest terms as the physical and chemical processing of matter, then what this particular sequence shows is the development, in the higher life forms, of an increasingly reflexive and conscious contact with the material world. At all levels of life such contact takes place through the coordinated components of the body and the nervous system, which provide respectively the technical interface with the external world and the organization of bodily movement in space:

> L'évolution se traduit, matériellement, par une double ligne de faits: d'une part le perfectionnement cumulative des structures cérébrales, d'autre part, l'adaptation des structures corporelles suivant des règles directement liées à l'équilibre mécanique de cette machine qu'est l'être vivant et mobile. (*GP*, I, p. 87)

While recognizing the necessary co-evolution of brain and body, this cybernetic understanding of living forms differs from that of evolutionists such as Teilhard de Chardin, for whom the significant fact is the ever-increasing development of the brain and nervous system.[4] For Leroi-Gourhan, this is an error of perspective based on the evolutionary success of *homo sapiens*, one which places the cart before the horse. He repeats his hypothesis of the delayed coupling of nervous system and body, in which the former follows the latter. Material proof of such a delay can be found in the sequence of palaeontological evidence presented in 'Le Cerveau', which shows the early emergence of the quadruped body plan coupled with an extremely small brain. With the stabilization of the different vertebrate groups, Leroi-Gourhan argues, one observes the progressive 'invasion' of the cranium by the brain, an expansion which takes advantage of the morphological changes in the vertebrate skull rather than directly determining them. In accordance with the rules of mechanical equilibrium governing the relationship between posture, dentition and skull shape, each species reaches an evolutionary ceiling as the brains fills the space available. Whereas for technically specialized species such as herbivores there is a mechanical limit to such expansion, species 'dont la structure corporelle correspond à la plus grande libération de la main sont aussi celles dont le crâne est susceptible de contenir le plus grand cerveau puisque libération manuelle et réduction des contraintes de la voûte crânienne sont deux termes de la même équation mécanique' (*GP*, I, p. 88). Within what may be described here as the *feedback circuit* established between brain and body, a more developed brain influences patterns of behaviour, which in their turn influence the development of body structure in response to the pressures of natural selection. In this sense, the brain does control the process of evolution, but in an indirect way, via selective adaptations brought about through changes in behaviour. In contrast to 'cerebralist' interpretations of evolution, such as that of Teilhard de Chardin, Leroi-Gourhan therefore insists that the brain cannot be treated as an abstract phenomenon, since its evolution is entirely dependent on the adaptive possibilities of body structure.

Stages of humanization

In terms of functional anatomy, the position of the four-handed primate in the evolutionary sequence described here seems very close to that of humans, for example, in terms of the potential complexity and flexibility of manual activity in the anterior field. However, despite their morphological similarities, for Leroi-Gourhan there is an evolutionary abyss between the ape and the human. The determining adaptive feature of the human form is bipedalism, which is anatomically dependent on the configuration of the toes, more like that of walking vertebrates, the construction of the leg bones and the shape of the pelvis, upon

---

4.   Pierre Teilhard de Chardin, *Le Phénomène humain* (Paris: Seuil, 1955).

which the full weight of the trunk is balanced (*en équilibre*). Other defining characteristics are a straightened spine, upon which the head is balanced (*en équilibre*), and a free hand, which is structurally similar to that of the ape but differs considerably in the proportions of its constituent parts (*GP*, I, pp. 91–2).

Despite the continuing obsession with the proximity of ape and human behaviour, Leroi-Gourhan insists on the evolutionary distance between the two forms, reminding us that speculations on the transition to bipedalism have no substantial supporting evidence. As far back in the palaeontological record as one is able to penetrate, one finds the anatomically distinct configuration of the human, described above, but no transitional forms. The more interesting question, in his view, is the diversity of human forms that precede what we now call anatomically modern humans. In the third and fourth chapters of *Le Geste*, he therefore attempts to reconstruct the different stages of *humanization*, the continued process of evolution within the hominid sequence which converges on *homo sapiens*, using the chronological categories of Australanthropian, Archanthropian, Palaeoanthropian and Neanthropian. Whereas human palaeontology until the mid-twentieth century had been based on documentation dating back to Archanthropian forms of the Lower Palaeolithic (200000–+/-1m years B.P.), the 'revolutionary' event in the five years preceding the publication of *Le Geste* was the discovery in Africa of much earlier human forms. What was disconcerting about these early human forms was the small size of the brain case (500cc), approximately one third that of anatomically modern humans. Here, Leroi-Gourhan repeatedly emphasizes the strangeness, the *uncanniness*, of what in the early 1960s was the earliest specimen of a proto-human skull, *Zinjanthropus boisei*:

> Aucun fossile relativement proche de nous ne laisse ce sentiment d'étrangeté, presque de gêne ou de discordance, aucun ne donne l'impression d'un homme inhumanisé plus que celle d'un singe qui s'humaniserait. Cette gêne vient de ce que les Australanthropes sont en réalité moins des hommes à face de singe que des hommes à boîte cérébrale défiant l'humanité. Nous étions préparés à tout admettre sauf d'avoir débuté par les pieds. (*GP*, I, p. 97)

At this lower limit of humanity there is already a clear separation between primate and human: *Zinjanthropus* is not the fabled missing link. At the same time, the human (s)he represents seems inhuman, unlike hominid remains from later periods – hence the sense of defamiliarization, of uncanniness. We find it difficult to accept that we started with the feet and not with the brain: bipedalism, which liberates the hand, is the mechanical condition of possibility of the human, but precedes advanced forms of cognition. *Zinjanthropus* is already (strangely) human because this small-brained biped was also a toolmaker. The implications of this apparent mismatch – a small brain accompanied by technical intelligence – are that we must radically revise our ideas about what constitutes humanity.

Zinjanthropus reveals that anatomically a form of humanity is possible before the full development of the brain: 'les instruments corporels sont apparus, humainement constitués, bien avant que l'évolution du cerveau soit terminée' (*GP*, I, p. 101). This confirms Leroi-Gourhan's previous hypothesis of the delayed coupling of brain and body in vertebrate evolution.

The principles of mechanical equilibrium derived from the study of the functional palaeontology of vertebrate forms also apply in the case of the evolution of the hominid forms that follow *Zinjanthropus*. Thus the palaeontological sequence from Australanthropian to Neanthropian indicates the recession and reduction of the teeth, a flattening of the face, and a corresponding increase in brain capacity, doubling from 500cc to 1000cc during the Middle Paleolithic (Archanthropian), with a further 50% increase in the Upper Paleolithic (Palaeoanthropian, Neanthropian). Leroi-Gourhan emphasizes that the enlargement of cranial capacity is not determined by some spontaneous 'expansive force' of the brain, but is simply the mechanical consequence of the evolutionarily prior event of upright posture, which determines the near-vertical entry of the vertebral column into the skull: the brain gradually occupies the space made available by the 'fanning out' of the brain case, culminating in the total 'liberation' of its frontal regions with *homo sapiens* (*GP*, I, p. 110).

The possibilities for direct study of the hominid brain are limited, restricted to the use of endocasts of the cranial cavity, which reveal something of the structure and proportions of the external parts of the brain. Leroi-Gourhan therefore turns to neurology, in particular studies of the middle cortex, which governs the motor functions of different parts of the body. He is particularly interested in those parts of the brain which control the technical activities of the anterior field. Again, the lexical field of his description is a cybernetic one: the body is described as a 'machine' and the primary motor region of the cortex as a 'tableau de régulation' (*GP*, I, p. 119). In humans, the control of body parts is not distributed equally across the pre-motor cortex, but is biased – in a proportion of approximately 80% – towards the head and the upper part of the body, with at least 50% of motor coordination devoted to the hands and the organs of speech. This differential distribution of neurological control is illustrated in a diagram in which the human body plan is flipped over, reflecting its spatially reversed representation in the cortex, and its different parts drawn to scale in relation to the amount of neural activity dedicated to them. In particular, Leroi-Gourhan notes the *contiguity* of the neural circuits governing the face and the hand:

> Un autre fait offre de l'intérêt, c'est la contiguïté des territoires de la face et de la main dans l'aire 4 [the primary motor cortex] et leur situation topographique commune. Une étroite coordination existe entre l'action de la main et celle des organes antérieurs de la face. Chez le singe cette liaison est de caractère surtout alimentaire, et cela aux proportions près est vrai aussi chez l'homme, mais en outre il faut constater

chez ce dernier une coordination non moins forte entre la main et la face dans l'exercice du langage. Cette coordination, qui s'exprime dans le geste comme commentaire de la parole reparaît dans l'écriture comme transcription des sons de la voix. (*GP*, I, pp. 121–2)

While apes and humans share virtually the same neurological configuration governing motor activities in the anterior field, there is a radical divergence between the two species in the modes of coordination of face and hand, to the extent that the human uses the hand for making things and the face for speaking. Primate tool use, argues Leroi-Gourhan, is a world apart from the technical activity of even the earliest of human forms. Assuming that the neurological correlation of gesture and speech in the middle cortex would have been the same in Australanthropians, he equally argues for some form of language competence in *Zinjanthropus*, whatever its level of intelligence (*GP*, I, pp. 126–7).

Without any direct evidence on the development of Anthropian intelligence, Leroi-Gourhan turns to the indirect evidence provided by the archaeological record, arguing for the parallel development of, or 'synchronism' between the cranial expansion of successive hominid forms and the lithic technology which accompanies them. Archaeological evidence indicates an increasing complexification and diversification of tool types through the different stages of humanity from Australanthropian to Neanthropian. The tools discovered with *Zinjanthropus* are very primitive but unmistakably human-made, corresponding to what prehistorians recognize as a *stereotype*. Like the natural organ in the biological world, the artificial organ of the tool must conform to certain constants of form. Here, Leroi-Gourhan repeats the reasoning of *Évolution et techniques* concerning the different kinds of determinism – material and functional – which come into play in the production of the object and delimit the field of the conscious human agent: 'il existe un stéréotype […] qui n'est pas simplement le produit d'une intélligence cohérente mais le produit de cette intélligence intégrée dans la matière et la fonction' (*GP*, I, pp. 132–3). The analysis of the Australanthropian stereotype, and that of the later hominid forms, is supported by the experimental reconstruction of the process of fabrication of lithic technology. Leroi-Gourhan refers to this process as the 'chaîne opératoire', the structured chain or sequence of actions necessary to extract a specific instrument from the raw material of the block of flint. The operational sequence therefore presupposes a certain intentionality, a capacity for anticipation in the agent of technology, from the earliest forms of human intelligence onwards. However, the form of intelligence that might be inferred from the technology of *Zinjanthropus* is a relatively limited one. Echoing his analysis of the elementary types of percussion in *L'Homme et la matière*, Leroi-Gourhan describes the basic chopping tool used by *Zinjanthropus* as the product of *one* type of gesture, the most simple type, which consists in striking the edge of the flint pebble at an angle of ninety degrees, producing *one* cutting edge. While this kind of technical behaviour is certainly human, involving a certain degree of technical consciousness, at the same time the tools of *Zinjanthropus* are described as being simply an extension of the zoological human, a natural 'secretion' of the body and mind of the Australanthropian. This potentially problematic interpretation is made with reference to the dimension of *time*: the industrial stereotype of the pebble culture remains unchanged for countless millennia, and there is no sign in *Zinjanthropus* of a system of 'creative thought' which might take it to another level of development (*GP*, I, pp. 133–4).

The palaeontological record indicates a doubling of cranial capacity between Australanthropians and the different Archanthropian forms of the Lower Palaeolithic period. The evolutionary distance between the two is manifested in more sophisticated techniques of tool production. With the Archanthropian stereotype, the single, perpendicular stroke used in the fabrication of the primitive chopper is supplemented by a second series of gestures in which the piece of stone from which the tool is extracted is struck obliquely, producing longer and thinner flakes. Leroi-Gourhan sees this additional series of gestures as representing a qualitative as well as a quantitative advance in techniques of fabrication, involving a higher degree of foresight and conscious choice, in terms of the selection of a suitable block of stone, the pre-conception of the form of the instrument, and the combination of the different sequences of gesture used to make it. Despite this advance, the typological range of Archanthropian technology is limited to forms such as the ax and biface. Again, this limitation is explained in relation to time, or the relative *tempo* of time. During the estimated 300 or 400 millennia of the Lower Palaeolithic, the 'rythme' of evolution of Archanthropian technology is extremely slow, introducing few new forms and minimal improvements in techniques of production. Again, the conservatism of the Archanthropian stereotype is seen as a direct expression of species behaviour, and the influence of individual innovation appears to have been negligible during this extremely long period: 'La technicité chez l'homme pendant la plus grande partie de sa durée chronologique [...] relèverait donc plus directement de la zoologie que de tout autre science' (*GP*, I, p. 140).

The timescale of Palaeoanthropians is relatively much shorter than that of preceding human forms, starting at approximately 200 or 300 years B.P. For prehistorians, there is considerably more data available on this particular stage of humanity, including information on habitat structures. The most studied form of Palaeoanthropian is Neanderthal, whose brain size is equivalent to or greater than that of modern humans, but whose frontal regions appear relatively less developed. The archaeological documentation relating to this period indicates a very high level of development of tool manufacture; correlated with the shorter timescale of Palaeoanthropians, this represents an *acceleration* of technical development. Compared with the two-step process of Archanthropian technology, the operational sequence necessary for the extraction of the tool has now been extended to at least six series of gestures, signifying a higher cognitive capacity. The other important development during this period relates to the utilization of raw materials, the block of stone from which the tool is extracted. Whereas previously this block would have formed the body of the projected tool, it now becomes the source of flakes of a predetermined form which themselves form the tool. This shift in the manufacturing process is an economic revolution, to the extent that it enables a significant increase in the quantity of tools extracted from a block, and therefore a greater degree of independence in relation to geographically fixed sources of raw materials. It is also accompanied by a considerable diversification of tool types (*GP*, I, pp. 140–6).

Leroi-Gourhan describes the Palaeoanthropian stereotype as representing an apogee of prehistoric technical development: all of the important problems of lithic tool manufacture have been solved. In this respect, it would be difficult to distinguish between the technical skill of the Palaeoanthropian and that of any contemporary artisan – one is very far here from the traditional image of Neanderthal as some transitional form between simian and human. At the same time, Leroi-Gourhan begins to draw a distinction between different types of intelligence. On the one hand, there is the technical intelligence which, from the Australanthropian onwards, distinguishes humans from the other higher primates. On the other hand, the interest of the Palaeoanthropian stage is that it appears to offer evidence of the emergence of another type of intelligence, not restricted to the elementary material activities relating to subsistence and survival. This 'reflective intelligence' is not only capable of comprehending the relationships between phenomena, but is also able to externalize these relationships in the form of symbolic representations. It is accompanied by evidence of behaviour of an aesthetic or religious kind:

> Les traces archéologiques de cette activité qui dépasse la motricité technique sont, pour le Quaternaire ancien, difficiles à saisir, mais au stade paléanthropien les premiers témoins archéologiques apparaissent. Ce sont les plus anciennes manifestations de caractère esthético-religieux et on pourrait les classer en deux groupes: celles qui témoignent de réactions à l'égard de la mort et celles qui témoignent de réactions à l'égard de l'insolite dans la forme. (*GP*, I, p. 153)

Leroi-Gourhan is referring to, first, the appearance, at a relatively late stage in the archaeological record, of the practice of inhumation, and, second, the presence of unusual natural objects with no clear utilitarian function, collected by Palaeoanthropians such as Neanderthal. He takes such non-utilitarian behaviour as evidence of an emergent aesthetic sensibility, an advanced form of pattern recognition anticipating the later explosion of artistic activity observed in *homo sapiens* during the Upper Palaeolithic period.

The distinction between different types of intelligence, between the kinds of reflexivity associated with technical activity and more abstract mental activities, may seem somewhat artificial. It is most constructive to view it as expressing not an opposition, or break, between different types of human, but as part of Leroi-Gourhan's more general attempt to conceptualize transitions between different stages of humanization – what makes successive hominid forms progressively more like *homo sapiens*. The extremely slow rate of technical development during the Australanthropian and Archanthropian stages leads him to the potentially paradoxical conclusion that the technical fact is more a 'zoological' than a fundamentally human fact. To use a previous image, it is as if the tool is a 'secretion', or a progressive 'exudation' of the Anthropian mind and body. This description is biologically deterministic to the extent that it refers on the one hand to the bodily anatomy without which human technics would be impossible, on the other hand to what Leroi-Gourhan considers to be the close correlation, or synchronism, between brain size, brain structure and degree of technical development during the different stages of human evolution. While, as we have seen, the basic body configuration stabilizes relatively early in the Anthropian sequence, the brain itself continues to evolve. This evolution is described as a series of *additions* or *accretions*, as the progressive layering of brain functions over time, culminating in the full development of the pre-frontal cortex in *homo sapiens*. The regions of the middle cortex governing technical motor function are already in place at the Australanthropian stage, whereas the frontal regions associated with reflexive thought and symbolic behaviour appear at a relatively late stage, with Neanderthal. These emergent cognitive capacities are seen to act as both a 'counterbalance' and a 'stimulant' to technical intelligence (*GP*, I, p. 152).

The question of different types of hominid intelligence inevitably introduces the question of language. Leroi-Gourhan argues for some form of language competence from the earliest human forms onwards at whatever level of intelligence. Without direct evidence of language, indirect confirmation can be found in the anatomical fact of the contiguity in the middle cortex of the neural circuits governing hand and face movements. According to Leroi-Gourhan, the fabrication of tools and the production of symbols are indissolubly linked, to the extent that both depend upon the same neurological infrastructure. Whereas tool use and vocal communication in primates are ephemeral and context-bound, human tool fabrication and language production share the properties of pre-existence and persistence: 'la permanence du concept est de nature différente mais comparable à celle de l'outil' (*GP*, I, p. 164). The guiding concept here is that of the operational sequence. The sequence of gestures which governs the fabrication of objects is compared to a 'syntax' which provides both fixity and flexibility to the process of fabrication. In accordance with his synchronistic reading of human evolution, Leroi-Gourhan argues for a roughly equivalent level of complexity of linguistic and technical behaviour at different stages of Anthropian development. Thus the linguistic ability of the Archanthropian would correspond to an operational sequence of two series of gestures applied to five or six tool stereotypes.

Such a language would probably be restricted to the expression of 'concrete' situations. The extension and complexification of the operational sequence observable at the Palaeoanthropian stage would then indicate a higher level of linguistic capability, symbolic thought applied to 'non-concrete' situations and time-independent narrative. Characteristically, Leroi-Gourhan qualifies that such capabilities would not have appeared spontaneously with Palaeoanthropians, but must have emerged gradually during the previous Archanthropian stage (*GP*, I, pp. 164–5).

The hypothesis of the co-emergence and co-evolution of language and technics is critical – formulated in opposition to the religious or rationalist humanist narrative according to which the intelligent (speaking) human appears fully-formed from the mind of God or the matrix of nature, the fully-conscious agent and originator of technics. *Le Geste*'s narrative of human evolution describes the incredibly slow development of human intelligence and culture, which up to Neanderthal seem to evolve at the rhythm of biological time, in step with the unfolding and superposition of the different cortical regions of the brain. The final stage of humanization, described as the final 'liberation', occurs with the Neanthropians, and is again presented first in anatomical and neuro-anatomical terms. The evolution of the brain follows the same principles as evolution in general: it builds upon the old in order to make the new. At each stage, there is therefore what Leroi-Gourhan describes as a stabilization, and then 'dépassement', of acquired structures. Whereas the anatomical structure of the hand stabilizes very early, the neuro-anatomical stabilization of the 'technical brain' does not occur until the end of the Archanthropian. The increase in brain size between Archanthropian and Palaeoanthropian also involves modifications in cranial structure: progressive 'invasion' of the frontal regions; further recession of the teeth; corresponding reduction in the massiveness of the face and an increased protrusion of the forehead. While there is no increase in brain size between Palaeoanthropian and Neanthropian, Leroi-Gourhan speculates that the qualitative difference between these two must have depended on a structural reorganization of the different parts of the brain, in particular with respect to the pre-frontal region. Drawing on neuro-anatomical research, he notes its division into the neo-cortex and the rhinencephalon, originally dedicated to smell but in the higher mammals becoming the 'centre of affective integration', regulating the emotions. The neo-cortex is mainly involved in operations involving control, prediction and lucid consciousness, and considered as a key component of individual personality. The combined system of the pre-frontal cortex therefore plays an essential regulatory role in relation to affect, motor functions and intellectual judgement, and its integral development in the Neanthropian is seen to mark the advent of reflexive intelligence in the fully human sense. The archaeological record reveals that the technical development of humanity, from its earliest forms, is precisely the effect of an increasingly 'controlling' intelligence. Importantly, for Leroi-Gourhan the

Neanthropian stage also marks the point at which the 'zoological' finally gives way to the 'sociological'. Whereas up to this point human evolution is played out within the triangle of biology, technics and language, with the liberation of the frontal regions of the brain, society increasingly plays a determining role in the development of the species (*GP*, I, pp. 167–87).

Neanthropian technical development appears equivalent to that of pre-industrial cultures with clear evidence of hut and tent construction, sophisticated preparation and sewing of animal skins, items of adornment made from animal teeth, shells and bone, and fine working of bone materials for both technical and non-technical objects. However, the most extensive evidence is supplied by lithic technology, which has become highly diversified, and undergone a considerable reduction in size. In addition to the ergonomic efficiency of such miniaturization, this tendency towards microlithism continues the technical and economic revolution begun with the Palaeoanthropians, enabling the increasingly efficient extraction of a greater number and range of flakes from the single block of stone. Consequently, the distance of Neanthropian habitats from their sources of raw materials is considerably extended (*GP*, I, pp. 188–94).

Because of its durability, lithic technology is the only category of archaeological evidence providing a continuous sequence of technical development since the origins of humanity. This shows an evolution of technical forms towards an increasingly effective adaptation of matter to function. The chronologically parallel sequence provided by the palaeontological evidence, though less extensive, indicates a steady increase in cranial capacity accompanied by an 'architectural drift' in the structure of the skull and face. While aware of the potential artificiality of the comparison, Leroi-Gourhan reiterates his hypothesis of a correlation or 'parallelism' between these two series of facts. However, the development of the brain is seen to reach a plateau following the decisive 'unblocking' of the pre-frontal cortex in *homo sapiens*. From this point onwards there is biological stabilization of the species, while the rate of technical development continues to increase. Leroi-Gourhan reads this divergence as a *dissociation* of the biological and the technical: 'La technique n'est plus liée chez l'*homo sapiens* au progrès cellulaire mais elle paraît s'extérioriser complètement et vivre en quelque sorte de sa vie propre' (*GP*, I, p. 197). This independent life is increasingly mediated through society.

From the zoological to the sociological

During the Upper Palaeolithic there are the first clear signs of regional variations in tool manufacture, and of distinct traditions in cave decoration. For Leroi-Gourhan, this type of ethnic diversification coincides with an acceleration in technical development, and is symptomatic of a transformed relationship between the individual and the social group. Diverging from the sociological tradition

(Durkheim, Mauss, Lévi-Strauss) which takes the social fact as the determining level of analysis, he proposes a 'bottom-up ethnology' (*ethnologie des profondeurs*), in which the social fact is first a general biological fact which has become totally 'humanized'. Just as his analysis of the conditions of possibility of human thought began with the feet, so his analysis of human social organization begins with the Anthropian digestive system, adapted to the consumption of a specific range of fleshy foods, both vegetable and animal. The geographical dispersal and seasonal variation of these food sources determines the structure of the primitive human group, in terms of its limited population density and its fixation and periodic displacement within a given territory. Distinctively, humans normally divide labour between male and female in the acquisition of animal and vegetal food sources, men tending to specialize in hunting and women in gathering. Consisting of a relatively limited number of conjugal couples and their children, as a unit of subsistence the primitive group must be technically polyvalent, that is, its members must have a complete practical knowledge of those elements of material culture which are vital to its continued survival. However, the group is not permanently isolated, to the extent that it is integrated into larger units composed of several groups through the exchange of women and material products. The 'symbiosis', as Leroi-Gourhan describes it, of complementary technical activities in the conjugal unit or 'cell' is therefore replicated at a higher level in the symbiotic federation of exchanging groups. The emergence of this more complex form of social organization marks the passage from the 'zoological species' to the 'ethnic species', and is already in evidence in the early stages of *homo sapiens* (*GP*, I, pp. 205–22).

While by the end of the Palaeolithic period the humanization of the biological imperatives of food acquisition and reproduction has already reached an advanced stage, the decisive techno-economic development during the Neolithic period is the appearance of animal domestication and agriculture. According to Leroi-Gourhan, this Neolithic 'revolution' (gradual in terms of human or technological, rather than geological, time) has exercised the most profound and lasting influence on human social organization. Developing recent archaeological research in the near-east, Leroi-Gourhan explores the different geographical and climatic conditions which would have led to the parallel emergence of these two techniques, reflecting the fundamental complementarity of a diet consisting of animal and vegetal components. Its effect is to completely transform the social structures of these human groups. While domestication initially replicates the nomadic patterns of primitive groups, the practice of agriculture produces the qualitatively new phenomenon of sedentarization, which has demographic and spatial effects, involving a relatively higher concentration of individuals grouped around food reserves and protected by defensive structures. Functionally, the relationship between agricultural and pastoral fractions is comparable to the symbiotic relationship of the primitive couple or group, but it is of a fundamentally different nature, since the fractions are not of the same culture or level of techno-economic development, forming two separate and, frequently, mutually closed groups. Leroi-Gourhan develops the biological analogy which is implicit in the concept of symbiosis to clarify this relationship:

> À la complémentarité du couple, à celle des groupes alliés dans un système d'échanges, se superpose une structure d'un échelon plus élevé où deux sociétés distinctes entretiennent des rapports d'un type analogue. Le fait qu'on retrouve ici est comparable à celui qui marque les organismes vivants dans lesquels, du bas au sommet de la série, les systèmes végétatifs passent de l'affrontement de cellules libres à celui d'organismes mettant en coordination un nombre considérable de cellules agrégées. (*GP*, I, p. 235)

The increased population density of the agricultural-pastoral society initiates a positive feedback cycle in which higher population levels both determine and enable increased food production, transforming the symbiotic relationship between agricultural and pastoral groups. Historically, this relationship is rarely equal or peaceful, and one group is habitually subordinated to the other. While aggression is considered an integral part of human behaviour, a *technique* fundamentally linked to the acquisition of food, its form and scale are completely transformed at the level of the large sedentary unit, where the practice of war is integrated into a process of technical innovation which becomes inseparable from the progress of society. The development of the sedentary society is therefore viewed as both an expression of the basic biological tendencies of the species and a *distortion* of them:

> Clefs de l'affranchissement de l'humanité primitive, les céréales et le bétail ouvrent la voie du progrès technique, mais ne libèrent nullement des servitudes génétiques et l'histoire se déroule sur trois plans discordants, celui de l'histoire naturelle qui fait que l'*homo sapiens* du XXe siècle n'est que très peu différent de l'*homo sapiens* du trois centième avant, celui de l'évolution sociale qui ajuste tant bien que mal les structures fondamentales du groupe biologique à celles qui naissent de l'évolution technique, et celui de l'évolution technique, excroissance prodigieuse d'où l'espèce *homo sapiens* tire son efficacité sans être biologiquement en possession de son contrôle. Entre ces deux extrêmes de l'homme physique et des techniques dont il finit par passer pour le simple instrument, la médiation s'opère par un édifice social dont les réponses sont toujours un peu en retard sur les questions posées, et par des concepts moraux, sanctionnés par des religions ou des idéologies dont les racines plongent dans la morale sociale. (*GP*, I, p. 237)

This passage reiterates a theme articulated in *Évolution et techniques*, that of the different rates of development of the internal milieu – the cumulative development of the technical milieu as opposed to the fluctuating development of moral, social or political systems. The complication here is that an additional level of determination has been introduced, that of the physical human, with its own rhythm of development in relation to the social and the technical domains – raising the problem of the potential discordance or mismatch between these different dimensions of the group.

Following the standard Marxist interpretation, Leroi-Gourhan sees a direct causal link between food storage, the accumulation of a surplus and the development of a stratified and exploitative social order in the agricultural-pastoral society. In particular, he is interested in the link between this new social configuration and technical innovation. Three major 'inventions' – ceramics, metallurgy and writing – appear almost instantaneously following the consolidation of the agricultural societies around 6000 B.C. The existence of a food surplus, combined with a higher population density, creates the 'favourable milieu' in which such an acceleration of technical progress can take place, as the time of the technician is freed and a greater number of specialized individuals are able to respond to the demand for innovation generated by a growing population. With the passage from the Neolithic to the Bronze Age, there is a gradual transition to urbanized existence, the start of 'civilization'. The basic functional plan of the city consists in villages grouped around an agglomeration ('the capital'), characterized by a marked social hierarchy with power and resources monopolized by a religious and military elite. The most important techno-economic development, however, is the emergence of the artisan, the principal agent of technical progress. Despite the importance of this function, the social position of the artisan within the city is a subordinate one, a feature of virtually all civilizations. This subordination is expressed in an ideology which valorizes the holy, the heroic and the noble as against the merely skillful, the intellectual and the reflective as against the merely technical. This ideology, Leroi-Gourhan speculates, may have deep psychological roots, deriving from a more fundamental distinction between the hand and the mind, technics and language. It is expressed in mythical figures such as Vulcan, the god of fire, all-powerful and marginal, feared and ridiculed by the other gods (*GP*, I, pp. 238–49).

The foundation of the first cities is seen as the point at which the evolution of technology takes off, social organization acting as mediator and multiplier of the dialogue between the physical human and the material world. Morphologically, the structural configuration of the city is compared to that of the biological organism, consisting of an aggregation of specialized cells forming organs serving the different sections of the vital economy, a body whose separate parts are increasingly subordinated to the whole, with overall power concentrated in the head. The archaeological evidence relating to proto-historical periods reveals a remarkable uniformity in this 'dispositif fonctionnel', one in which 'l'injustice sociale est l'image négative du triomphe sur le milieu naturel' (*GP*, I, p. 250). While structurally the city will change its form during the industrial revolution – breaking up into geographically dispersed industrial cities linked to a traditional centre – functionally the system will continue to operate as a stratified 'artificial socio-technical organism' in which the individual is increasingly subservient to the ends of the collective. The exploitation of the individual by the social organism – or *super*-organism, as it becomes in the post-industrial-revolution period – is mirrored in its exploitation of the natural environment. While the social unit of the primitive group is presented as existing 'in equilibrium' with its environment, the increasingly effective exploitation of natural resources by industrial civilization creates a chronic disequilibrium: 'Les rapports entre production, consommation et matière laissent prévoir que l'homme consomme de mieux en mieux, mais de manière irrémédiable, sa propre substance, c'est-à-dire ce qui lui vient du milieu naturel' (*GP*, I, p. 259). Leroi-Gourhan concludes that the 'zoological equilibrium' achieved during the long process of human evolution has been replaced, from the Upper Palaeolithic onwards, by a 'new equilibrium', mediated by the ethnic group or 'nation'. The problem is the mismatch between the physical human, which by the stage of *homo sapiens* has reached the limits of its physiological and mental evolution, and the socio-technical infrastructure which both protects (envelops) and exploits the human. Essentially a predatory mammal, in society the human animal becomes alternately hunter and prey, the effects of natural aggression magnified through technical creations. While these technical achievements, projected into the future, are likely to ensure the complete triumph of humanity over the natural environment, the result will not be some materialist utopia but an ecological dystopia: 'la dernière poche de pétrole vidée pour cuire la dernière poignée d'herbe mangée avec le dernier rat' (*GP*, I, p. 260).

Leroi-Gourhan's analysis of the city as both super-organism and machine (*dispositif*) continues from the point of view of the 'humanization' or 'domestication' of time and space. In common with many animals, the human relationship to space is characterized by two tendencies: the construction of a shelter offering a refuge from the external environment; and the periodic exploration of the environment for the acquisition of resources. The separation and alternation between internal and external space, shelter and territory, provide the fundamental spatial and temporal coordinates within which humans and animals with similar patterns of behaviour are able to achieve a degree of physical and psychical 'equilibrium'. However, for humans the relationship between the two modes of spatial behaviour is historically a variable one, depending on the stage of technical and social development. Up to the Palaeolithic, their perception of space is predominantly *itinerant*: 'Le nomade chasseur-cueilleur saisit la surface de son territoire à travers ses trajets'. Following the introduction of agriculture, this perception becomes a *radial* one: 'l'agriculteur sédentaire construit le monde en cercles concentriques autour de son grenier' (*GP*, II, p. 157). The spatial perception of agricultural-pastoral societies informs the architectural plan of cities, organized geometrically in relation to the natural coordinates of sky, earth and the four cardinal directions. With the progress of urbanization, this humanization of space is accompanied by the increasing domestication of time. While in pre- and early agricultural societies the measurement of time remains calibrated on the concrete reference points of seasonal variation and astronomical time, the social and spatial organization of the city permits the emergence of a more abstract treatment of time in which the duration of daily existence is divided into increasingly smaller units. Quite logically, the social groups in which this regulation of time is most developed are the religious and military elites (*GP*, II, pp. 145–6).

Leroi-Gourhan notes the remarkable consistency of the basic topographical configuration of the city, from its earliest recorded forms to the present day. However, a decisive threshold is crossed in the eighteenth century and the beginnings of the industrial revolution. In terms of perceptions of time and space, this has to do with the individual's mode of 'integration' into the urban landscape. In the eighteenth century, such integration remains relatively balanced: even in the largest cities the daily existence of the inhabitant unfolds at a rhythm limited by the distance one is able to walk or travel by horse. The industrial revolution, with its defining technology of steam power, transforms both the shape and scale of urban topography. In particular, the revolution in transportation leads to the formation of the industrial city and the delocalization of the worker – the city becomes a utilitarian 'agglomeration', consisting of 'd'immenses espaces humanisés de manière inhumaine, dans lesquels les individus subissent le double effet de leur désintégration technique et spatiale' (*GP*, II, p. 177). While it is an efficient instrument of the social organism, the nineteenth-century city creates a 'pathological disequilibrium' through its alienation of the human individual and its extensive pollution of the environment. This dystopic development of the city continues into the present day, where there is not only a reduction in the vital space available to the individual, but also a generalization of urban time, first through the extension of transportation systems, and more recently through the normalization of a time aligned to the rhythms of mass communication. Following the logic of this trajectory, Leroi-Gourhan's vision of the potential future of urbanized humanity is a singularly dark one:

> Un temps et un espace surhumanisé correspondraient au fonctionnement idéalement synchrone de tous les individus spécialisés chacun dans sa fonction et son espace. Par le biais du symbolisme spatio-temporel la société humaine retrouverait l'organisation des sociétés animales les plus parfaites, celles où l'individu n'existe que comme cellule. L'évolution corporelle et cérébrale de l'espèce humaine paraissait la faire échapper par l'extériorisation de l'outil et de la mémoire au sort du polypier ou de la fourmi; il n'est pas interdit de penser que la liberté de l'individu ne représente qu'une étape et que la domestication du temps et de l'espace entraîne l'assujettissement parfait de toutes les particules de l'organisme supra-individuel. (*GP*, II, p. 186)

Thus the idea of humanization appears progressively to take on a different sense and value as the exposition of *Le Geste* develops. In early chapters, humanization refers to the gradual evolution, within the hominid sequence, towards *homo sapiens*, an evolution inseparably biological and cultural. In this phase of human development, humanization is something which happens, reflexively, to the human animal, and ends with the biological stabilization of the species with *homo sapiens*. From this point onwards, the process of humanization is increasingly 'externalized', in terms of more complex forms of social organization and a more extensive integration of groups into the environment. Leroi-Gourhan's evaluation of this phase of human development is not entirely positive. While the forms of social organization that develop in the wake of the agricultural-pastoral revolution provide the conditions for an exponential increase in technical development, their negative counterpart is the systematic exploitation of the individual and, especially following the industrial revolution, the decimation of the natural environment. Humanization in the post-agricultural phase is therefore equated with domestication, not simply the transitive domestication of plant and animal life, but also the reflexive self-domestication of human life in time and space. In its extreme development, as projected in the passage above, it results in the paradoxical reversal of the process of 'liberation' which has characterized the general evolution of human and technical systems. We shall return to this question of freedom in the conclusion of this article, but first we shall analyze what Leroi-Gourhan says about the history of technology itself, in particular with reference to his concept of *externalization*, applied to the key domains of human memory and human gesture.

Operational memory and the history of technology

Leroi-Gourhan's account of the co-evolution of language, technology and society in the first part of *Le Geste* draws on palaeontology, comparative anatomy, neurology, archaeology, ethnology and comparative technology to provide empirical facts – in some cases very recently discovered facts – against which Leroi-Gourhan's analysis of human evolution is constantly checked. In terms of conceptualization, this analysis is informed by the biological analogy which was critical to the description of technical systems in *Évolution et techniques*: the evolution of technology *imitates* the evolution of living systems; the historical development of human society is *like* the growth of an organism. However, there is another layer of conceptualization at work in *Le Geste* which both complements and complicates the biological analogy. This second level of conceptualization is influenced by developments in post-war scientific and technological culture which are most clearly formalized in the discourse of *cybernetics*.

The best short definition of cybernetics is provided in the subtitle of Norbert Wiener's seminal book, *Cybernetics, or Control and Communication in the Animal and the Machine* (1948, 1961).[5] Cybernetics originated in the convergent

---

5. Norbert Wiener, *Cybernetics or Control and Communication in the Animal and the Machine* (New York: Technology Press, 1948).

developments of communications and engineering technologies in the first half of the twentieth century. In cybernetic systems, the small quantities of energy required for the transmission of information (communication) are used to activate and direct (control) the relatively higher magnitudes of energy powering the movement and articulation of different types of *mechanism*. Expressed schematically, the cybernetic system involves a coupling of the *programme* (a set of instructions for a given sequence of actions or events) and the mechanism via a channel of communication, the essential requirement being that (i) the message or signal transmitted through the channel is expressed in the right language; (ii) the channel itself is relatively free of 'noise'. The simple, linear control system, consisting of programme plus mechanism plus channel of communication, is closed to its environment: it is 'senseless', the programme is 'unaware' of the effects of its execution. In the real world, the effects of environmental variation and perturbation mean that a form of real-time adjustment is necessary in order to maintain the ideal execution of the programme. This is achieved by circularizing the channel of communication between programme and mechanism: part of the output of the mechanism is 'fed back' to its input from the programme, thus providing the latter with a kind of 'sensing' of its effects and a means of measuring and, if necessary, reducing the divergence between (ideal) input and (actual) output. Properly cybernetic control therefore consists not simply in a linear chain of cause and effect from programme to mechanism, but more specifically in a circular or reflexive process of regulation described as *feedback*.

Wiener describes the new generation of reflex mechanisms typical of cybernetics as a Second Industrial Revolution, in which the defining technology is *electronics*. While the history of automatic control systems predates the twentieth century, the remarkable advances in electronics in the years preceding and following the Second World War enabled an increasingly effective integration of the electronic circuit into automatic systems, allowing for greater flexibility in the coupling of programme and mechanism and faster and more precise regulation of the mechanism. By the mid-1960s, the 'component revolution' in electronics had seen an evolution in circuit components from valve to solid state (transistor) to integrated (monolithic) circuits over a period of less than 20 years. This revolution permitted a marked increase in the speed, reliability and durability of circuit components, and also a dramatic reduction in their size.

It is important to remember that for Wiener the aim of cybernetics was not simply to describe the technological revolution of the post-war years, but also to generalize it. As the subtitle of his book indicates, cybernetics is about control and communication in the *animal* as well as the machine. The increasing complexity of 'intelligent' or reflexive machine systems also has a revealing effect, to the extent that it throws light on the functional centrality of control, communication and feedback in biological systems, from the cell to the central nervous system to the brain. Equally importantly for our reading of Leroi-Gourhan, Wiener's book does not simply describe the realms of the animal and the machine as homologous but separate instances of cybernetic function, but also looks at the *coupling* of the human and the machine, an association which had assumed entirely new levels of complexity.

The intellectual and cultural impact of cybernetics in post-war France was extensive. The information-theoretical side of cybernetics played an important role in the early development of structuralism; more generally, cybernetics contributed to the growth in theoretical reflection on technology and the history of technology which was a specific feature of the post-war years. Cybernetics is never explicitly referenced in *Le Geste*, but its influence on Leroi-Gourhan's conceptualization of the evolution and history of technology in his post-war work is clear. We have already noted the cybernetically-inflected vocabulary (*command*, *control*, *coordination*) of the description of the coupling of nervous system and body articulation in vertebrate evolution, and the closeness of the analysis of the circular relationship between brain, hand and tool in human evolution to the concept of feedback. In the second part of *Le Geste*, the conceptual input of cybernetics becomes still more apparent as the focus of analysis shifts from the question of language and technics to the question of *memory* and technics.

In the seventh chapter, 'La Libération de la mémoire', Leroi-Gourhan turns to the question of *operational* memory, which underlies the behaviour of the zoological group in activities necessary to its material subsistence and development. Here, the concept of the *chaîne opératoire*, previously applied to human technical activity, is extended to animal behaviour in general. Every zoological group has its own 'traditions', or collective memory, in which specific operational sequences are stored. This type of memory storage is described as a *programme*: a specific stimulus or situation will lead to the activation (*déclenchement*) and unfolding (*déroulement*) of the sequence (*chaîne*) of actions prescribed in the programme. This cybernetic conceptualization of species behaviour complicates the traditional opposition between intelligence and instinct, human and animal behaviour. From this perspective, the nervous system is viewed as a collection of programmes mediating between internal and external environments:

> Il s'agit donc plus d'une question d'appareillage nerveux que de la présence d'une vertu propre à la condition animale. Plus précisément le système nerveux n'est pas une machine à fabriquer de l'instinct, mais à répondre aux sollicitations internes et externes stimuli en construisant des programmes. (*GP*, II, p. 13)

The difference between animal forms is therefore conceived in terms of relative degrees of *programming*. In the most elementary forms of invertebrate, the programme consists in short sequences determining a limited range of stereotyped actions which maintain the organism in relative equilibrium with its environment.

In higher forms such as insects – for example, bees or ants – there is evidence of considerably more complex, genetically predetermined programmes which result in highly organized patterns of behaviour. Finally, while the behaviour of most vertebrate forms remains highly predetermined, in the higher vertebrates, especially in carnivores and primates, there is the possibility of *selection* between operational sequences and the *checking* (*contrôle*) of their appropriateness to a given situation, in other words, the possibility of individual learning and experience. For each of these levels of animate life, especially its more elementary forms, Leroi-Gourhan suggests that it should be possible to construct an electronic mechanism simulating relative degrees of reflex behaviour. This kind of modelling of biological systems, typical of cybernetics, draws attention to the functional similarities between animal and mechanical systems, in particular with respect to automatic processes. Its rhetorical purpose in Leroi-Gourhan's argument is to clarify the somewhat vague and vitalistic concept of 'instinct' by attempting to provide a more precise and articulated image of levels of automatism in living systems.

Leroi-Gourhan distinguishes between three levels of operational behaviour in humans. The first level is described as *automatic*, relating to those elements of reflex behaviour which are thoroughly predetermined by the genetic heritage of the species. In psychological terms, this level of behaviour is part of the individual unconscious, it is not accessible to direct perception or intuition. It forms the biological bedrock upon which ethnic groups superimpose their distinct traditions through education. The second level of operational behaviour is described as *machinal*, and refers to the operational sequences acquired through individual experience and education and embedded in gestural behaviour and language. This kind of behaviour is subconscious, consisting of the stereotyped gestures which ensure the individual's balanced integration into the social group: bodily posture, eating habits, hygiene, professional practices, interpersonal relations. The elementary operational sequences supporting these different categories of everyday behaviour are acquired early, through imitation, experimentation and verbal communication. Leroi-Gourhan describes them as unfolding in a 'pénombre psychique' of which the individual subject is only subliminally aware. They constitute a kind of second nature, vital to the survival of the individual and the group in the sense that they replace the automatisms of biological 'instinct'. It would be impossible to exercise an entirely conscious control of these operational sequences, since this would entail the perpetual reinvention of each gesture. Thus these programmes represent an economy of thought, freeing the mind from the burden of constant attention. On the other hand, they are deeply implanted in the everyday behaviour of individuals, never able entirely to escape their initial conditioning by the ethnic group (*GP*, II, pp. 26–30).

Mechanical behaviour is already distinctively human, involving the substitution or supplementation of genetic determination by ethnic determination. However, this second level of operational behaviour is a necessary but not sufficient condition of human development. The third and definitively human level is fully conscious, *lucid* behaviour, in which language is predominant, necessary for the higher-level supervision or maintenance of operational sequences. If the majority of the individual's daily actions are governed by the subconscious execution of programmes elaborated by the group, accidental breaks in the operating sequence, or *chain* of gestures, do occur. In these cases, to continue the metaphor, lucid intervention is required in order to adjust and repair the defective chains in the sequence. Leroi-Gourhan links this reflexive component of operational behaviour with what he describes as the distinctive feature of the (modern) human brain, the ability to make comparisons (*confrontations*), which is in turn dependent on the capacity for symbolic thought. This means that not only is lucid behaviour involved in the cybernetic regulation of the operational sequence – it checks deviations from the sequence – its correcting function also carries within it the potential for *improvement*. This circular relationship between the instances of mechanical and lucid behaviour is therefore proposed as the essential condition for the social and technical development of human societies. Whereas the function of the social group is basically a conservative one – to preserve and perpetuate the programmes governing operational behaviour – the lucid intervention of the individual subject generates new programmes, leading to innovation. This dialectic, or rather, *circuit*, between individual and group is made possible and maintained through the mediation of language, which allows humans to place the programme outside of the individual, in a social memory. If the tool is characterized by its separation and detachment from the human body, even more fundamentally the symbol represents a detachment and *mise à distance* from lived experience. With this analogy and distinction in mind, Leroi-Gourhan therefore qualifies and reformulates what has been one of the guiding arguments of *Le Geste*:

> Toute l'évolution humaine concourt à placer en dehors de l'homme ce qui, dans le reste du monde animal, répond à l'adaptation spécifique. Le fait matériel le plus frappant est certainement la 'libération' de l'outil, mais en réalité le fait fondamental est la libération du verbe et cette propriété unique que l'homme possède de placer sa mémoire en dehors de lui-même, dans l'organisme social. (*GP*, II, p. 34)

Leroi-Gourhan proceeds to explore this human phenomenon of *externalization* with reference to the historical evolution of the tool and the accompanying expansion of human memory.

In its most general form the cybernetic system consists of the programme and the mechanism, linked by a channel of communication. Leroi-Gourhan's examination of operational behaviour first focuses on the programmatic component of the system, viewing the operational sequence as a kind of virtual memory written into the nervous system or deposited in the social organism. He then moves to the mechanism, to the physical interface between the programme and the material environment. Typically, Leroi-Gourhan's analysis is a 'bottom-up' one, returning to the elementary forms of mechanism found in the animal world. In primates and humans, the primary interface for technical activity in the anterior field is the hand. The hand itself is an evolutionary archaism, to the extent that it has not become as narrowly specialized as the organs of other species, but this relative lack of specialization is also the condition of its flexibility as a technical instrument. In both primates and humans, the essential gestural operation is prehension, the grasping of objects between the fingers or the palm and fingers. The hand can also be used as a weapon and, as an articulated extension of the arm, to impart movements of rotation and translation.

Leroi-Gourhan repeats that there is no fundamental difference in the anatomical configuration of the hand or its range of operational possibilities in primates and humans. The essential difference lies not in the mechanism, but between the mechanism and the programme, in increased tactile sensitivity and neuromotor control in humans. This qualitative difference is evident in the technical behaviour of early Anthropians, which marks the progressive 'emigration' of the mechanical operations of the hand into the tool: 'la main humaine est humaine par ce qui s'en détache et non par ce qu'elle est' (*GP*, II, pp. 40–1). From this point onwards, the hand enters into an extended dialogue with the material world mediated by increasingly more complex mechanisms, culminating in the automatic (cybernetic) machines of the mid-twentieth century. This history is presented as a sequence of 'externalizations', and therefore, 'liberations' of human manual activity, consisting of five main stages, which may be represented schematically as follows:

• Hand tool (direct manual operation)
• Manual machine (mediated amplification of manual gesture)
• Naturally-powered machine (animal or elemental motors; human control)
• Industrial machine (artificial motors; mainly human control)
• Cybernetic machine (artificial motors; automatic control)

The first stage of manual-technical evolution involves the direct engagement of the hand in the operation of the tool, orienting the tool and providing the motor force necessary for its percussive action – here, Leroi-Gourhan refers back to his analysis of the elementary categories of percussion in *L'Homme et la matière*. This stage of technical development covers the major part of human evolution up to and including the Upper Palaeolithic. The second stage is, according to Leroi-Gourhan, decisive, probably coincident with the rise of *homo sapiens*. This is the stage of the simple 'manual machine', in which part of the motor gesture is transferred to the mechanism – for example, the lever, later the sling, followed by the bow, traps, pulleys. These are devices which extend and amplify human gesture but still require manual intervention. The third stage of technical development, beginning in the Neolithic period, corresponds with the use of animal, and later elemental forces (wind, water) to drive more complex machines. This is a decisive stage of motor liberation: the role of the hand becomes that of initiator and controller of a sequence of operations programmed into the machine. In historical times, the systematic harnessing of animal and elemental energy is the basis of the techno-economic domination of the major civilizations up to the eighteenth century. However, there are physical and geographical limits to the use of these natural sources of power. The next major stage of technical development is the artificial motor, corresponding with the industrial revolution and the invention of the steam engine, which permits an exponential increase in the generation of power and a liberation of the machine from naturally (geographically) determined sources of power. This advanced stage of technical civilization is, however, not the ultimate stage: the machines of the industrial revolution are powerful but not 'intelligent', they lack a 'nervous system', and still require a high degree of human supervision; while they are automotive, their mechanism is powered by a single, centralized motor (*GP*, II, pp. 43–51).

A new generation of machines emerges in the twentieth century which do not require human intervention or control, and are activated by a number of power sources. If previous stages of technical evolution marked the progressive externalization of human gesture, its movement from the tool to an ever-proliferating family of machines, then the current age appears to represent a final stage of externalization, that of the human muscular and nervous system, and indeed the brain itself, in the fully programmed, automatic machine:

> Les perfectionnements dans l'usage de l'électricité et surtout le développement de l'électronique ont suscité, à moins d'un siècle de la mutation des machines automotrices, une mutation au-delà de laquelle il ne reste plus grand-chose à extérioriser dans l'être humain. Une transformation radicale s'est produite dans la machine par le développement des petits moteurs, celui des cellules sensibles à l'action lumineuse, celui des mémoires, des transistors, de tous les dispositifs miniaturisés. Cet arsenal disparate fournit, par pièces détachées, les éléments d'un assemblage étrangement comparable à l'assemblage biologique. Alors que la machinerie du XIXᵉ siècle, avec ses sources d'énergie volumineuses, conduisait la force unique par d'énormes systèmes de transmission vers des organes aveugles, la mécanique actuelle construit, en multipliant les sources de force, un véritable système musculaire, commandé par un véritable système nerveux, dont les connexions avec un organe qui est un véritable cerveau sensito-moteur assure le déroulement d'un programme opératoire complexe. (*GP*, II, pp. 51–2)

From the vantage point of the mid-1960s, one can see a century of accelerated technical development, in which the 'mutation' of steam power, the defining technology of the Industrial Revolution, is superseded by electrical power and the proliferation of electronic devices, from motors to sensors to operating programmes. This is the Second Industrial Revolution described in Wiener's *Cybernetics*, characterized by the progressive miniaturization and differentiation of machine components. The result is an uncanny resemblance of cybernetic machines to the biological organism: the distributed operation of the power source in increasingly small electrical motors is compared to a muscular system; the development of different forms of electronic sensor provides the machine with the equivalent of a sensory system; in their turn, these motor and sensory systems are connected to a 'nervous system' which both controls the machine and responds to information from its sensory organs, its field of action determined by a higher-level operating programme which constitutes the machine's 'memory'. This is more than a simple analogy: it expresses a functional homology, a structural and ontological continuity between living and artificial systems. As Leroi-Gourhan remarks: 'Il est bien difficile, pour un biologiste, de ne pas mettre en parallèle la mécanique d'animaux déjà évolués avec ces organismes qui ont fini par constituer un monde vivant parallèle' (*GP*, II, p. 56).

While the miniaturization of the motor and the development of the sensor are important in this technological revolution, the determining role is attributed to the automatic programme. The history of the programme is relatively recent, dating back to the European Middle Ages and the development of more precise techniques for measuring time. From the medieval period, clockwork technology provides the 'favourable milieu' for the construction of programmed machines capable of executing a series of predetermined actions, culminating in sophisticated eighteenth-century automata. However, these programmes are part of the mechanism, written into the relationships between the parts of the machine, and cannot be changed. A decisive stage in the history of automation is reached when the programme is separated from the mechanism. The classic example of this development, at the start of the nineteenth century, is the Jacquard loom, operated by punched cards external to the mechanism and constituting a central 'memory' which can be modified at will to direct different operational sequences. However, only in the previous twenty years, claims Leroi-Gourhan, thanks to unprecedented advances in electronics, has the automatic programme been able to achieve a level of complexity and flexibility approaching that of the nervous system, in the new generation of cybernetic machines (*GP*, II, pp. 53–6).

The comparatively short history of the automatic programme can be situated within the considerably longer history of the externalization of human memory. Here, Leroi-Gourhan delineates five periods or stages of development, corresponding to the progressive delegation of collective memory to external supports. The first and universal stage consists in the oral transmission of a society's intellectual capital, the preservation and replication of the operational sequences essential to its material survival. The verbal transmission of a tradition of techniques remains the predominant mode of memorization until relatively late. A further stage of externalization occurs with the appearance of writing, which Leroi-Gourhan associates historically with the invention of metallurgy, the emergence of the first urbanized centres and the formation of highly hierarchical societies. At first the preserve of an elite, the technology of writing permits an exponential increase in the recording and conservation of collective memory, in particular following the introduction of printing. For the individual, this massive expansion of social memory brings with it the problem of orientation – by the eighteenth century, it has become impossible to navigate the ever-growing, diversifying corpus of human knowledge deposited in the book. The technical response to this problem is a further extension of the technology of writing through the introduction of peripheral devices – marginal notes, alphabetical indexes, analytical tables of contents, encyclopedias, dictionaries. This is followed, in the nineteenth century, by the development of sophisticated filing systems enabling the operator to access and cross-reference information from a multiplicity of sources. If the book is comparable to the hand-tool, the filing system is like a manual machine: both require the animating presence of the human subject. With the introduction of punched-card filing systems, the externalization of human memory enters a new phase, comparable to that of the first automatic machines. The qualitative advance of these systems is that, like the human mind, they are not only capable of holding memories, but also of making correlations between these memories. Unlike the human mind, their capacity for storage and correlation is virtually infinite. Using different technical means, but following the same principles, the 'electronic brains' of the contemporary period are able to perform the logical operations of comparison, judgement and decision based on an accumulated 'experience', with a speed and precision that is beyond human measure. As Leroi-Gourhan notes, this technology is still in its early phases, and there is no reason why, supported by the continued progress in electronics, this particular tendency in human externalization should not ultimately lead to the integral simulation and replacement of the higher faculties of the mind (*GP*, II, pp. 63–76).

While not teleological, Leroi-Gourhan's history of technology is deterministic to the extent that the sequence of externalizations is not an arbitrary development but the necessary product of the intersection of the human organism and the material world. It expresses what, in *Milieu et techniques*, Leroi-Gourhan described as the technical tendency, the technological determinism which dictates that humans will engage with their external environment in predictable and convergent ways, and that the aggregate tendency of technical evolution will be towards an increasingly effective engagement with that environment. The difference in *Le Geste* is that this process of technical development is re-conceptualized in cybernetic terms, as a series of shifts in the instance of control, coordination and computation from the human to the machine, the machine finally replicating and integrating the functions of the human nervous system and even the brain. Like all histories of technology, this account is historically determined to the extent that it is written from the viewpoint of the defining technologies of the time. Yet, there is a sense in which the cybernetic paradigm could be conceptually definitive, describing universal features of both living and artificial systems: the coupling of programme and mechanism through the processes of control, communication and feedback. Consequently, the advanced externalizations of body and mind described in *Le Geste* are revealing, throwing retrospective light on the history of technology alongside the biological evolution which preceded it.

Leroi-Gourhan insists on the neutrality of this history of technology: 'Il n'y a aucun jugement de valeur à émettre sur un processus évolutif' (*GP*, II, p. 59). However, just as the value attached to the process of 'humanization' appears to shift as one moves from pre- and protohistorical to historical times, so here the process of externalization and its correlate, *liberation*, are viewed with increasing ambivalence, in particular within the context of modern machine civilization. This ambivalence relates not simply to the subordination of the individual to the socio-technical organism and the decimation of the natural environment, but more fundamentally to what Leroi-Gourhan believes to be the progressive divergence of the biological reality of the human, described as a 'living fossil', from the technological world which has become, quite literally, its material externalization. Although there is biological stabilization of the human species with the appearance of *homo sapiens*, this does not mean a fixed, internal 'essence' of the human in relation to the externalized world. If humans remain biologically the same through the different stages of technological evolution described above, nevertheless at each stage it could be said that humanity is *affected* by the world it has created – in Leroi-Gourhan's words, it becomes more or less a different species (*GP*, II, p. 50).

The question is, therefore, what effects successive modes of technological substitution may have on the human animal, and more precisely on the cybernetic circuit of gesture and speech, hand and brain, which has defined the human. On the one hand, it is logical that the process of externalization that is specific to human evolution should affect what is traditionally considered to be the motor of that evolution, the brain or mind. Here, Leroi-Gourhan clearly does not subscribe to the conventional humanist or essentialist critique of the mechanization of human functions, nor does he give any credence to the science-fictional scenario of an intelligent machine revolution that would replace humans – as always, the ultimate threat of violence lies within the species itself (*GP*, II, p. 52). On the other hand, his diagnosis of the current state of *homo sapiens* is that there is something out of balance, a mismatch between the biological infrastructure of the human as it has evolved in concert with the tool, and the technological world itself which, in every sense of the word, exceeds the human. This brings us back to the concept of *equilibrium*, which was a central, if unarticulated, element of Leroi-Gourhan's account of the evolution of forms. This concept is especially important as Leroi-Gourhan begins to extrapolate from the past and present of human evolution to its future, to the possible forms that *l'homme du futur* might assume. Inevitably, his extrapolation is based on what he believes humanity has become in the present, a species out of step with its externalized world: 'l'ajustement des individus qui conservent le cerveau et la carcasse corporelle de l'homme de Cro-Magnon se fait par une distorsion grandissante' (*GP*, II, pp. 57–8). In particular, there is the question of what happens, or has happened, to the hand. The body plan, especially the hand turned to technical production, are the evolutionary singularities which enable human cognition. With the advent of advanced computing and control systems, the externalization of body functions has reached a point where one can envisage their ultimate subsumption in machine systems, rendering the body redundant. The atrophy of the body, particularly the hand, is, for Leroi-Gourhan, the atrophy of thought. He describes the 'regression' of the hand, which clearly troubles him:

> Il serait de peu d'importance que diminue le rôle de cet organe de fortune qu'est la main si tout ne montrait pas que son activité est étroitement solidaire de l'équilibre des territoires cérébraux qui l'intéressent. [...] Ne pas avoir à penser avec ses dix doigts équivaut à manquer d'une partie de sa pensée normalement, philogénétiquement humaine. Il existe donc à l'échelle des individus sinon à celle de l'espèce, dès à présent, un problème de la régression de la main. (*GP*, II, pp. 61–2)

The withdrawal of the hand from articulated interaction with the world threatens to become a species-wide phenomenon, ultimately affecting the future evolution of the human body and nervous system. Whether or not one shares Leroi-Gourhan's views about the redundancy of the hand, or indeed the future development of human evolution, it is interesting that he conceives such a shift in terms of a *disequilibrium* – under this scenario, neurologically the 'equilibrium' between the areas of the pre-motor cortex that control manual articulation is disrupted. The atrophy of digital manipulation means the loss of an evolved, and uniquely human, capacity for thought. At this future stage, paradoxically the human will no longer be properly human – it will have become something else.

   This pessimism regarding the future of humanity haunts the concluding chapter, appropriately titled 'La Liberté imaginaire et le sort de l'*Homo sapiens*'. Leroi-Gourhan anticipates four potential outcomes for the human species:

1. Atomic annihilation. This particular threat is a corollary of the evolutionary 'mismatch' described above. According to Leroi-Gourhan, the advanced technological knowledge that has allowed us to master atomic energy is not matched by the capacity to master our own aggression, an effective adaptation for the hunter-predator of prehistoric times, but a dangerous residual trait in contemporary humanity.
2. The end of evolution. This refers not to biological extinction as such, but to the Jesuit philosopher-paleontologist Teilhard de Chardin's 'Omega point', the idea of an apocalyptical termination of the evolutionary process. This mystical vision of the fate of humankind has the limitation of all

apocalyptical thought: even as one waits for the end of history, there remains the mundane task of organizing the world.

3. Genetic alteration. In other words, the long-term adaptation to the evolutionary 'mismatch' between a phylogenetically stable *homo sapiens* and the metamorphic evolution of its artefacts. For Leroi-Gourhan, such an adaptation would signal the ultimate disappearance of *homo sapiens* as we know it.

4. Active intervention. This final alternative is an existential one involving a conscious *prise de conscience* of the situation of humanity and an assertion of its desire to remain human. This means rethinking both the relationship between individual and society and our relationship with the natural world, in particular with respect to demographic growth and environmental change. Actively addressing these problems amounts to a readjustment, or *rebalancing* of the disparate forces which determine the contemporary situation of *homo sapiens*. (*GP*, II, pp. 267–8)

While the first three scenarios envisaged in the conclusion of *Le Geste* are in their different ways *passive* responses to the fate of humankind, the fourth scenario is a pragmatic and voluntarist one. It is visibly the solution favoured by Leroi-Gourhan; indeed, he claims that it is inevitable. This is because – in the very last words of the book – 'l'espèce est encore trop liée à ses fondements pour ne pas chercher spontanément l'équilibre qui l'a portée à devenir humaine' (*GP*, II, p. 268). While one might agree with Leroi-Gourhan's quasi-existentialist view of human evolution, which emphasizes our collective responsibility for managing the material world and (therefore) our own future within it, nevertheless the formulation of this final sentence remains conceptually problematic. This is due to the conceptual stress placed upon the term 'equilibrium', which, by the conclusion of *Le Geste*, has become thoroughly overdetermined. The concept of equilibrium is operative throughout Leroi-Gourhan's narrative, governing descriptions of structural and functional adaptation in vertebrate and hominid anatomies, neurological complexification relating to human manual articulation, the cybernetic relationship between hand and tool and the relationship between individuals and the different forms of social organization mediating technological change. Yet, unlike more explicitly marked concepts such as externalization, liberation or humanization, 'equilibrium' is never properly foregrounded; while this concept may be effective in describing aspects of biological form and functional adaptation, its extension to qualitatively different levels of human organization is not self-evident. The implication of the final sentence of *Le Geste* is that humanity possesses a *natural* point of bio-cultural equilibrium to which it must spontaneously seek to return, whereas the macroscopic narrative of the book has in fact described a series of departures from equilibrium which have at each stage *altered* the mental and physiological configuration of the human animal.

It is important to remember, however, that Leroi-Gourhan's analysis of human technical evolution is intentionally a two-dimensional one, focusing on the attributes which may distinguish humans from the higher primates, but which paradoxically, in the age of cybernetics, may not ultimately distinguish them from their machines. As he notes, the field of discussion of the first two parts of *Le Geste* works primarily within 'un triangle main-langage-cortex sensito-moteur' (*GP*, II, p. 76). The third dimension of human evolution is that of aesthetics. In a further recalibration of his definition of the human, Leroi-Gourhan will argue that 'l'art est un meilleur instrument de mesure de l'humanité que la technique' (*GP*, II, p. 218).[6]

---

6.   Aesthetics is the subject of the following (fourth) chapter in Johnson's book 'The Evolution of Forms'. [JS]

Nottingham French Studies 59.3 (2020): 289–310
DOI: 10.3366/nfs.2020.0292
© University of Nottingham
www.euppublishing.com/nfs

LA TÉLÉ-COMMANDE

YVES GILONNE ⓘ

O Captain! my Captain!

L'oubli de l'analogie

Christopher Johnson, l'un des premiers à révéler l'importance de la cybernétique et son impact sur le champ épistémologique de la pensée française, dévoile son statut paradoxal: « pervasive in its influence on contemporary theory and relatively forgotten as an event »[1]. Si l'influence de la cybernétique se mesure ainsi à son oubli, un certain nombre d'études[2] commencent à en éclairer les circonstances historiques que ce soit les conditions technoscientifiques de son développement autour du paradigme central d'*information* et ses implications philosophiques et sociales[3]; l'influence de la cybernétique sur le paysage intellectuel contemporain, du structuralisme au postmodernisme[4]; son rôle déterminant dans la genèse des sciences cognitives et de l'intelligence artificielle[5]; ou plus récemment, son impact sur la redéfinition des pratiques de modélisation interdisciplinaire dans la France des Trente Glorieuses[6]. D'aucuns évoquent l'acte de nomination de cette science émergente par Norbert Wiener en 1948[7] lors de la publication de son ouvrage éponyme *Cybernetics, or Control and Communication in the Animal and the Machine*, se contentant de rappeler, de façon anecdotique, l'étymologie du mot officiellement adopté en 1949 par les organisateurs des fameuses conférences Macy[8], sans mentionner l'analogie fondamentale entre *gouverner* et *piloter* qui la sous-tend et reste à ce jour inquestionnée.

---

1. Christopher Johnson, « Analogue Apollo, Cybernetics and the Space Age », *Paragraph*, 31: 3 (2008), 304–26 (p. 304).

2. Liste qui ne saurait être exhaustive, mais indique l'importance du champ conceptuel de la cybernétique.

3. Mathieu Triclot, *Le Moment cybernétique* (Paris: Champ-Vallon, 2008).

4. Céline Lafontaine, *L'Empire cybernétique* (Paris: Seuil, 2004).

5. Jean-Pierre Dupuy, *Aux origines des sciences cognitives* (Paris: La Découverte, 1999).

6. Ronan le Roux, *Une histoire de la cybernétique en France* (Paris: Classiques Garnier, 2018).

7. Triclot, *Le Moment cybernétique*, p. 13; Dupuy, *Aux origines des sciences cognitives*, p. 69; Lafontaine, *L'Empire cybernétique*, p. 40.

8. Lafontaine, *L'Empire cybernétique*, p. 40.

Cela est d'autant plus surprenant que l'usage de l'analogie ne se limite pas à l'acte de nomination de la cybernétique ou à un simple effet de style mais se situe au cœur de la « puissance performative »[9] de sa démarche comme l'indique notamment Pierre Dubarle dès 1948: « la science nouvelle suppose essentiellement la découverte et l'exploitation systématique des analogies. »[10] La cybernétique aurait notamment été conçue comme « science des analogies maitrisées entre organismes et machines »[11] et pour Katherine Hayles « across the range of Wiener's writings, the rhetorical trope that figures most importantly is analogy »[12], attirant souvent le reproche de manque de rigueur scientifique qu'il réfutera dans un fragment de 1950 intitulé « The Nature of Analogy »[13]. Ainsi, pour Johnson, la cybernétique introduit « an influential set of analogies between brain and machine [which] is both taken for granted and so pervasive that its history and the set of circumstances which favoured its acceptance has received little attention »[14]. L'oubli de l'analogie découle de son omniprésence acceptée au cœur de pratiques épistémiques contemporaines qui influent sur nos modes de représentation de la pensée et en régule un certain usage.

Ainsi, selon nous, le terme *cybernétique*, loin de se réduire à l'acte de nomination insignifiant que les études lui réservent, place la pensée au sein d'une analogie déterminante entre *gouverner* et *piloter* qui mérite attention d'autant plus que celle-ci a une histoire attestée au moins depuis Platon[15]. Sans doute l'étymologie était-elle un obstacle dans la mesure où elle offrait la caution d'un « naturel » à une analogie toujours déjà intégrée à la langue, allant de soi. Ainsi *gouverner* vit de l'oubli de l'analogie qui pourtant le fonde puisqu'il vient du grec *kybernao* (diriger un navire) qui donne *kybernetès* (capitaine, pilote). C'est donc « tout naturellement » que le terme a dû s'imposer à Wiener pour designer l'approche épistémologique émergente qui vise à déterminer des processus de contrôle *analogues* aux vivants et aux machines. Wiener lui-même reprend les deux éléments (gouverner, diriger un navire) de l'analogie puisqu'il explique que le

---

9.   Christopher Johnson, « "French" Cybernetics », *French Studies*, 69:1 (2015), 60–78 (p. 60).

10. Père Dominique Dubarle, 'Une nouvelle science: la cybernétique. Vers une machine à gouverner le monde', *Le Monde*, 28 December 1948, p. 47.

11. Dupuy, *Aux origines des sciences cognitives*, p. 42.

12. N. Katherine Hayles, *How We Became Posthuman* (Chicago: University of Chicago Press, 1999), p. 91.

13. Ibid., p. 97.

14. Johnson, « Analogue Apollo », p. 318.

15. On notera l'absence d'étude approfondie de sa genèse chez Platon: « Though Plato's use of the simile regularly earns a footnote in books on political philosophy, it has not received the attention accorded the central similes in the *Republic*. » Davit Keyt, « Plato and the Ship of State » dans *The Blackwell Guide to Plato's Republic*, dir. par Gerasimos Santas (Oxford: Blackwell, 2006), p.189.

terme *cybernétique* fut créé à la fois en hommage à l'article « *On Governors* » de Clerk Maxwell sur le comportement des régulateurs (dispositifs de contrôle de la vitesse des moteurs à vapeur), et car « the steering engines of a ship are one of the earliest and best-developed forms of feedback mechanisms. »[16] Par ailleurs, comme le rappelle Johnson, deux des principaux médiateurs de la cybernétique en France, Guilbauld et Ducroq, « refer to the analogy of the ship as a principle of explanation »[17] et chez Ducroq « the general structure of the cybernetic system [is] based on his analogy of the command sequence of the ship »[18], semblant indiquer un schème de penser qui ne se limite pas à sa simple valeur illustrative.

Cette surdétermination de l'analogie nautique découle aussi du fait que toute analogie repose sur une *logistique des transports*, cherchant à *véhiculer* un sens d'un domaine à l'autre et à s'assurer de son *arrivée à bon port*. L'analogie nautique sert donc de matrice à toute analogie et le *couplage* capitaine-navire/pensée-corps, génère d'autres appareils analogiques tels que animal-machine, cerveau-ordinateur, grâce auxquels la cybernétique souhaite abolir la distance entre disciplines, entre le concret et l'abstrait, entre le corps et le monde. Or si la cybernétique croit *piloter* l'analogie à ses fins, nous verrons que la cybernétique est à son tour portée par cette analogie qui échappe à son contrôle.

L'analogie nautique est donc bien un paradigme technique et théorique central pour la cybernétique qui efface l'écart entre *gouverner* et *piloter* au nom d'une universalité qui commande de loin ce que penser veut dire jusqu'à ce jour. L'analogie nautique, sacrifiée au profit de dispositifs formels communs aux deux domaines, aurait été intégrée à la raison qui en fait un usage univoque, réduit à une simple information dans l'oubli de la valeur différentielle de toute analogie qui tient précisément en la non-coïncidence de ses termes. L'*oubli de l'analogie* entraine l'interchangeabilité entre commandement (raison) et pilotage (technique), selon une même indifférenciation des fins et des moyens qui s'étend aux autres analogies. Ainsi la cybernétique « s'emploie à déceler un même dispositif formel de feedback dans un animal et dans une machine »[19] et pour Wiener « a uniform behavioristic analysis is applicable to both machines and living organisms, regardless of the complexity of behaviour »[20], de tel sorte que « dans la représentation du monde par la cybernétique, la différence entre les machines automatiques et les êtres vivants est abolie »[21].

---

16. Norbert Wiener, *Cybernetics* (Cambridge: MIT Press, 1961), pp. 11–12; p. 7.

17. Johnson, « "French" Cybernetics », p. 64.

18. Ibid., pp. 66–7.

19. Dupuy, *Aux origines des sciences cognitives*, pp. 38–9.

20. Wiener, Rosenblueth and Bigelow, « Behaviour, Purpose and Teleology » dans *Philosophy of Science*, 10:1 (January 1943), pp. 18–24 (p. 22).

21. Martin Heidegger, « La Provenance de l'art et la destination de la pensée » dans *Cahier de l'Herne, Heidegger* (Paris: Poche, 1983), p. 88.

L'analogie semble donc traitée par le cybernéticien comme un *homéostat*, icône de la cybernétique, régulant *input* (piloter) et *output* (gouverner) par un mécanisme de *feedback* qui de façon symptomatique corrige les écarts (ici de sens) afin d'assurer l'*arrivée à bon port* de son propre projet: « the equation between organism and machine works because it is seen from a position formulated precisely so that it will work. »[22] Par ailleurs, si les machines ressemblent aux organismes vivants, cette ressemblance éclaire en retour l'appareil biologique selon ce que Johnson nomme « a retroactive analogy, typical of cybernetics ».[23] La rétroaction (feedback) est une boucle informationnelle qui *contrôle la distance* (*télé-commande*) entre l'état actuel et l'état final d'un système. Appliqué à l'usage de l'analogie par la cybernétique, nous verrons que le concept de *contrôle* résulte de la réduction de la *marge d'erreur* qui sépare piloter de gouverner, entrainant l'érosion de ces deux concepts et notamment de tout ce qui « fait corps » avec leur domaine d'origine. Nous montrerons comment le traitement cybernéticien du concept-source de *pilote* se caractérise paradoxalement par l'effacement de son appareil technique (capitaine, gouvernail, navire), entrainant la virtualisation de son appareil symbolique (pensée, langage, corps) et donc la réduction du sens du concept-cible (*gouverner*) à la notion de contrôle. La cybernétique opérerait un transfert de matérialité entre source et cible qui fait de *gouverner* un simple appareil technique.

Or, « le phénomène du gouverner est devenu à l'époque de la cybernétique, si fondamental qu'il met en cause et détermine toutes les sciences de la nature et le comportement de l'homme; d'où l'obligation pour nous de l'éclaircir davantage »[24], comme y invite Heidegger. Dès 1948, Dubarle – pour qui « l'une des perspectives les plus fascinantes ainsi ouvertes est celle de la conduite rationnelle des processus humains » – envisage la construction future « d'une machine à gouverner » anticipant une réduction du champ conceptuel de *gouvernement* à celui de *contrôle* qui influe sur nos débats contemporains[25]. Néanmoins, si le projet cybernétique partage les craintes et espoirs d'une société se cherchant un nouveau cap au terme d'une guerre qui aura marqué l'échec des idéologies et du projet rationaliste, on ne saurait le réduire à un simple

---

22.　Hayles, *How We Became Posthuman*, p. 94.

23.　Christopher Johnson, « Leroi-Gourhan and the Limits of the Human », *French Studies*, 65:4 (2011), 471–87 (p. 483).

24.　Martin Heidegger et Eugen Fink, *Héraclite: séminaire du semestre d'hiver 1966–1967*, (Paris: Gallimard, 1973), p. 23.

25.　L'effacement de la notion de *gouvernement* au profit de celle de *contrôle* dans le discours politique contemporain mériterait une analyse plus poussée; que ce soit autour du récent succès du slogan « take back control », ou le *contrôle* illicite du débat politique par Cambridge Analytica, indiquant une réduction du politique et de l'éthique à une technicité télé-commandée, et la gestion du capital cognitif humain envisagé comme une série d'inputs-outputs qui peuvent être contrôlés à distance.

antihumanisme, d'autant plus que Wiener envisageait les dérives technocratiques de la société[26]. Ainsi, loin d'interpréter la cybernétique comme la fin de la raison (philosophique) suppléée par une technologie triomphante perçue comme son autre, nous voudrions au contraire montrer que la cybernétique en poursuit le programme, symbolisée par la continuité de l'analogie nautique.

Nous questionnerons l'unité présupposée d'une analogie qui *commande de loin* à la fois le programme de la raison philosophique et celui de la cybernétique et régule et asservit un certain usage de la pensée. Nous nommons *télé-commande* universelle, le contrôle du programme de la raison réduite à une intelligence devenue artificielle, la commodification d'une pensée appareillée, et l'intégrisme de son circuit d'opération qui se renvoie un monde à son image. Ce mode de pensée repose sur l'équivalence entre *arkhè* et *telos*, *input-output*, source et cible et le *contrôle* de la *distance* (télé-commande) qui les sépare. Nous montrerons enfin que la notion de contrôle, reposant sur une érosion de la différence analogique entre piloter et gouverner, s'avère insuffisante pour modéliser le gouvernement de soi, des autres et du monde, invitant à une redéfinition de la notion de commandement en sa portée éthique.

Changement de *cap*?
On rappelle souvent que la cybernétique est issue de recherches sur la défense anti-aérienne[27] et la construction du *AA predictor*, appareil dédié au suivi du trajet de la cible et l'anticipation de sa position future tout en minimisant la *marge d'erreur* due aux limites de cette autre *machine réflexe* qu'est l'opérateur humain. Le paradigme de la conduite de tir émancipée de son interface humaine autorise par analogie de considérer l'opérateur lui-même comme un *servomécanisme* qui adapte son action et corrige ses écarts en fonction d'un but. Il détermine la conduite de l'homme comme un comportement finalisé régi par un feedback négatif qui trouvera sa formulation en 1943 dans un des premiers articles cybernétiques, « Purpose, Behavior and Teleology ». Le feedback suppose donc « qu'un but soit assigné au comportement; pas de feedback sans projet, forme finale régulatrice »[28]. La conduite de tir, celle de l'avion ou de l'opérateur semblent donc gouvernés par l'anticipation d'une *fin* sans autre *finalité* que la réconciliation entre *input* et *output*, l'*arrivée à bon port* de son programme. Par extension, la cybernétique – visant à travers l'analogie une identité de rapports – *corrige le tir* et cherche à réduire l'écart entre source (piloter) et cible (gouverner) et à prédire la dérive aléatoire du sens afin de mieux le contrôler.

26. Voir notamment Mathieu Triclot, « Les Implications politiques de la cybernétique américaine », *Araben*, no. 3 (janvier 2006), pp. 54–63.
27. Wiener, *Cybernetics*, pp. 5–6; Triclot, *Le Moment cybernétique*, pp. 78–9.
28. Triclot, *Le Moment cybernétique*, p. 91.

Sans doute pourrait-on conclure à un anti-humanisme technocratique si l'analogie nautique, loin d'annoncer une simple rupture épistémologique, ne s'intégrait dans une tradition philosophique basée sur le modèle de la conduite raisonnable assignée à un cap. Dans un entretien sur la nature du gouverner à l'ère cybernétique où il joue le rôle de timonier de Heidegger, répondant à sa commande, Eugen Fink reprend l'analogie sans la questionner: « le gouverner est le mouvement d'un homme qui conduit un navire dans une direction souhaitée. C'est la direction d'un mouvement produite par un homme raisonnable. »[29] La raison *télé-commande* donc la pensée en régulant la distance (*télé-*) entre *telos* et *arkhè* depuis son origine comme l'indique Derrida:

> L'idée d'une pointe avancée de *l'exemplarité* est *l'idée de l'idée* européenne, son *eidos*, à la fois comme *arkhè* – idée de commencement mais aussi de commandement (le cap comme la tête, lieu de mémoire capitalisante et de décision, encore le capitaine) – et comme *telos* – idée de la fin, d'une limite qui accomplit ou met un terme, au bout de l'achèvement, au but de l'aboutissement. La pointe avancée est à la fois commencement et fin, elle se divise comme commencement et fin; c'est le lieu depuis lequel ou en vue duquel tout à lieu.[30]

La raison n'attend donc pas la cybernétique pour asseoir sa puissance sur le contrôle input-output. Fin et commencement ont toujours été associés à l'idée de contrôle puisque le terme *arkhè* « signifie aussi bien origine, principe, que commandement, ordre »[31] et *telos* indique par son étymologie la puissance, l'autorité. La raison aurait toujours voulu asseoir sa puissance en orientant son action dans la parfaite réunification de *l'arkhè* (*input*) et du *telos* (*output*), circularité exemplaire (*feedback*) d'un *principe de raison*[32] qui donne raison au monde pour mieux se le rendre, qui ne multiplie les départs que pour mieux se retrouver dans la vision inaltérée de son *eidos* (essence). « Faire cap », dans cette optique, loin d'indiquer un départ, serait « faire raison », c'est-à-dire établir la raison comme *telos* et *arkhè* « depuis lequel ou en vue duquel tout a lieu »: raison absolue offrant une vue en

---

29. Heidegger-Fink, *Héraclite*, p. 23.

30. Derrida, *L'Autre Cap; suivi de La Démocratie ajournée* (Paris: Éditions de Minuit, 1991), p. 29. Par « pointe avancée » et « exemplarité » Derrida indique que l'Europe s'est toujours identifiée comme un cap spirituel, projet universel exemplaire pour la civilisation mondiale ou la culture humaine.

31. Giorgio Agamben, *Qu'est-ce que le commandement?* (Paris: Payot, 2013), p. 10.

32. « Sous la forme de l'information, dit Heidegger, le *principe de raison suffisante* domine toute notre représentation. » Jacques Derrida, *Du Droit à la philosophie* (Paris: Galilée, 1990), pp. 485–6. Ce principe fut formulé par Leibniz considéré par Wiener comme « saint-patron de la cybernétique » (Wiener, *Cybernetics*, p. 12) et indique que pour toute chose il existe une raison qui doit être rendue (*ratio reddenda*). La *ratio*, telle une boucle de rétroaction, rend raison du monde, lui prête un sens (*telos*) qui lui est rendu (*arkhè*) selon la circularité du retour à l'envoyeur.

surplomb (*télé-*) et de survol (*commanding view*), qui réduit le réel à un point, qui fait le point et ne le valide que par le télescopage du début et de la fin, leur présence immédiate, leur ponctualité. Ainsi, avant le contrôle cybernétique, la raison impliquait déjà un *asservissement* de la pensée, une régulation en vue d'un but qui n'est pas sans violence comme le rappelle Eugene Fink pour qui « un navire sans gouvernail et sans pilote est le jouet des vagues et des vents. Gouverner est un mouvement […] qui oblige le navire à prendre un cours déterminé. Il comporte le moment de la domination. Il faut donc voir et impliquer dans le phénomène du gouvernement le moment de la violence. »[33]

Or Heidegger, afin de soustraire la pensée à la contrainte cybernétique, appellera à entendre une autre origine du commandement et donc de la pensée: « n'y a-t-il pas aussi un gouverner sans contrainte? Le moment de la contrainte fait-il essentiellement partie du phénomène du gouvernement? »[34] Pour Heidegger, il y aurait un commandement du commandement, un envoi pré-originaire de la cybernétique, « quelque chose qui a été émis et envoyé par une *arkhè*, par un commencement qui demeure caché et reste cependant opérant dans ce qu'il a envoyé et commandé »[35]. Il identifiera, notamment dans *Der Satz von Grund*, l'accélération d'un *principe de raison* devenu omnipotent et commandant de loin une certaine tradition philosophique jusqu'à son avènement cybernétique. Selon lui, reconduire la raison cybernétique à son envoi pré-originaire permettrait de retrouver le sens véritable d'une pensée qui échappe à la contrainte de la technique moderne.

Derrida, tout en offrant une lecture attentive de la pensée Heideggérienne, s'éloignera de cette vision qui selon lui se replie encore trop sur une prétendue origine (*arkhè*) de la pensée qui se retrouverait intacte au terme (*telos*) de ses envois et de ses re-*commandés*[36] et qui ne serait donc pas aussi distante de la cybernétique qu'elle y prétend. Derrida appelle à *changer de cap*, à penser autrement la nature du commandement et à se soustraire à la contrainte du *telos* et de *l'arkhè*: « au-delà de *notre cap*, il ne faut pas seulement se rappeler à *l'autre cap* et surtout au *cap de l'autre*, mais peut-être à *l'autre du cap*, c'est-à-dire à un rapport de l'identité à l'autre qui n'obéisse plus à la forme, au signe ou à la logique du cap, pas même de

---

33. Heidegger-Fink, *Héraclite*, pp. 23–4.
34. Ibid., p. 24.
35. Agamben, *Qu'est-ce que le commandement?*, pp. 17–18.
36. À *l'envoi* pré-originaire heideggérien, Derrida opposera le *renvoi*: « J'ai tenté de retracer une voie ouverte sur une pensée de l'envoi qui […] ne se rassemblait pas encore avec lui-même comme envoi de l'être […]. Cet envoi pré-ontologique, en quelque sorte, ne se rassemble pas. Il ne se rassemble qu'en se divisant, en se différant […]. Il n'émet qu'en renvoyant déjà, il n'émet qu'à partir de l'autre. Tout commence par le renvoi, c'est-à-dire ne commence pas. » Jacques Derrida, « Envoi », dans *Psyché* (Paris: Galilée, 1987), p. 141. Selon nous, l'analogie est *renvoi*, elle n'*émet* une identité de sens qu'*à partir de l'autre*, donc *en se divisant, en se différant*.

l'anti-cap – ou de la décapitation. »[37] Il faudrait donc ouvrir la pensée à ce qui résiste à sa commande, à ce qui l'éloigne d'elle-même pour accueillir l'altérité irréductible du réel. Ce mouvement n'est pas le simple rejet du *cap*, car rejeter c'est encore se placer sous sa dépendance (fut-elle conflictuelle), mais *l'autre du cap* c'est-à-dire un rapport qui modifie le mode d'opération d'une pensée régulée par la raison en remettant en cause ses principes d'identité, de non-contradiction et la logique de sa *télé-commande:*

> L'histoire d'une culture suppose sans doute un cap identifiable, un *telos* vers lequel le mouvement, la mémoire et la promesse, l'identité, fut-ce comme différence à soi, rêve de se rassembler: *en prenant les devants* dans *l'anticipation*. Mais l'histoire suppose aussi que le cap ne soit pas *donné*, identifiable d'avance et une fois pour toutes. L'irruption du nouveau [...] devrait être anticipée *comme l'imprévisible*, l'*inanticipable*, le non-maitrisable, le non-identifiable, bref, comme ce dont on n'a pas encore la mémoire.[38]

Là où le *AA predictor* de Wiener offrait le modèle de « l'anticipation » d'une raison obsédée par l'arrivée à bon port de ses intentions, veillant de loin sur la logistique de ses transferts entre *telos* et *arkhè*, sur leur ponctualité, Derrida oppose l'injonction imprescriptible et inassignable du « tout autre » qui seul brise la circularité d'une pensée qui veut se donner raison. Commandement sans contrainte, avant tout commandement, c'est-à-dire proprement ana-chronique, qui interrompt le mythe de la présence à soi par l'irruption de « l'imprévisible et de l'inanticipable ». Aux *fins* sans *finalité* de la Cybernétique s'opposerait donc la *finalité* sans *fin* d'une philosophie à venir qui reposerait sur un tout autre usage de l'analogie qui empêche source (pilote) et cible (gouverner) « de se rassembler » sous une simple identité fonctionnelle.

Le dispositif technique de l'analogie: capitaine, gouvernail, navire

Pour Derrida et toute une génération de penseurs, la raison n'est plus le *capitaine* de la pensée car ils perçoivent à l'orée de la cybernétique que *rendre raison* (*principium reddendae rationis sufficientis*) risque de répondre au schème déceptif d'une capitulation de la pensée (se rendre à la raison) entérinant son acte de reddition, en succombant à son autorité et à la *suffisance* de son principe de commande. Le *cap-* signifie tête, le chef, le capitaine mais aussi tire son origine de la racine indoeuropéenne informant les mouvements de saisissement (*-cep*) et donc de prise comme de méprise. Peut-on penser sans saisir, en se dessaisissant de sa propre emprise, sans succomber aux mouvements parfois saisissants de la raison? Il s'agirait de soustraire la pensée à son programme de *télé-commande universelle*, « la télécommande remplaçant progressivement non seulement la

---

37. Derrida, *L'Autre Cap*, p. 21.
38. Ibid., p. 23.

commande, le commandement immédiat, mais surtout l'éthique (les dix commandements) »³⁹ car elle plie le commandement à ses fins (*telos*), selon la logique
d'une intégration toujours plus grande, qui réponde au programme de l'univocité
de la raison, à son intégrisme. Le langage universel du *contrôle* maintient alors le
commandement naturel, politique, éthique *à distance* (*télé-*).

Derrida, afin de mieux rejeter l'intégrisme d'une raison univoque dénoncera
l'intégration du pouvoir de commandement par la caricature d'un homme solitaire
(chef, tête, voire Führer) qui concentre tout son savoir dans la prise en main
symbolique de la barre:

> Le mot de « cap » (*caput*, *capitis*), qui signifie, vous le savez bien, la tête ou
> l'extrémité de l'extrême, le but et le bout, l'ultime, le dernier, la dernière extrémité,
> l'*eskhaton* en général, voici qu'à la navigation il assigne le pôle, la fin, le *telos* d'un
> mouvement orienté, calculé, délibéré, volontaire, ordonné […] c'est un homme qui
> décide du cap, de la pointe avancée qu'il est lui-même, la proue, en tête du navire ou
> de l'avion, qu'il pilote. L'eschatologie et la téléologie, c'est l'homme. C'est *lui* qui
> donne les ordres à l'équipage, il tient la barre ou le manche, bref, il se trouve à la tête,
> la tête qu'il est lui-même, de l'équipage et de la machine – et on le nomme
> souvent *capitaine*.⁴⁰

Le *cap* symbolise la circularité du système puisqu'il est à la fois *arkhè* (en tête)
et telos (but et bout), faisant de l'homme l'origine et la fin d'un monde à son
image. Penser *l'autre de tout cap* impliquerait donc un autre rapport au
commandement qui évite la concentration des pouvoirs en un seul homme qui
« tient la barre et le manche » symbole de la force rectiligne d'une volonté
« calculée, délibérée, orientée ». Néanmoins cap, capitaine et barre sont au cœur de
l'appareillage de l'analogie entre piloter et gouverner puisque le pouvoir aura
toujours porté sur:

> La détermination du meilleur levier. Le *mochlos* pouvait être une barre de bois, un
> levier pour déplacer un navire, une sorte de pieu pour ouvrir ou fermer une porte,
> bref ce sur quoi l'on s'appuie pour forcer et déplacer. Or quand on demande
> comment s'orienter dans l'histoire, la morale, la politique, les désaccords et
> les décisions les plus graves portent moins souvent, me semble-t-il, sur les *fins*
> que sur les *leviers*.⁴¹

Si pour Derrida gouverner implique traditionnellement la subordination des *fins* au
levier, la cybernétique semble offrir un processus d'extériorisation par la technique
du principe de commandement symbolisé par la subordination du *levier* aux *fins*.

---

39. Paul Virilio, *L'Inertie polaire* (Paris: Christian Bourgeois, 2002), p. 147.

40. Derrida, *L'Autre Cap*, pp. 19–20.

41. Derrida, Jacques Derrida, « Mochlos ou le conflit des facultés », in *Du droit à la philosophie* (Paris: Galilée, 1990), pp. 397–438, (p. 436).

La télécommande représente l'évolution de cette forme prototypique du pouvoir qu'est le bâton de commandement[42], le *mochlos*, ce « levier, qui se dit aussi de n'importe quelle barre, par exemple, celle avec laquelle Ulysse crève l'œil du Cyclope »[43]. Il y aurait donc un *passage de bâton* déterminant au sein de l'analogie nautique qui porte sur le gouvernail, bâton de commandement supplanté par la télécommande cybernétique que Johnson relève dans le cadre des séquences de commande de la mission Apollo. Là où le *joystick* du cosmonaute représentait « an *analogue operation*, to the extent that its effects on the spacecraft reproduces the human body's basic sense of orientation in space »[44], l'essentiel du pilotage du navire spatial est subordonné aux « *opérations numériques* » de l'ordinateur de bord. La télécommande, icône de la technologie moderne, ne garde du bâton de commandement que sa forme symbolique, subordonnant le *levier* aux *fins* préprogrammées de son circuit interne. On retient seulement l'illusion d'un contrôle virtuel qui se limite à la *commande à distance* de quelques touches prédéterminées. Par analogie, la perte du levier (*leverage*) change le rapport au gouvernement de soi, des autres et du monde, et donc modifie radicalement la façon dont on « s'oriente dans l'histoire, la morale, la politique ».

Sans *mochlos*, le capitaine ne fait plus *corps* avec son navire, menaçant l'identité même de l'analogie pensée-corps/capitaine-navire sur laquelle repose pourtant la cybernétique et l'intelligence artificielle. La perte du gouvernail entraine la modification du statut du capitaine au sein de l'analogie. Guilbauld, l'un des médiateurs de la cybernétique en France, nous dit:

> La fonction du *pilote* est de veiller à ce que les *timoniers* suivent exactement la route que le *capitaine* leur ordonne. Peu importe que le pilotage ait pu prendre d'autres formes, ici le pilote est un intermédiaire: il ne tient pas la barre du gouvernail, ni les autres manœuvres, il ne commande pas non plus, il contrôle, il règle les moyens selon la fin ordonnée par le capitaine.[45]

L'analogie est ici pliée aux fins de la cybernétique qui réduit l'écart pourtant irréductible entre comparant et comparé au prix d'un escamotage (« peu importe que ») de la différence analogique. Le *kybernetès* n'est plus ici la figure tutélaire du commandeur, cœur de l'analogie classique: « tel Ulysse, le *polymètis*, gouvernant son navire en maitre, assis près de la barre: le chef, tout à sa besogne, au gouvernail de la cité, tient la barre en main, sans laisser dormir ses

---

42. Le *bâton de commandement* est attesté dès la préhistoire sous la forme de bâtons percés à usage indéterminé, vraisemblablement polyvalents.

43. Pierre Chantraine, *Dictionnaire étymologique de la langue grecque* (Paris: Klinkseick, 2009).

44. Johnson, « Analogue Apollo », p. 317.

45. Georges Guilbaud, *La Cybernétique* (Paris: Presses universitaires de France, 1954), p. 120. Cité dans Johnson, « "French" Cybernetics », p. 66.

paupières »[46]. Dans le modèle cybernétique « il ne tient pas la barre du gouvernail » et ne « commande pas non plus » il se contente de « réguler » les opérations de bord.

La cybernétique semble donc initier un effacement de l'appareillage technique du *pilote* (perte du *mochlos*, du capitaine) qui, par analogie, modifie l'interprétation de *gouverner*. Le passage de la commande à sa virtualisation (*télé-commande*) entérine le « remplacement progressif de la commande, du commandement et de l'éthique » par le contrôle, la régulation et l'asservissement. L'analogique cède le pas à la logique, la différence étant sacrifiée au nom de l'identité des rapports recherchée. Il y aurait perte de l'appareil analogique du corps humain au profit de cette « centrale de commande » qu'est la raison. Il semblerait donc que loin de constituer un simple changement de programme, la cybernétique poursuit le logiciel du *principe de raison* et ne fait qu'accentuer la rupture traditionnelle entre intelligence pratique, stochastique (*mètis*) et intelligence rationnelle (*logos*) au cœur de l'analogie nautique:

> Se montrer prévoyant, faire preuve de vigilance, mener droit le navire, ce sont quelques-uns des aspects essentiels de la *mètis* du navigateur. [...] Le bon timonier doit avoir pesé tous les coups, en bon joueur de trictrac: il lui faut prévoir les sautes de vent, opposer ruse à ruse, guetter l'occasion fugitive d'inverser le rapport des forces. Jeté dans le *pontos*, plongé dans la mouvance de la mer, l'homme de barre met toute son intelligence à corriger les écarts du navire à coups de gouvernail et à diriger sa course en se guidant sur les points de repères que les astres lui tracent sur la voute du ciel. Diriger, redresser, mener droit, *ithunein*, [...] soulign[ent] dans l'art du pilote l'importance d'un projet qui est tout autant habileté à prévoir la route que capacité de fixer le regard sur le terme ultime de la course. À travers un cheminement tout en détours, en tracés obliques et en circuits tortueux, [...] l'intelligence navigatrice sait mener droit le navire, sans jamais dévier de la route qu'elle a par avance médité de suivre.[47]

À l'origine, l'art du *kybernetès* fait appel à cette pensée pratique, quasi instinctive qu'est la *mètis*, cette intelligence des grecs polymorphique, sollicitant la prudence et la temporalité du *kairos* (« occasion fugitive »), une intelligence « rusée » qui tout en s'appliquant à maintenir l'unité d'un cap et la logique de la ligne droite fait appel à la flexibilité hasardeuse d'un « cheminement tout en détours » que la raison aura tôt fait de rejeter comme simple « jeu de trictrac ». La philosophie évacuera ainsi tout un pan de l'intelligence au profit du simple exercice de la rationalité; schisme qui se ressent ici dans l'opposition entre deux champs lexicaux: d'une part « diriger, redresser, mener droit » d'autre part l'« oblique, le tortueux, le détour » de la pensée elle-même; autant d'écarts qui seront soumis aux corrections du *feedback* cybernétique.

---

46. Marcel Detienne et Jean-Pierre Vernant, *Les Ruses de l'intelligence, la mètis des grecs* (Paris: Champs/Flammarion, 1974), p. 216, note.

47. Détienne et Vernant, *Les Ruses de l'intelligence*, pp. 216–17.

Si Platon évoque donc souvent l'analogie du *kybernetès* dans sa recherche du bon modèle de gouvernement, il s'en détachera en raison du caractère limité de ce savoir de *mètis* que le philosophe considère comme essentiellement technique, pratique et stochastique. Platon dénoncera l'aspect conjectural de ce mode de connaissance qui « procède par le détour d'une comparaison qui permet de deviner une similitude entre des choses à première vue profondément différentes. C'est une opération intellectuelle à mi-chemin entre le raisonnement par analogie et la capacité à déchiffrer les signes qui relient le visible à l'invisible. »[48] Comme le montrent Détienne et Vernant:

> Sans aucune ambiguïté, Platon condamne les savoirs et les techniques qui relèvent de l'intelligence stochastique [...] le *Philèbe* distingue parmi les productions humaines celles qui dépendent d'un savoir incertain et celles qui ressortissent à l'exactitude: d'un côté, les arts stochastiques, de l'autre les productions qui sont objets de calcul (*artithmos*), de mesure (*metron*) et de pesée *(stathmos)*. Seul ce qui est mesurable peut faire partie de la science exacte, de l'*épistème*, et appartenir au domaine de la vérité.[49]

L'ambiguïté de l'évocation du *kybernetès* se ressentira par ailleurs dans *République I* (364a, b) et *Gorgias* (512a, b) où le *kybernetès* ne détient pas le savoir nécessaire au gouvernement véritable puisque sa conduite ne se règle pas sur le cap du bien. S'il y a donc bien *passage de bâton* entre la cybernétique et la tradition philosophique, celui-ci découlerait d'un malentendu puisque Platon éloigne la figure du *kybernetès* et son savoir analogique au nom même d'une science exacte par laquelle la cybernétique annonce sa réhabilitation. Pilote trop technique pour la philosophie car astreint aux limites de la « connaissance des règles de son art » dans l'ignorance des principes éternels qui la commandent de loin; pilote pas assez technique pour la cybernétique car limité aux outils rudimentaires de son temps et à leurs interfaces tributaires du système analogique du corps humain. Platon accentue la différence analogique au profit du concept-cible (*gouverner*). La cybernétique efface la différence au profit du concept-source (*pilote*). Là où la tradition métaphysique accélère la séparation des systèmes de commande entre méta- et physique, tête (*cap-*) et corps, intelligible et sensible pour mieux asseoir le commandement de l'un à raison du contrôle de l'autre, la cybernétique cherche à « déloger en elle tous les concepts métaphysiques – et jusqu'à ceux d'âme, de vie, de valeur, de choix, de mémoire – qui servaient naguère à opposer la machine à l'homme »[50], entraînant l'équivalence du commandement et du contrôle.

Néanmoins, en se plaçant dans la continuité du rejet de la *mètis*, l'épistémè moderne entérine « le fossé séparant les hommes des bêtes [qui] ne pouvait que se

---

48.   Ibid., p. 302.
49.   Ibid., p. 304.
50.   Jacques Derrida, *De la grammatologie* (Paris: Éditions de Minuit, 1967), p. 19.

creuser davantage et la raison humaine apparaitre plus nettement encore que pour les Anciens séparée des aptitudes animales […] reléguant dans l'ombre tout un plan de l'intelligence avec ses façons propres de comprendre »[51]. Puisque le mode de pensée analogique qu'est la *mètis* empruntait bien de ces métaphores à l'observation du monde animal[52], au moment où l'accélération de la perte de la diversité des espèces s'accélère, peut-être faudrait-il entrevoir au-delà de la réduction du monde naturel télécommandée par l'avènement de la toute-puissance de la raison humaine (l'anthropocène), une perte de cet autre écosystème qu'est la pensée qui se formait jadis dans l'échange *ana-logique* (autrement que logique) avec son environnement. L'homme saura-t-il encore trouver les mots pour se dire après la disparition de ce qu'il considère comme Autre? Force est de remarquer que:

> L'ignorance est la condition moyenne de l'homme aujourd'hui, le rapport à l'objet technique est de réaction à des stimuli programmés. Il y a donc une différence essentielle dans le rapport à l'objet technique. […] Le propre du manœuvre est de *s'y connaitre*, et c'est justement parce qu'il s'y connait qu'il peut s'en sortir en toutes circonstances, et que la technique au sens ancien est toujours une forme de ruse. Tout au contraire, dans mon rapport quotidien à l'objet je *n'y connais rien*, je me contente de suivre docilement le réseau de la signalétique, c'est-à-dire d'intégrer de nouvelles normes.[53]

La perte symbolique du *mochlos* fait de l'homme un spectateur déqualifié, réduit au rôle d'opérateur d'un système qu'il ne commande plus mais qui le commande de loin. Là où l'*homme de barre* (« le manœuvre »), doué de *mètis*, « s'y connaissait » – expression où il faudrait entendre au-delà de la maitrise externe d'un savoir technique, le processus interne de la connaissance de soi – l'homme moderne « n'y connait rien », c'est-à-dire qu'il n'a plus accès à la connaissance du monde (fût-il technique). La perte du *mochlos* entraine l'oubli de la *mètis*, cette « forme de ruse » qui permet de s'en sortir. On rappellera alors que le *mochlos* est le cœur analogique de la ruse d'Ulysse qui lui permet d'échapper au Cyclope par l'articulation d'un stratagème linguistique (la *pointe* d'esprit, jeu de mot grâce auquel il trompe sa vigilance) et technique (la *pointe* aiguisée avec laquelle il l'aveugle)[54]. Le *mochlos* est donc un levier polyvalent (qui se prête à la *polymètis*) puisqu'il peut à la fois servir ou renverser le pouvoir. Il ne se réduit pas à l'univocité de la *télécommande universelle* initiée par la cybernétique mais appelle la

---

51. Détienne et Vernant, *Les Ruses de l'intelligence*, p. 306.

52. Voir Détienne et Vernant, « Le Renard et le poulpe », dans *Les Ruses de l'intelligence*, pp. 32–57.

53. Jean Vioulac, *L'Époque de la technique: Marx, Heidegger et l'accomplissement de la métaphysique* (Paris: Epiméthée, 2009), p. 149.

54. Cf. l'article « Mètis » dans Barbara Cassin, *Vocabulaire européen des philosophies* (Paris: Seuil/Robert, 2004).

différence analogique qui lui permet de se réinventer d'un domaine à l'autre. Il permet d'échapper au piège de la raison univoque – symbolisé par l'œil unique du cyclope – qui se manifeste dans la cybernétique par la réduction du sens au *signal* dont « la structure n'est pas le renvoi mais le commandement. »[55] Le *renvoi* (analogique) vers un autre domaine de connaissance permet la sortie vers une réalité extérieure au système; or la cybernétique assigne le sens à résidence et aux limites d'un système interne qui asservi la réalité à ses fins. Le commandement cybernétique se limite au *contrôle* et institue un rapport de maitre à esclave: « il s'agit non pas de comprendre l'injonction, mais de percevoir le signal » et de « placer les corps dans un petit monde de signaux à chacun desquels est attaché une réponse obligée et une seule »[56] dans l'oubli de la différence analogique. La cybernétique *perçoit* dans l'analogie nautique *un seul signal*: le *contrôle*. L'écart entre source (*piloter*) et cible (*gouverner*) est alors réduit dans la poursuite de cet objectif unique, effaçant par *rétroaction* l'écart homme-machine.

Le dispositif symbolique de l'analogie: pensée, langage, corps virtuels

L'effacement par la cybernétique de l'appareillage technique (capitaine, gouvernail, navire) du concept-cible (pilote), entraine une virtualisation des rapports symboliques associés (pensée, langage, corps) qui modifie le sens du concept-cible (gouverner). En retirant *la barre* qui lie/sépare le capitaine de son navire on efface l'écart entre homme et machine. De même, le langage, réduit au signal, affecte la relation pensée-corps. L'analogie concrète est remplacée par sa virtualisation qui lui donne le don d'ubiquité au sein de la cybernétique. *Contrôler* signifie alors réduire la distance qui sépare du but fixé:

> Il n'y a plus de distance. On est si près des choses qu'elles ne vous concernent plus du tout […] Là où il s'agissait uniquement d'*aménager* l'environnement pour y loger nos activités corporelles, il s'agit maintenant de *contrôler* ce même environnement, grâce aux techniques de l'interactivité *en temps réel*. […] On condense en un point, on concentre toutes ses activités, grâce à la télécommande, pour éviter à l'usager de se déplacer.[57]

La *télé-commande* serait le symbole d'une virtualisation des distances, omniprésente dans les dérivés de la cybernétique contemporaine qu'est la télé-présence (satellites, caméras de surveillance, écrans tactiles, etc.) qui, comme le montre Virilio dans l'*Inertie polaire*, sous couvert de 'téléprésence' se manifeste paradoxalement par une *absence* des corps. En effet, le *kybernetès* aurait non seulement perdu la commande de son *mochlos* mais aussi de son embarcation puisque « la fin du siècle annonce une dernière mutation avec la venue prochaine du

---

55. Vioulac, *L'Époque de la technique*, p. 157.
56. Ibid., p. 148.
57. Virilio, *L'Inertie polaire*, p. 120.

véhicule audiovisuel, véhicule statique, substitut de nos déplacements physiques »[58]. Le corps du commandant de bord lui-même est devenu superflu, remplacé par ce que l'on nomme aujourd'hui un *système embarqué*. Heidegger aurait perçu dès le départ la perte de distance qu'annonçait l'avènement de la cybernétique: « toutes les manières d'accroître la vitesse auxquelles nous prenons part aujourd'hui de gré ou de force poussent à surmonter l'être éloigné. Avec la TSF, par exemple, le Dasein est en train d'opérer un deséloignement du monde. »[59] La *télé-commande* repose donc sur un paradoxe, car si elle *commande de loin* le *socius* humain elle n'institue pas un éloignement du monde mais ce que Heidegger nomme dés-éloignement (*Entfernung*). Éloigner c'est introduire l'écart qui permet le surgissement du proche, la distance qui permet de mieux voir et de trouver sa place dans la proximité du monde. « L'éloignement est la désintimisation du proche dont il libère par là-même la proximité. »[60] Le dés-éloignement serait au contraire l'un des effets du système de *télé-commande* qui, en effaçant la distance, offre un monde à portée de main mais bloque aussi le mécanisme d'approche du proche. *Télé-commander*, c'est contrôler le système d'éloignement sur lequel repose la pensée vivante. Sans éloignement il n'y a plus de place pour l'Autre et nous voilà soumis à la tyrannie du Même symbolisé par les « télécommunications, autre nom de cette soudaine confusion du proche et du lointain, du dedans et du dehors, non-séparabilité médiatique affectant gravement […] la stabilité morphologique du réel »[61]. L'oubli de l'analogie par la cybernétique est symbolique de cette perte de l'éloignement, de la différence entre gouverner et piloter, écart nécessaire à la pensée.

En prenant le relais du processus de rationalisation du réel préinscrit dans la philosophie métaphysique, la cybernétique opère un nivellement des différences (*non-séparabilité, dés-éloignement*), un *appareillage* du réel qui le pourvoit certes d'appareils mais qui opère sa réduction à des pièces équivalentes (*bits*), donc substituables au sein du système. L'homme lui-même risque de n'être qu'une pièce défectueuse dans un processus qui tend à évacuer l'erreur humaine. La redondance de l'humain (de son corps, de son *mochlos*) se retrouve chez Virilio pour qui « le valide suréquipé de l'aviation militaire ressembl[e], trait pour trait, à l'invalide équipé […] capable de piloter son environnement domestique grâce à un reste de performance corporelle »[62]. Il fait écho à Lyotard décrivant la logique suppressive du système: « quand il s'agit d'étendre les capacités de la monade, il semble raisonnable d'abandonner, voir même de détruire activement, ces parties de

---

58. Ibid., p. 42.

59. Jean-Philippe Milet, « L'Inassignable » dans *Le Passage des frontières, autour de Jacques Derrida* (Paris: Galilée, 1994), pp. 285–96 (p. 295).

60. Ibid., p. 294.

61. Virilio, *L'Inertie polaire*, p. 65.

62. Ibid., p. 127.

l'espèce humaine qui paraissent superflues, sans emploi pour cette fin. »[63] La monade est alors le symbole d'une pensée réduite à un *principe de raison* univoque, panoptique, cyclopéen.

Le dispositif de *télé-commande* initié par la cybernétique aura donc opéré une mise à distance de la commande, le retrait successif du bâton de commandement, du véhicule, du corps pour nous exposer à la réalité virtuelle d'une pensée sans corps, télé-présente. La *télé-présence* « pose qu'un cerveau pourrait commander un autre corps, n'importe quel corps, et qu'il n'y a donc pas de corps propre »[64] et « les ordres de locomotion sont transférés d'un corps à un autre, d'un appareil à un autre, *sans contact aucun avec une quelconque surface:* l'interface homme-machine éliminant les uns après les autres tous les supports physiques. »[65] Les technosciences en quelque sorte réduisent le corps au rang de *hardware* du dispositif complexe de la pensée, brisant sa co-dépendance avec le langage humain qui n'est plus qu'un *software*, dans la recherche d'une pensée sans corps indépendante des conditions de vie terrestre. La pensée est ainsi abstraite de son corps, instituant un transfert de commandement qui informe la cybernétique puisque celle-ci « parle de *systèmes formels* dont la qualité principale est l'indépendance des supports d'existence réelle »[66]. Cette tentation d'une pensée sans corps se ressent dans l'hésitation au moment de l'acte de nomination de la *cybernétique*: « Wiener relates how the importance of the concept of communication first led him to consider the Greek word *angelos* (messenger). »[67]

La perte du corps soumet la pensée à une réduction de son champ d'action, un passage de l'*ana-logique* à la simple *logique* rationnelle. Loin de commander, elle est aujourd'hui « ramenée aux consternantes théories du choix rationnel, qui tente de modéliser les décisions de l'opérateur dans un système donné. La pensée se trouve ainsi intégrée aux réquisits de fonctionnement de l'appareil [...] elle obéit aux commandements. »[68] N'est-ce pas alors ce que Levinas identifie, dans *Liberté et commandement*, comme étant la forme prototypique du gouvernement tyrannique? « Cette violence » que l'on croit être « l'application directe d'une force à un être », serait en réalité ce qui refuse « à l'être toute son individualité, en le saisissant comme élément de son calcul, et comme cas

---

63. Jean-François Lyotard, « Le Temps aujourd'hui », dans *L'Inhumain* (Paris: Klincksieck, 2014), p. 80.

64. Bernard Stiegler, « Quand faire c'est dire: de la technique comme différance de toute frontière », dans *Le Passage des frontières*, p. 273.

65. Virilio, *L'Inertie polaire*, p. 132.

66. Bernard Claverie et Gilles Desclaux, « Commande, contrôle, communication: gestion cybernétique des systèmes d'information », *Hermès*, 71 (2015), 70–77 (p. 73).

67. Johnson, « "French" Cybernetics », p. 61.

68. Vioulac, *L'Époque de la technique*, p. 158.

particulier d'un concept »[69]. L'homme cybernétique n'est qu'une autre machine, qu'un *cas particulier du concept* de contrôle. Qu'aurait dit Levinas, penseur de « l'éthique du visage », d'un monde réduit à la modalité de l'*interface* et au visage impersonnel d'un centre de commande? Pour lui, « le fait de ne pas regarder en face ce à quoi s'applique l'action […] le fait de ne pas lui trouver de face »[70], c'est la tyrannie. L'*interface* tend à présenter un monde à visage unique qui se plie aux désirs de l'usager et donc à l'illusion d'un monde à son image, réduit à la circularité du principe de raison:

> La pensée aujourd'hui parait requise de prendre part au procès de rationalisation. Tout autre manière de penser est condamnée, isolée et rejetée comme irrationnelle […] Le langage est-il un instrument destiné par excellence à doter l'esprit de la connaissance la plus exacte de la réalité et d'en contrôler autant que possible la transformation? La vraie tâche du philosophe consiste alors à aider la science à se soustraire aux inconsistances que comportent les langues naturelles, en construisant une langue symbolique pure et univoque.[71]

On voit ici toute l'étendue du transfert de commandement déclenché par la cybernétique, puisque la pensée n'est plus le mandataire mais le mandaté dans un « procès de rationalisation » qui réduit à son tour le *logos* au rang d'*information*, terme clef de la cybernétique. L'*information* donne une forme « pure et univoque », « exacte » au réel mais en même temps elle l'*in-forme*, c'est-à-dire la soustrait à sa forme (à son corps) précisément par le rejet de ces « inconsistances » qui leur donnent leur « individualité ». Or pour Levinas, « la réalité soumise à la tyrannie est une réalité *informée*; elle est déjà absente de la relation que l'agent entretient avec elle »[72], la tyrannie apparait « même lorsque la hiérarchie fonctionne parfaitement, lorsque tout le monde se plie aux idées universelles [et] à la nécessité de l'ordre raisonnable »[73]. Le commandement de la raison peut donc s'avérer tyrannique dans la mesure où il ne laisse plus de place à l'Autre qu'il réduit au rang de simple inconsistance dans ce programme qui *commande de loin* la pensée. Or pour Lyotard, « une rationalité ne mérite pas son nom si elle dénie sa part à ce qu'il y a de passibilité ouverte et de créativité incontrôlée dans la plupart des langages y compris cognitif. »[74] En (*re*)*commandant* le modèle du *logos* cybernétique aux autres langages (humain, politique, éthique) la pensée se plie à une rationalité étroite perçue comme idéale au nom de la seule valeur de performativité. Pensée

---

69. Emmanuel Levinas, *Liberté et commandement* (Paris: Folio, 1999), p. 47.
70. Ibid., p. 45.
71. Lyotard, « Le Temps aujourd'hui », p. 75.
72. Levinas, *Liberté et commandement*, p. 48.
73. Ibid., p. 97.
74. Lyotard, « Le Temps aujourd'hui », p. 77.

unique, sans corps puisqu'elle propose de s'appliquer indifféremment à tous les corps:

> La déception procurée par ces organes de pensée sans corps provient de ce qu'ils opèrent en logique binaire, celle qui s'est imposée avec la logique mathématique de Russell et Whitehead, la machine de Turing, le modelé neuronal de McCulloch et Pitts, la cybernétique de Wiener et von Neumann, l'algèbre de Boole, l'informatique de Shannon. Or, la pensée humaine ne pense pas en binaire. Elle ne travaille pas sur des unités d'information (les bits), mais sur des configurations intuitives et hypothétiques. Elle accepte des données imprécises, ambiguës, qui ne semblent pas sélectionnées selon un code ou une capacité de lecture préétablis. Elle ne néglige pas les à-côtés, les marges d'une situation. Elle n'est pas seulement focalisée, mais aussi latérale.[75]

La *logique* cybernétique qui travaille sur des « unités d'information » discrètes et interchangeables (*bits*[76]) correspond à l'évacuation du langage *ana-logique* de la pensée corporelle au même titre que le *logos* orthothétique de l'*épistémè* platonicienne rejetait la pensée stochastique. À la logique cyclopéenne de la pensée unique « focalisée » sur les *bits* s'oppose la pensée « latérale » de la *mètis* qui « s'applique à des réalités fugaces, mouvantes, déconcertantes et ambiguës, qui ne se prêtent ni à la mesure précise, ni au calcul exact, ni au raisonnement rigoureux »[77]. On rappellera que le Cyclope fut vaincu par l'esprit plein de ressources (*lateral thinking*) d'Ulysse précisément car sa vision unifocale ne lui aurait pas permis de saisir le double-entendre (*mètis – outis*) par lequel Ulysse le trompe. Là où le Cyclope travaille sur des « unités d'information », Ulysse exploite les ressources analogiques du langage et *pense à bras le corps*; son expédient allie de façon inséparable pensée (le jeu de mot déroutant) et corps (le *mochlos* qui crève l'œil du cyclope). Ainsi:

> Ce qui rend inséparable la pensée et le corps, ce n'est plus simplement que celui-ci soit l'indispensable hardware de celle-là, sa condition matérielle d'existence, c'est que chacun d'eux est *analogue* à l'autre dans son rapport avec son environnement respectif (sensible, symbolique), ce rapport étant lui-même de type *analogique* dans les deux cas […]. Si l'on parle *d'analogique* sérieusement, c'est cette expérience qu'on connote, ce flou, cet incertain, et cette foi dans l'inépuisable sensible, et pas seulement un mode de report du donné sur une surface d'inscription qui n'est pas

---

75. Lyotard, « Si l'on peut penser sans corps », dans *L'Inhumain*, pp. 23–4.
76. Lyotard précise alors dans « Réécrire la modernité » (*L'Inhumain*, p. 42): « Avec les *bits*, il n'est plus question de formes libres données ici et maintenant à la sensibilité et à l'imagination. Ils sont au contraire des unités d'information conçues par l'ingénierie de l'ordinateur et définissables à tous les niveaux de langage: lexical, syntaxique, rhétorique, et le reste. Ils sont assemblés en systèmes selon un ensemble de possibilités (un menu) sous le contrôle d'un programmeur. »
77. Détienne et Vernant, *Les Ruses de l'intelligence*, p. 10.

originairement la sienne [...]. La vraie « *analogie* » requiert que la machine à penser
ou à représenter soit elle-même au milieu de ses « données » *comme* l'œil est dans le
visuel ou l'écriture dans la langue.[78]

La pensée et le corps ne sont jamais entièrement commandés ou soumis à une
volonté, à une raison préinscrite dans leur programme, mais cherchent par leur
navigation « ce qu'elles veulent dire » sans encore le savoir. La pensée véritable se
« représente au milieu de ses données » c'est-à-dire qu'elle pense en s'exprimant
dans la matérialité de la langue, elle ne peut se dire en dehors de ses mots, mais
s'éprouve dans l'interdépendance analogique d'une pensé qui travaille le corps et
d'un corps qui travaille la pensée. Pensée et corps sont « analogues à l'autre dans leur
rapport avec leur environnement respectif »; il faut (contrainte, obligation) qu'ils
pâtissent, c'est-à-dire qu'ils ressentent la résistance d'une force contraire à leur
volonté, comme le timonier éprouve la force du courant dans le manche du
gouvernail (*mochlos*). À condition de saisir l'écart *analogique* qui empêche la
pensée de se réduire au simple *feedback* cybernétique. Si la pensée est « plongée dans
le champ des phrases », juge de la force de leur contre-courant, éprouve sa résistance,
c'est pour faire cap sur un sens « latent » qui ne préexiste pas à sa navigation.

Pour Lyotard, il y aurait « une imbrication du penser et du souffrir. Ces mots,
phrases et instances d'écriture [...] disent autre chose que ce qu'on voulait dire,
parce qu'ils sont plus vieux que l'intention actuelle, surchargés d'usages. »[79]
L'expérience analogique du langage ne saurait donc se réduire au concept
d'*information* cybernétique et à sa logique binaire (*bits*) qui soumet le réel à la
volonté d'un programme prédéterminé. On aura vu que la cybernétique réduit
l'analogie nautique à un usage univoque (*bit*) qui pourtant « nous dit autre chose
que ce que [la cybernétique] voulait dire. » L'évacuation successive de son
dispositif technique (le capitaine, la barre, le navire) et symbolique (pensée,
langage, corps) modifie aussi celui de commandement entrainant d'importantes
conséquences philosophiques, politiques et éthiques dans l'oubli de l'art véritable
du pilote. Or l'analogique ne disparait pas dans l'analogue (le même), le capitaine
ne se réduit pas à sa fonction de pilote, le commandement ne se limite pas à la
télé-commande mais vivent de l'écart entre leurs deux termes, souffrent et jouissent
de leur irréconciliation.

L'analogie du gouvernement: l'art véritable du pilote
Comme le rappelle Descartes, la pensée *en souffrance*, en attente de sa finalité,
distingue l'homme de la machine:

> Je ne suis pas seulement logé dans mon corps ainsi qu'un pilote en son navire [...] car
> si cela n'était, lorsque mon corps est blessé, je ne sentirais pas pour cela de la douleur

---

78.   Lyotard, « Si l'on peut penser sans corps », pp. 26–7.
79.   Ibid., p. 27.

[…] mais j'apercevrais cette blessure par le seul entendement, comme un pilote aperçoit par la vue si quelque chose se rompt dans son vaisseau.[80]

La pensée ne répond donc pas à la *télé*-pathie cybernétique (transfert de pensée dans un corps substituable, sans souffrance) mais plutôt à la télé-*pathie*, pensée *en souffrance*, c'est-à-dire en attente de son sens qu'elle doit à la fois placer dans le courant du toujours-déjà inscrit et l'y soustraire pour que « vienne ce qui n'est pas encore pensé et s'inscrive ce qui doit l'être. »[81] Selon Lyotard:

> La douleur de penser n'est pas un symptôme, qui viendrait d'ailleurs s'inscrire sur l'esprit à la place de son lieu véritable. Elle est la pensée elle-même en tant qu'elle se résout à l'irrésolution, décide d'être patiente, et veut ne pas vouloir, veut, justement ne pas vouloir dire à la place de ce qui *doit* être signifié. […] J'abrège: vos machines à représenter, à penser, souffriront-elles?[82]

Il y aurait donc une autre forme de commandement qui se soustrait à la simple application d'une volonté, qui n'a pas d'origine, qui échappe au *telos* comme à *l'arkhè* et donc ne peut être télé-programmé. Pensée qui, à l'épreuve de forces contradictoires (« vouloir ne pas vouloir »), se retrouve en défaut et se laisse guider par ce qui « n'est pas encore nommé ». Pour qu'une machine puisse véritablement penser, il faudrait donc qu'elle puisse souffrir, ressentir sa propre inadéquation; soit l'écart au programme qui lui commande de se donner d'autres résolutions encore inimaginées. Le transfert analogique du *contrôle* cybernétique au modèle du gouvernement (de soi, des autres, du monde) porte à son paroxysme la tyrannie du vouloir. Puisqu'on peut, on doit le vouloir ce qui, dans son application politique, s'annonce par la *croissance à outrance*, pouvoir d'accroissement d'un vouloir, *fin sans finalité*, qui commande de loin tous nos modes de vie: « cet entrelacement des trois verbes modaux [*on doit pouvoir vouloir*] définit l'espace de la modernité et l'impossibilité d'articuler en lui quelque chose comme une éthique » dit Agamben qui y entend: « *je dois vouloir pouvoir, c'est-à-dire: je me donne l'ordre d'obéir* »[83] comme autant de reformulations de la notion de contrôle. Au contraire, le commandement éthique implique précisément un « vouloir [qui] échappe au vouloir […]. Je ne suis pas entièrement ce que je veux faire. »[84] L'éthique fait ainsi appel à un commandement qui nous expose à

---

80. René Descartes, *Œuvres et lettres* (Paris: Gallimard-Pléiade, 1937), p. 326.
81. Ibid., p. 29.
82. Ibid., p. 28.
83. Agamben, *Qu'est-ce que le commandement?*, pp. 57–8.
84. Emmanuel Levinas, *Totalité et infini* (Paris: Folio, 1990), p. 252.

l'imprescriptible c'est-à-dire à ce qu'on ne saurait prescrire ou pré-inscrire dans un programme:

> Avant de se placer au sein d'une raison impersonnelle, ne faut-il pas que les libertés puissent s'entendre librement sans que cette entente soit, d'ores et déjà, présente au sein de cette raison? [...] Autrement dit, n'y a-t-il pas déjà, de volonté à volonté, un rapport de commandement sans tyrannie, qui n'est pas encore obéissance à une loi impersonnelle, mais condition indispensable à une telle loi?[85]

L'éthique implique un commencement avant tout *arkhè* (commandement avant tout commandement), raison *sans* raison, qui se soustrait au *contrôle* du *principe de raison*, à toute volonté particulière, dans la préséance d'un dire avant tout dit. Il s'agit d'un rapport préalable à toute loi rationnelle, par lequel on participe au discours, sans contrainte, librement:

> Platon y fait allusion au moment où Thrasymaque se refuse à parler, consent à faire signe de la tête, oui et non, et finalement est entraîné par Socrate dans la discussion. Et Socrate se réjouit de constater que Thrasymaque ne fait pas que scander le discours de Socrate par oui et par non.[86]

Il y aurait donc une *navigation* du discours qui se soustrait à la simple scansion programmatique d'un langage binaire (*bits*) par « oui ou par non » (1 ou 0), qui ne se limite pas au vouloir d'un chef (*cap*-), à ses *signes de la tête*, ou à une raison qui *n'en fait qu'à sa tête*, dans l'oubli de son corps et de celui de l'Autre. Ce commandement éthique à partir de la responsabilité pour Autrui, « à rebours de l'intentionnalité et du vouloir », interrompt le programme du Même par la « tension extrême du commandement exercé par autrui en moi sur moi, l'emprise traumatique de L'Autre sur le Même »[87]. Le gouvernement de soi et aussi celui d'un moi en souffrance c'est-à-dire en attente d'une réponse qui n'est pas entièrement de sa volonté: « commandement venu *on ne sait d'où* »[88], « comme d'un passé immémorial, qui ne fut jamais présent, qui n'a commencé dans aucune liberté »[89]. Ce commandement se soustrait à toute *arkhè* comme à tout *telos*, brise l'unité et la quiétude du Même et lui interdit de se reposer dans la satisfaction d'un *principe* fut-il de *raison*. L'an-archie du commandement trouvera son écho chez de nombreux auteurs qui cherchent à se soustraire à l'emprise d'une pensée ratiocinante réduite à son modèle cybernétique. Le commandement éthique expose

---

85. Levinas, *Liberté et commandement*, p. 42.
86. Ibid., p. 43.
87. Emmanuel Levinas, *Autrement qu'être ou au-delà de l'essence* (La Haye: Martinus Nijhoff, 1974), pp. 180–2.
88. Emmanuel Levinas, *De Dieu qui vient à l'idée* (Paris: J. Vrin, 1986), p. 11.
89. Levinas, *Autrement qu'être*, p. 112.

la pensée à une *finalité* (eschatologie) *sans fin* (sans téléologie) qui se soustrait à ses attentes, et à son questionnement; contrairement aux *fins* sans *finalité* du *principe de raison* téléguidé par « cette façon de questionner qui se précipite à sa fin – la réponse – [et] comporte une sorte d'impatience en ce seul présupposé qu'en tout cas l'on peut toujours trouver une raison ou une cause à toute question »[90]. Toute pensée digne de ce nom nécessite que quelque chose arrive dont la raison ne soit pas connue. Le commandement éthique expose donc à une double contrainte: pas de pensée sans le connu; pas non plus sans inconnu. *Il faut* cette *défaillance*, étonnante in-jonction d'une pensée qui *doit* faire *défaut*, qui se retire devant l'Autre pour « être apte à accueillir ce que la pensée n'est pas préparée à penser »[91].

Commander consisterait alors à répondre d'un *mochlos* étrange, barre-espace, suspension du programme, trait d'union qui sépare le Même de l'Autre, écart entre comparant et comparé (dans l'analogie nautique) que la raison-cybernétique n'aura eu de cesse de corriger par son principe de *feedback*. Or un bon barreur sait ménager les espaces. Ainsi « dans ce que nous appelons penser, on ne dirige pas l'esprit, on le suspend. On ne lui donne pas des règles, on lui enseigne à accueillir. »[92] Penser à accueillir, accueillir la pensée, art véritable du pilote qui raisonne encore en moi de façon télépathique et que désormais je ne peux pas ne pas entendre sans la voix chaleureuse de Christopher, saint-patron des navigateurs, dont la bienveillance aura su, plus que tout autre, ménager des espaces de pensée entre disciplines et entre collègues et, générosité des plus rares, offrir à chacun le temps de penser.

> *I hope to see my Pilot face to face*
> *When I have crossed the bar…*

ORCID

Yves Gilonne ⓘ https://orcid.org/0000-0002-1812-4066

---

90. Lyotard, « Le Temps aujourd'hui », pp. 77–8.
91. Ibid., p. 77.
92. Lyotard, « Si l'on peut penser sans corps », p. 28.

Nottingham French Studies 59.3 (2020): 311–332
DOI: 10.3366/nfs.2020.0293
© University of Nottingham
www.euppublishing.com/nfs

ENCOUNTERS BETWEEN LIFE AND LANGUAGE: CODES, BOOKS, MACHINES AND CYBERNETICS

BRIGITTE NERLICH Ⓘ

Introduction

This article explores questions around life and language, a subject that interested Chris Johnson throughout his academic life. I will look at this topic through the lens of language itself, namely metaphor. A key moment in the conceptualization of life and language occurred in France in the 1950s and 1960s, and two pioneers of molecular biology, François Jacob and Jacques Monod, were at the centre of both scientific and conceptual developments in this field. Their use of terms such as 'feedback', 'control' and 'regulation' to analyse the transcription of DNA sequences drew directly on a scientific context in which cybernetics, focusing on the regulation and control of dynamic systems, played a central role in the study of life: this was the fertile intellectual ground on which molecular biology began to flourish. The important influence of cybernetics on the biological sciences at that time also connected in intricate ways with the analysis of language as a system, something that I will explore further by examining a 1967 conference called 'Vivre et parler' in which Jacob participated, together with an eminent linguist and anthropologist.[1]

While Jacob and Monod shared an interest in cybernetics, their use of linguistic insights differed. Both used metaphors such as 'information', 'code' and also 'programme', but ultimately Jacob had more of a feeling for the advantages and disadvantages of such metaphors, not only for studying life but also for thinking about the development of the sciences of life. They both tried to unravel the mysteries of life, but, as Alfred Fabre-Luce said in 1971: 'En comparant Jacques Monod et François Jacob, il m'a semblé trouver chez le second un sens plus vif de ces possibilités futures de la science.'[2] Jacob's openness to other disciplines and dimensions meant that he was aware that the conceptual framework of messages,

---

The author would like to thank John Marks for all his help with this article.

1. François Jacob, Roman Jakobson, Claude Lévi-Strauss, Pierre L'Héritier, Michel Tréguer, 'Vivre et Parler', *Les Lettres françaises*, 1221 (1968), 3–7, and 1222 (1968), 4–5.

2. Alfred Fabre-Luce, 'La Philosophie de Jacques Monod', *Revue des Deux Mondes* (1829–1971) (1971), 50–62 (p. 52).

codes and information would eventually be displaced. As he put it, new, as yet invisible, 'Russian dolls', of life and of language, would be revealed.[3] In the 1970s and early 1980s it seemed that the future Russian dolls in the field of molecular biology would be genetic engineering, manipulation and in vitro recombination. Of course, forty years later, we now have to add genomics, synthetic biology, gene editing and gene writing and much more. In linguistics we have come a long way from structuralism to contextualism and beyond. The question is: have the metaphors changed as the Russian dolls have changed or do they stay the same? This is a question I want to explore in this essay.

Cybernetics is the study of the regulation and 'control' of dynamic systems, be they mechanical, organic or electronic.[4] Biology is the study of living organisms, often regarded as dynamic systems. There should, one might think, be a lot of cross-fertilization between these fields. However, such cross-fertilization is constrained historically and linguistically. While cybernetics inspired the founders of molecular biology, modern students of biology have 'limited pedagogical training in the theory of dynamical systems'.[5] Another barrier to interactions between cybernetics and biology may be the language used to talk about biological systems. I shall focus here on one aspect of such biological systems: genetics and genomics.

As I will show, most of the metaphors used to understand and talk about genes, genomes and DNA that emerged during the heyday of cybernetics and genetics in the 1940s and 50s have highlighted static rather than dynamic, product rather than process aspects of these phenomena.[6] This in turn has contributed to popular (mis)understandings of genes, DNA or genomes as one-dimensional, deterministic, linear and fixed, rather than complex, flexible, random and dynamic.

As a consequence of side-lining the more complex, processual and dynamic aspects of cybernetics as a source for metaphors, scientists and lay people are trapped in a set of metaphors, and thus ways of thinking, which highlight the description of what DNA, genes or genomes *are*, or are supposed to be (a code, a book, a machine) rather than what they *do*. These metaphors also pervade speculations about what scientists, having achieved mastery over genes or genomes, are supposed to be able to do with genes and genomes (to code, to read, to edit,

---

3.   François Jacob, *La Logique du vivant: une histoire de l'hérédité* (Paris: Gallimard, 1970), p. 345.

4.   Matthew Cobb, *Life's Greatest Secret: The Race to Crack the Genetic Code* (London: Profile Books, 2015), p. 316.

5.   Paul Miller, 'Dynamical Systems, Attractors, and Neural Circuits', *F1000research*, 5 (2016), 1–18 (p. 9).

6.   Daniel J. Nicholson and John Dupré (eds), *Everything Flows: Towards a Processual Philosophy of Biology* (Oxford: Oxford University Press, 2018).

to write, to engineer).[7] This overemphasizes the influence of genes on what makes us human and the supposed control that scientists have over genes.

In the following, I shall investigate three metaphors, whose roots are in the 1940s and 50s, that have shaped the way in which genetics and genomics have been researched and communicated between the 1960s and now: life as a code and hence as information (discovery of the structure of DNA, development of molecular biology); life as a book (the Human Genome Project, synthetic biology, gene editing); life as a machine (molecular biology, systems biology, synthetic biology). For reasons of space, I shall not discuss other metaphors, such as programme, map and blueprint.[8] I end with a quick excursion into the metaphor of life as a signal, a metaphor, if indeed it is a metaphor, which promises to be more cybernetic than the others, but has, so far, not entered the public sphere. I will propose that one cybernetically inspired metaphor that should be but is rarely, if ever, used is life as a dynamic and continuous feedback loop or adaptive self-organization.[9] This vision of life has been in the foreground of many scientists' work, but has been pushed to the background in the language they speak and the language used to speak about them.

In 2005, Evelyn Fox Keller argued in her seminal article 'The Century of the Gene' that, although biologists now generally agreed that it was necessary to focus on the interaction between and among individual parts, she felt that they were still 'handicapped by ingrained habits of thought and speech that give ontological priority to those parts'.[10] She therefore stressed that we need 'new ways of talking'.[11] This view is shared by Jon Turney, who asked in 2009:

> How can language and indeed metaphor start to reflect this more fragmented, complex and context-dependent view of genes, which focuses no longer on what genes are but rather asks what they do within a biological system that changes and develops over time?[12]

A decade later Philip Ball, also a science writer, noted in an article on the non-existence of 'the gay gene': 'we lack a language – we have no good metaphors – for talking about what the role of genes is. The problems arise

---

7.   See Sheila Jasanoff, *Can Science Make Sense of Life?* (Cambridge: Polity Press, 2018).

8.   See John Marks's article in this special number.

9.   For a rare exception, see Jamie Davies, 'A Closed Loop', *Aeon* <https://aeon.co/essays/the-feedback-loop-is-a-better-symbol-of-life-than-the-helix> [accessed 4 August 2019].

10. Evelyn Fox Keller, 'The Century Beyond the Gene', *Journal of Biosciences*, 30:1 (2005), 3–10 (p. 9).

11. Ibid., p. 8.

12. John Turney, 'Genes, Genomes and What to Make of Them', in *Communicating Biological Sciences: Ethical and Metaphorical Dimensions*, ed. by B. Nerlich, R. Elliott and B. Larson (Farnham: Ashgate, 2009), pp. 131–44.

because we thought we did'.[13] As I will show, we thought we did have that language in the 1960s, in the context of the emergence of molecular biology, and in the 1990s and early 2000s, during the birth of genomics. But to quote the neurogeneticist Kevin Mitchell:

> To make real progress, we will need a different language, based on a different conceptual footing, with different tools and methods that can be brought to bear. Fortunately, such concepts and tools already exist, derived from cybernetics, information theory, dynamic systems theory, decision-making theory, semiotics, and many other areas.[14]

Let us now see how such a new language failed to develop when cybernetics and information theory were all the rage, not only in molecular biology and genetics but also in, especially French, linguistics. We then have to ask whether a new language steeped in this tradition might be possible today and might be able to rejuvenate biology.

Life as a code (and as information)
The dominant current understanding of genetics, both in research and popular understanding, is based on a number of metaphors, such as DNA or the genome as a *code, book, blueprint, programme, recipe, map* and so on.[15] The most pervasive metaphor for DNA and the human genome is the *code* metaphor. Without it, we would not have genetics, as we know it. The code metaphor started life in 1943, gathered pace in 1953 and then spread through genetics unstoppably.

In 1943, at Trinity College Dublin, the Nobel Prize-winning physicist Erwin Schrödinger gave lectures entitled 'What is Life?', in which he explored relations between quantum physics, thermodynamics and life in the context of recent discoveries in biology, coining the metaphor of 'the code script'.[16] As Matthew Cobb points out in his book *Life's Greatest Secret: The Race to Crack the Genetic Code* (2015), Schrödinger, a physicist, was one of the first to speculate about what is contained in a gene. His guess was that it was a kind of 'code script', a pattern for

---

13. Philip Ball, 'Now we've Dispensed with the Nonsense "Gay Gene" Trope, Let's Interrogate the Way we talk about Genetics and Traits Full Stop', *Prospect Magazine*, 4 (September 2019), <https://www.prospectmagazine.co.uk/WP_SITEURL/blogs/philip-ball/now-weve-dispensed-with-the-nonsense-gay-gene-trope-lets-interrogate-the-way-we-talk-about-genetics-and-traits-full-stop> [accessed 4 August 2019].

14. Kevin Mitchell, 'What are the Laws of Biology?', *The Biologist*, 64:6 (2019), 6.

15. Carmen McLeod and Brigitte Nerlich, 'Synthetic Biology, Metaphors and Responsibility', *Life Sciences, Society and Policy*, 13:13 (2017), <https://lsspjournal.biomedcentral.com/articles/10.1186/s40504-017-0061-y> [accessed 20 April 2020].

16. Cobb, *Life's Greatest Secret*, pp. 11–13.

future development. As Cobb puts it: 'This was the first time that anyone had clearly suggested that genes might contain, or even could simply be, a code.'[17]

One concept Schrödinger did not use was that of 'information',[18] a concept not yet in circulation at the time, neither in physics nor in biology, although any biologist today, if asked what the genetic code contains, would say, according to Cobb: information. Information would come to dominate biological thinking together with the code metaphor, and I shall discuss both in this section. The two concepts have distinct meanings and complex histories, a detailed discussion of which would go beyond the scope of this article.[19]

Schrödinger also wrote before the structure of DNA was discovered. However, in 1944, the year that his 1943 talk was published, *The Journal of Experimental Medicine* published an account by Oswald Avery, Colin MacLeod and Maclyn McCarty of an experiment, which showed for the first time that DNA is a carrier of what we now call 'genetic information'. A decade later, in 1953, Francis Crick wrote a letter to his son and proclaimed that DNA was 'like a code'.[20] He sent this letter in the context of the discovery of the structure of DNA by James Watson, Crick himself, Maurice Wilkins and Rosalind Franklin, for which Watson, Crick and Wilkins received the Nobel Prize in 1962. When writing to his son, Crick (and his colleagues, of course) also had in mind something like the Morse code.

DNA, as discovered at that time, is strung together by pairs of nucleotide bases: adenine and thymine, and guanine and cytosine. It became the convention to represent the nucleotides by the letters A, T, C and G. It has also become conventional to say that each of these bases or units is like a letter in a book (we shall come back to this metaphor). As Carl Zimmer put it in a recent article: 'Each living thing carries a book made up of these bases in us in the shape of the genome. In the case of the gorilla, that book is 3.04 billion letters long, comprising 21,000 genes'. In this context, the genetic code is understood to be different from the genome, which corresponds to an organism's specific genetic sequence: 'To translate the gorilla's genes into the corresponding proteins that build and do almost everything in the gorilla's body, its cells use a set of rules: the genetic code.'[21]

17. Ibid., p. 14

18. Lily E. Kay, *Who Wrote the Book of Life? A History of the Genetic Code* (Stanford: Stanford University Press, 2000), p. 66.

19. U.E. Stegmann, '"Genetic Coding" Reconsidered: An Analysis of Actual Usage', *British Journal for the Philosophy of Science*, 67:3 (2016), 707–30.

20. Francis Crick, 'Letter to his Son' (1953), *Letters of Note*, <http://lettersofnote.com/2015/07/a-most-important-discovery.html> [accessed 15 January 2019].

21. Carl Zimmer, 'Creating Life as We Don't Know It', *Nautilus Magazine*, 6 (2013) <http://nautil.us/issue/6//secret-codes/creating-life-as-we-dont-know-it> [accessed 16 January 2019].

George Gamow, who, like Crick, Watson and others, attempted to solve the problem of how the ordering of four different bases A, C, T and G in DNA chains might control the synthesis of proteins from their constituent amino acids, the so-called 'coding-problem', used the word 'code' in 1954, a use that can be traced back directly to Schrödinger's 'code script'. That was also the time when Crick started to use the term 'information' to refer to what was passed (via the code) between nucleotides and amino acids.[22]

In popular discourse, the phrase 'the genetic code' has assumed a rather deterministic meaning, based on some over-hyped pronouncements by famous geneticists like James Watson, for example, who stated that our fate is in our genes.[23] Such claims of genes and the genetic code controlling our destiny are now largely disputed,[24] highlighting the need for different metaphors and different ways of talking about biology.[25] As we have seen, Schrödinger wrote at a time when the concept of 'information' did not yet circulate in science and technology discourses. As D. J. Nicholson points out, after Second World War ideas from cybernetics, information theory, and computer science inspired a new vision of the cell as a machine that fed into the research programme of what came to be known as 'molecular biology'.[26]

In 1948, Norbert Wiener published his hugely popular book *Cybernetics or Control and Communication in the Animal and the Machine*.[27] He conceived the book in Paris, inspired by interactions with people like Alan Turing, John B. S. Haldane and the University of Manchester computer pioneers.[28] Wiener coined the term 'cybernetics' initially for the study of messages as a means of controlling machinery (for example, anti-aircraft control).[29] In this context, the issue of 'control' became highly important, something that Wiener tried to encapsulate in the word 'cybernetics' itself, derived from the Greek for 'steersman'.

---

22. Cobb, *Life's Greatest Secret*, pp. 113–17.

23. See Linda L. McCabe and Edward R. B. McCabe, *DNA: Promise and Peril* (Berkeley: University of California Press, 2008), p. 32.

24. See Kevin Mitchell, 'Wired That Way: Genes Do Shape Behaviours but It's Complicated', *Princeton University Press Blog*, December 2018, <http://blog.press.princeton.edu/2018/12/04/kevin-mitchell-wired-that-way-genes-do-shape-behaviours-but-its-complicated/> [accessed 3 January 2019].

25. Nicholson and Dupré (eds), *Everything Flows*.

26. Daniel J. Nicholson, 'Is the Cell Really a Machine?', *Journal of Theoretical Biology*, 477 (2019), 108–26 (p. 109).

27. Norbert Wiener, *Cybernetics or Control and Communication in the Animal and the Machine* (New York: Technology Press, 1948).

28. Cobb, *Life's Greatest Secret*, p. 74 and Christopher Johnson, '"French" Cybernetics', *French Studies*, 69:1 (2015), 60–78.

29. August W. Smith, 'Information Theory and Cybernetics', *Journal of Cybernetics*, 4:3 (1974), 1–5.

Cybernetics became the study of control and apparently purposive behaviour in animals and machines, as Wiener had suggested that living systems should be viewed as systems governed by feedback control.[30] The concept of control is linked to concepts such as negative feedback, homeostasis, self-regulation, and checks and balances (think of the 'governor' in a steam engine, for example). Control in cybernetics involves the coupling of two systems in 'control' and 'effector' components. 'In the generation of machines that informed Wiener's theorization of cybernetics, such control is effected by way of an information-bearing signal defining the actions to be performed.'[31] And so we come to information.

Wiener's book brought the vocabulary of information to bear on genetics, but he was not alone in this. This was the era of information theory, 'a subfield of communication engineering dedicated to the study of how improved encryption codes enabled more efficient and error resistant data transmission'.[32] In 1948, Claude Shannon, who had completed a PhD thesis entitled, 'An Algebra for Theoretical Genetics', published two seminal articles on communication systems,[33] followed in 1949 by the famous book with Warren Weaver, *The Mathematical Theory of Communication*.[34] Shannon and Weaver's model, indeed diagrammatic depiction of communication, represented a linear (information) flow of a signal from an information source through a transmitter to a receiver and a destination with 'noise' lurking in the background potentially disrupting efficient transmission of messages.

In mathematical communications theory, the definition of information is simply a measure of, for example, the accuracy or probability of transmitting signals or symbols: 'It may have nothing to do with knowledge or meaning inherent in the content of the symbols.'[35] This is important, as 'communication theories' in linguistics, which involve meaning, were later inspired by this model. Moreover, in a mathematical model of communication, the concept of information is linked to that of entropy and the second law of thermodynamics (thus linking back to Schrödinger). The concept is also related to that of 'organization' which became extremely important for molecular biologists like François Jacob, as we shall see.

30. Cobb, *Life's Greatest Secret*, p. 306.

31. Johnson, '"French" Cybernetics', p. 65.

32. Barry D. Geoghegan, 'From Information Theory to French Theory: Jakobson, Lévi-Strauss, and the Cybernetic Apparatus', *Critical Inquiry*, 38:1 (2011), 96–126 (p. 97).

33. Claude E. Shannon, 'A Mathematical Theory of Communication', *Bell System Technical Journal*, 27:3 (1948), 379–423, and Claude E. Shannon, 'Communication Theory of Secrecy Systems', *Bell System Technical Journal*, 28:4 (1949), 656–715.

34. Claude E. Shannon and Warren Weaver, *The Mathematical Theory of Communication* (Urbana: University of Illinois Press, 1949).

35. Charles De Quincey, *Radical Nature: The Soul of Matter* (New York: Simon and Schuster, 2010).

As Wiener pointed out: 'Just as the amount of information in a system is a measure of its degree of organization, so the entropy of a system is a measure of its degree of disorganization; and one is simply the negative of the other.'[36] Information is negative entropy, just as, according to Schrödinger, life is negative entropy.

Shannon and Weaver's theory of information and communication was initially developed not to examine human communication (and certainly not semantic meaning), but to separate 'noise' from 'information' carrying signals and to evaluate the efficiency of communication channels and communication codes. The model also had no room for feedback.[37] The model was further developed by Colin Cherry, a cognitive scientist interested in radar engineering, in his 1957 book *On Human Communication*.[38] This influenced the establishment in linguistics of a linear model of communication that became, after various iterations and transmutations, the dominant model of communication popularized by linguists such as Roman Jakobson.[39]

At the same time as cybernetically-inspired linear models of communication and information were emerging, molecular biologists developed a rather mechanistic model of life in general and of the cell in particular. Jacques Monod, the Nobel prize-winning French biologist, 'argued that organisms should be thought of as cybernetic structures, governed by patterns of control and feedback.' 'He also argued that the components of many cellular molecular networks interact in a way that is based on information, not on chemical structure.'[40] The 'code' (metaphor) was as important to him as the 'machine' (metaphor), to which we shall turn later in this article. He felt that the research in the field of molecular biology had revealed a 'cybernetic network' in the heart of the cell that assured the coherent functioning of the intracellular chemical machinery.[41]

In the 1960s and 70s, both linguists and biologists were completely aware of the dynamic aspects of cybernetics but these were sidelined in popular models of communication and of life, which were rather deterministic. We shall now see how a linguist and a biologist came together to talk about life and language and what this can show us about the confluence of thinking about language and life at a time when the code metaphor (and related metaphors) dominated the scene.

---

36. Wiener, *Cybernetics*, p. 43.

37. Cobb, *Life's Greatest Secret*, p. 78.

38. Colin Cherry, *On Human Communication: A Review, A Survey, and A Criticism* (Cambridge, MA: MIT Press, 1957).

39. Colin Cherry, Morris Halle and Roman Jakobson, 'Toward the Logical Description of Languages in their Phonemic Aspect', *Language*, 29:1 (1953), 34–46.

40. Cobb, *Life's Greatest Secret*, pp. 306–7.

41. Jacques Monod, *Le Hasard et le nécessité: essai sur la philosophie naturelle de la biologie moderne* (Paris: Seuil, 1970), pp. 77–8.

Encounter between life as a code and language as a code

During the 1950s and 60s one can observe a gradual intertwining of linguistics and genetics, which owed much to the enthusiasm of two people: the linguist Roman Jakobson, and, at least initially, the geneticist François Jacob, both interested in cybernetics.[42] The field of cybernetics flourished for a time when concepts of information, feedback and control were generalized from specific applications to systems in general, including systems of living organisms and systems of language. In France, cybernetics became fashionable through the work of people like Albert Ducrocq, a prolific science communicator, who wrote popular books in which he discussed the newest discoveries in biology, such as *Découverte de la cybernétique* (1955) and *Le Roman de Vie* (1966), the second part of his *Cybernétique et univers.*[43] Shortly after the publication of this book, in 1967, cybernetics made its appearance in a televized discussion between a linguist, a geneticist, a biologist and an anthropologist. I shall here focus on the contribution to this debate by two people: François Jacob and Roman Jakobson, a biologist and a linguist.

Inspired by cybernetics and information theory, Jacob had elaborated with Monod and others a new model of how cells organize, control and regulate the processes of life within themselves to maintain homeostasis and ensure survival, focusing especially on how genes are expressed and regulated. To put it in more detail, they discovered how bacteria controlled the production of the enzyme beta-galactosidase: 'This system of feedback and negative regulation became the lac operon and was the first model for the control of protein production.'[44] Together with Monod, Jacob also discovered messenger RNA, which transmits information encoded in the base sequence to ribosomes, the sites of protein synthesis. It is not surprising that Monod wrote an unpublished manuscript entitled *Enzymatic Cybernetics* (1959) in which he used cybernetics to understand bacteria through the lens of, for example, 'regulator genes' 'controlling' structural genes through 'feedback loops'.[45]

Around the same time as Jacob and Monod began to establish molecular biology, Jakobson, a linguist, inspired by cybernetics and biology, as well as, of course, the work of general linguist and father of structuralism, Ferdinand de Saussure, developed theories of language as a (hierarchical) system of systems and of communication as the (linear) transmission of messages via a code between an

---

42. See Kay, *Who Wrote the Book of Life?*

43. See Johnson, '"French" Cybernetics'. Albert Ducrocq, *Découverte de la cybernétique* (Paris: Julliard, 1955) and Albert Ducrocq, *Le Roman de la vie: cybernétique et univers II* (Paris: Julliard, 1966).

44. I take this description from <https://www.dnalc.org/view/15884-The-lac-operon.html> [accessed 4 April 2019].

45. See Kay, *Who Wrote the Book of Life?*, p. 311.

encoder and a decoder.[46] He contributed to establishing the school of structural linguistics, sharing with Jacob an emphasis on the central importance of concepts such as system, structure, organization and regulation, together with information and communication.

Jakobson and Jacob met during a televized debate entitled 'Vivre et parler', aired in France in September 1967 and subsequently published under that title in the journal, *Les Lettres françaises*.[47] The printed version of the debate contains a figure derived from Ducrocq's book *Le Roman de la vie*. Two other scholars participated in the debate, the famous anthropologist Claude Lévi-Strauss and the not so well-known geneticist Philippe L'Héritier. Like Jakobson's work in linguistics, Lévi-Strauss's work in anthropology had been influenced by cybernetics, as was indeed the whole French tradition of linguistic structuralism and post-structuralism. I cannot analyse the whole text in this section of the article. I will focus instead on some seminal pronouncements by Jacob and Jakobson with a focus on their metaphorical framing of life and language.

The debate was largely Jacob's brainchild. When the moderator, Michel Treguer, asks him to explain how he came up with the idea for this debate, Jacob draws an analogy between genetic information and the functioning of language:

> [...] ce que nous appelons l'information génétique, c'est-à-dire l'ensemble des caractères d'un individu – et portée par une substance chimique et on connaît, l'acide désoxyribonucléique, qui est une longue fibre polymétrique et on sait que cette information est véritablement inscrite dans le chromosome, à l'aide d'éléments très simples, de quatre éléments simples qui sont répétés et permutés par millions le long de la fibre, exactement comme dans la phrase d'un texte [...].[48]

They then talk about language as a system, organization and structure and agree on something rather profound proposed by Jacob, namely that one of the easiest ways to make something complicated or complex is to combine something simple. This applies to sentences as well as to genetic sequences (and indeed the Morse code, for example).

Jakobson then points out that there is a real analogy between 'le système de la génétique moléculaire et le système linquistique' and that this is based on the fact that both are hierarchical. Next, he talks about the genetic alphabet, focusing on the linear rather than the hierarchical, namely 'les codons ou bien, comme le disent au moins certains généticiens américains, les mots du code'.[49] They move on to reflect on the similarity in structure between molecules and language and the origins of

---

46. See Geoghegan, 'From Information Theory to French Theory'.
47. Jacob et al., 'Vivre et Parler', 1221, 3–7, and 1222, 4–5.
48. Jacob et al., 'Vivre et Parler', 1221 (1968), p. 3.
49. Jacob et al., 'Vivre et Parler', 1221 (1968), p. 6.

language. This leads them to debate the status of 'signification' or meaning in the genetic and linguistic code.

One question, especially pushed by L'Héritier, is that of the decoder, who, in human language extracts meaning from an encoded message; but what is the status of the decoder in genetics where we observe the translation of 'le langage nucléique en langage protéique'? That question is not really resolved. They do not mention Shannon's shunning of 'meaning' for example. However, they do raise the issue of how we get from linearity to architecture and from the simple to the complex. In this context, L'Héritier points out that 'à partir de cette espèce d'information codée que réçoit un organisme à l'origine de son existence, il bâtit une structure qui, elle, n'est pas linéaire, qui est une espèce d'idéogramme en fait'.[50]

Cybernetics only enters the discussion towards the end, when Jakobson talks about various books and people that have influenced his work and mentions Norbert Wiener as having had quite a bit of influence on American biologists. This then prompts Jacob to talk more about molecular biology and cybernetics and to claim that 'tout organisme procède de la traduction et de l'exécution d'un programme' and that an organism is in fact a programmed machine.[51] One thing is puzzling him though, and that is how a programme evolves and becomes more complicated over time. These reflections happen in the context of speculating about the issue of teleology in biology, a topic on which Jacob's colleague Monod reflected in depth in 1970 in his book on chance and necessity and a topic still current today.[52] Throughout the discussion the focus seems to have been on the structural aspects of language and life, both linear and hierarchical, on how complicated and complex structures emerge on the basis of something simple, mechanistic and algorithmic, such as a code or a programme. Dynamic aspects of language and life are not really touched upon.

Around the time of this debate, scientists began to publish books with titles such as *The Code of Life* (1965), *The Language of Life* (1966), and *The Book of Life* (1967) that promoted the new science of genetics.[53] As this indicates, language and life intersected strongly at this time. Indeed, while Jakobson was a visiting professor at the Salk Institute for Biological Studies in California in 1969, he delivered a paper entitled 'Language of Life and the Life of Language' at a meeting in which biology was put forward as a bridge between the 'two cultures'. Proposing that

---

50. Jacob et al., 'Vivre et Parler', 1221 (1968), p. 7.

51. Jacob et al., 'Vivre et Parler', 1222 (1968), p. 5.

52. Monod, *Le Hasard et la nécessité*.

53. Ernest Borek, *The Code of Life* (New York: Columbia University Press, 1965); George W. Beadle and Muriel Beadle, *The Language of Life: An Introduction to the Science of Genetics* (Chicago: Chicago University Press, 1966); Robert Sinsheimer, *The Book of Life* (Boston, MA: Adison-Wesley, 1967).

language was the link between the natural sciences and the humanities and referring to George and Muriel Beadle's recent book, he stated:

> The title of the book by George and Muriel Beadle, *The Language of Life*, is not mere figurative expression, and the extraordinary degree of analogy between the systems of genetic and verbal information fully justifies the guiding statement of the volume: 'The deciphering of the DNA code has revealed our possession of a language much older than hieroglyphics, a language as old as life itself, a language that is the most living language of all.[54]

Language, code and information metaphors were dominant in these encounters between linguists and geneticists in the 1960s and 70s. And yet, despite the fact that they were important for their work, linguists and biologist seem not to have used cybernetic concepts like feedback, regulation and control in their public discourse, which is a shame.

By the 1970s Jacob began to question the deeper analogies between language (conceptualized as code) and genetics. However, this emerging scepticism never destroyed the strong appeal of coding and information metaphors in genetics and genomics. It might nonetheless have been opportune to listen to Jacob when he mused about the dilemmas of scientific representation: 'Mais enfermée dans son système d'applications, la science ne peut s'en évader. Aujourd'hui le monde est messages, codes, information. Quelle dissection demain disloquera nos objets pour les recomposer en un espace neuf? Quelle nouvelle poupée russe en émergera?'[55]

The code and information metaphors that were used for life and language between around 1948 and 1968 emerged at a time when cybernetics was in vogue and with it the study of dynamic systems. Despite this, visions of linearity, necessity and determinism dominated text and talk about genes and us. This was not helped by the overuse of our next metaphor, that of 'the book of life', which emerged at the same time but came to dominate public talk about genomes in the early 2000s.[56] Interestingly, linear and static concepts of language and communication have been replaced in linguistics by more dynamic and context sensitive models, models that, however, have had no influence yet on reconceptualizing genes and genomes.

---

54. Roman Jakobson, *Main Trends in the Science of Language* (London: George Allen and IJnwin, 1973), p. 49, quoted by Kay, *Who Wrote the Book of Life?*, p. 310.

55. Jacob, *La Logique du vivant*, p. 345.

56. See Brigitte Nerlich, Richard Dingwall, and David D. Clarke, 'The Book of Life: How the Completion of the Human Genome Project was Revealed to the Public', *Health*, 6:4 (2002), 445–69.

Life as a book

While code and information metaphors dominated the period when the structure and function of DNA were discovered, the book metaphor dominated the period when scientists sequenced the entire human genome; a genome being the complete set of genes or genetic material present in a cell or organism.

The Human Genome Project (or sequencing project) began in 1990 and was completed in 2003. As it turned out, there were fewer protein-coding genes in the human genome than expected, only around 20–25,000 instead of the expected 100,000. Overall, the project revealed a vast amount of unexpected complexity and many unknowns – we still do not know, for example, what a large number of genes actually do. At the time when the project was almost constantly in the press, the early code metaphor and its cryptographic connotations were still alive. For example, in June 2000 the then Vice President of the United States, Al Gore, having noted that some genetic sequences predispose to cancer, compared the human genetic code to the 'Nazi's secret code', before proclaiming: 'With the completion of the Human Genome, we are on the verge of cracking another enemy's secret code.'[57]

However, another metaphor for the genome was in the ascendant, namely the metaphor of the 'book of life', a metaphor that is grounded in layers of cultural knowledge that go much deeper than twentieth-century information discourse and that almost obliterated all references to cybernetics. In 2000, when the human genome was almost completely sequenced, the then President of the United States, Bill Clinton, quoted Alexander Pope's rhetorical question: 'What more powerful form of study of mankind could there be than to read our own instruction book?'. Clinton concluded: 'Today, we celebrate the revelation of the first draft of the human book of life.'[58] At the same press conference, Francis Collins, one of the leaders of the Human Genome Project, said: 'It is humbling for me and awe inspiring to realize that we have caught the first glimpse of our own instruction book, previously known only to God.'[59] The human genome was hence framed as an almost biblical book of instructions about how to make a human.

Whereas the code metaphor links genetic discourse to information theory, cryptanalysis, mathematics, cybernetics and modern science, the book, letter and

---

57. Quoted by George J. Annas, 'The Limits of State Laws to Protect Genetic Information', *New England Journal of Medicine*, 345 (2001), 385–8 (p. 385).

58. Bill Clinton, 'June 2000 White House Event', *National Human Research Institute Archives*, <https://www.genome.gov/10001356/june-2000-white-house-event/> [accessed 23 January 2019].

59. Francis Collins, 'June 2000 White House Event', *National Human Research Institute Archives*, <https://www.genome.gov/10001356/june-2000-white-house-event/> [accessed 23 January 2019].

word metaphors anchor genetic and later genomic discourse to older technologies, such as the printing press, as well as deep-seated cultural knowledge of religion, the mystical and the supernatural, giving them added rhetorical power. These connotations also project additional images of design, determinism and destiny onto the complex and dynamic world of the human genome.

It is difficult to say who used the 'book of life' metaphor for the first time. One of the first uses appears to be in Robert Sinsheimer's booklet entitled precisely *The Book of Life* from 1967, in which he stated:

> In this book are instructions, in a curious and wonderful code, for making a human being. In one sense – on a subconscious level – every human being is born knowing how to read this book in every cell of his body. But on the level of conscious knowledge it is a major triumph of biology in the past two decades that we have begun to understand the content of these books and the language in which they are written.[60]

In the political speeches of Clinton and even Collins, the book of life is linked to God in what is surely an attempt to appeal to the American public. In Sinsheimer, by contrast, we find no reference to God. The 'instruction book' is democratized and embodied (albeit only in a male body!): 'every human being is born knowing how to read this book in every cell of his body'.

In 1966, one year before the publication of Sinsheimer's booklet, his colleague, George Beadle, had published, together with his wife Muriel, *The Language of Life*, in which they speculated that errors could be erased from the gene pool, in an active intervention into the book of life that goes beyond being able to read or decipher it.[61] It would take a few decades to flesh out this metaphor of editing the genome and achieve what we now call 'gene/genome editing' – an attempt to alleviate human suffering, especially related to monogenetic diseases, that some call 'playing God'. In 2015 the book of life was resurrected in the context of genome editing, which involves a range of new technologies, such as CRISPR Cas9, and which allows experts to edit genomes with much greater precision than before, that is, to engage in almost literal cutting and pasting using so-called molecular scissors.

As Anjana Ahuja, wrote in the *Financial Times*, in an article entitled 'Geneticists' Quest for Crisper Prose in the Book of Life': 'Imagining ourselves as glorified books, penned in the language of genes, is a fitting analogy as we muddle on. At some point, society must decide whether any person deserves to be a perfect piece of prose, or whether we should each remain an unedited thriller with

---

60. Sinsheimer, *The Book of Life*, pp. 5–6.
61. Kay, *Who Wrote the Book of Life?*, p. 291.

an unpredictable ending.'[62] Given the progress in digital and computer technologies, it is no surprise that other metaphors beyond the older book/editing ones are also being used in this context. The first popular science book on gene/genome editing harks back to the code metaphor and is entitled *Hacking the Code of Life: How Gene Editing will Rewrite our Futures* (2019).[63] Jennifer Doudna, one of the discoverers of gene editing, chose to give her book the title *A Crack in Creation: Gene Editing and the Unthinkable Power to Control Evolution* (2017), linking this new technology, unfortunately, to the metaphor of scientists 'playing God' and controlling life – a rather misleading control metaphor.[64]

All of these images overlook the extraordinary complexity of the genome and the dynamics, chance and randomness that structure it. As Steven Pinker said: 'Genetic editing would be a droplet in the maelstrom of naturally churning genomes.'[65] The idea that editing is a straightforward act also side-lines the issue of (cybernetic) 'self-organization' that makes organisms what they are. As Cohen et al. pointed out in 2009 in their article detailing the limits of the Human Genome Project:

> [...] an organism is built and operates with the help of its genome, but the genome is only one element in a recursive process. The iterating cycle of genes that form proteins that form genes is the self-organizing process from which the organism emerges. If there be a genetic programme, then such a program writes itself collectively. The action, as it were, precedes the plan.[66]

And this, I assume, applies not only to the programme of life, but also to 'the code' and 'the book', something that Jacob had already felt in the 1970s.

The book of life, like human language, will always be complex, complicated and messy, and reading, writing or editing it will never be as straightforward as it might appear to be or to become. Metaphors like 'the book of life' or 'genome editing' are useful in encapsulating all this complexity, but they can only afford us glimpses of

62. Anjana Ahuja, 'Geneticists' Quest for Crisper Prose in the Book of Life', *Financial Times*, 28 June 2015, <https://www.ft.com/content/18b4b484-1c1f-11e5-8201-cbdb03d71480> [accessed 24 January 2019].

63. Nessa Carey, *Hacking the Code of Life: How Gene Editing will Rewrite our Futures* (London: Faber & Faber, 2019).

64. Jennifer A. Doudna and Samuel H. Sternberg, *A Crack in Creation: Gene Editing and the Unthinkable Power to Control Evolution* (New York: Houghton Mifflin Harcourt, 2015).

65. Quoted in Patrick Skerrett, 'Experts Debate: Are We Playing With Fire When We Edit Human Genes?', *STAT News* (2015), <https://www.statnews.com/2015/11/17/gene-editing-embryo-crispr/> [accessed 15 January 2019].

66. Irun R. Cohen, Henri Atlan and Sol Efroni, 'Genetics as Explanation: Limits to the Human Genome Project', in *Encyclopedia of Life Sciences* (Chichester: John Wiley, 2009), pp. 1–8.

what is going on. They should not be taken as literal representations. Some early social science critics of the Human Genome Project elaborated on this insight. Colin Tudge wrote:

> To map the genes is merely to create a lexicon. How the genome works - its metaphorical syntax - is another matter again; and truly to understand the genome, we must come to terms with its literature - the ambiguities, the nuances, the subtexts. They are in there somewhere, and when the genome mapping is finished we will still be centuries from understanding them. [...] 'The literature of the genome' will take centuries to unfold.[67]

Uncertainties, ambiguities and nuances are aspects of genes and genomes, of how they work in context, that are only gradually coming to the metaphorical fore again in modern biology.

Life as a (digital) machine

So far, we have looked at two periods in the study of genes and genomes: a first one when scientists discovered the structure and function of DNA as a double-stranded sequence of nucleotides coding for proteins, and a second when they found out how to read whole genome sequences. During the next period, reading was gradually replaced by writing in the context of synthetic biology.[68] As we have seen, DNA was sometimes framed as the language in which God wrote the book of life. With the advent of synthetic biology, scientists began to 'play God' and to write or rewrite the 'code of life'; or, in modern terms, they began to 'reprogramme' life, using digital computers. Not only that, they were also able to build whole biological 'machines'.

Synthetic biology has its roots in many disciplines, but is mainly based on a convergence of engineering, computing and modelling with systems biology (and through systems biology, cybernetics), evolutionary genomics, and biotechnology. It continues a tradition of work started by scientists engaged in 'recombinant' DNA in the 1970s, but its roots also reach back to attempts to create artificial life in the 1920s.[69] It is sometimes defined as the 'application of rigorous engineering

---

67. Colin Tudge, 'The Language of the Future', *Index on Censorship*, 28:3 (1999), 172–80.

68. See Iina Hellsten and Brigitte Nerlich, 'Synthetic Biology: Building the Language for a New Science Brick by Metaphorical Brick'm *New Genetics and Society*, 30:4 (2011), 375–97, and Carmen McLeod and Brigitte Nerlich, 'Synthetic Biology, Metaphors and Responsibility', *Life Sciences, Society and Policy*, 13:1 (2017), <https://lsspjournal. biomedcentral.com/articles/10.1186/s40504-017-0061-y> [accessed 20 April 2020].

69. Manuel Porcar and Juli Pereró, 'Creating Life and the Media: Translations and Echoes', *Life Sciences, Society and Policy*, 14:1 (2018), <https://lsspjournal.biomedcentral. com/articles/10.1186/s40504-018-0087-9> [accessed 20 April 2020].

principles to biological system design and development', such as designing, modularizing, and standardizing.[70]

We should not forget that it also has strong roots in molecular biology and with this in cybernetics, although this is rarely mentioned in current synthetic biology work using metaphors of machines, bio-factories and so on, metaphors that were around in the 1960s, as the following quotation shows:

> Taking then, as an engineering definition of a living cell, 'A completely automatic factory for fabricating automatic factories like itself', we may profitably consider what components might be found in such a system. Passing over such trivia as a power station for utilizing whatever energy source might be available, it is clear that a large computer would be the control mechanism at the centre of our design. In its store would be an encyclopaedia of programmes which would give the proper response to all possible sets of external circumstances, and these would be activated by input devices which would record the external conditions and the supply position. Other input channels would monitor the progress of the various factory processes, forming the feedback loops which are essential to control mechanisms. Output from the computer would go [...] to a set of automatic machine tools which would perform the various operations required for construction of a duplicate factory. Here the complex task of converting the information stored in the computer into solid matter would be performed.[71]

The link between biology and cybernetics, control and feedback loops is clear here, but has faded into the background in current popular representations of synthetic biology. Some argue that cybernetics actually entrenched machine metaphors in biology, thus partially side-lining more dynamic aspects of biological system.[72] Monod, one of the founders of molecular biology, talked for example about the 'microscopic clockwork function' that assures a resolutely non-dialectical relationship between DNA and protein: 'Il est foncièrement cartésien et non hégélien: la cellule est bien une *machine*.'[73]

In 2010 Craig Venter, one of the pioneers involved in the Human Genome Project, managed to create a first synthetic or artificial cell, often referred to in the press as creating artificial life. In an interview he said:

> As the industrial age is drawing to a close, I think that we're witnessing the dawn of the era of biological design. DNA, as digitised information, is accumulating in computer databases. Thanks to genetic engineering, and now the field of synthetic

---

70. The Royal Academy of Engineering, Synthetic Biology: Scope, Applications and Implications (May 2009), <https://www.raeng.org.uk/publications/reports/synthetic-biology-report> [accessed 20 April 2020].

71. David M. Blow, 'The Molecular Approach to Biology', *Contemporary Physics*, 3 (1962), 177–93 (p. 177).

72. Nicholson, 'Is the Cell Really a Machine?'.

73. Monod, *Le Hasard et la nécessité*, p. 125.

> biology, we can manipulate DNA to an unprecedented extent, just as we can edit software in a computer.

And, more importantly:

> All the information needed to make a living, self-replicating cell is locked up within the spirals of DNA's double helix. As we read and interpret that software of life, we should be able to completely understand how cells work, then change and improve them by writing new cellular software.[74]

Here the book of life has become the software of life, and supercomputers can now sequence, decipher, as well as (re)assemble life – they can write and rewrite it.

Using such 'software', synthetic biology has the ambition to build or create biological machines or devices that do not yet exist and to make them programmable and able to perform certain tasks. Hence, 'single cell organisms are described as "genetically engineered machines" [...], intracellular molecular processes are "genetic circuits" [...], and genetically engineered organisms are referred to as "platform organisms"'.[75] Sometimes synthetic biology is described as designing 'bio-factories'.

In their most elementary form, synthetic biological machines are in fact 'circuits'. Through the 'metaphor' of 'circuits' a link is re-established with bio-cybernetics within synthetic biology. However, while the circuit metaphor is ubiquitous, references to cybernetics are relatively rare or rather indirect. As a recent article on synthetic biological circuits has highlighted, a 'central design problem in synthetic biology is to devise circuits that combine biological parts such as genes, RNAs, or proteins to achieve pre-defined dynamic behavior'.[76] These circuits can be assembled into larger systems 'in order to obtain more complex circuit behaviors with controlled features such as switches, amplifiers, and pulse generators'. And that brings us back to 'systematic, model-based design methods using systems and control theory concepts', that is, cybernetics.[77] As some synthetic biologists have explained: 'Biological systems are cybernetic machines in that they hold a history and the history or experience changes the outputs even though the input is the same' – feedback loops, learning (from past experience/history), self-organization and self-correction are

---

74. Quoted in Roger Highfield, 'J. Craig Venter Sequenced the Human Genome. Now he Wants to Convert DNA into a Digital Signal (Interview)', *Wired Magazine*, November 2013, <https://www.wired.co.uk/article/j-craig-venter-interview> [accessed 13 January 2019].

75. John Boldt, 'Machine Metaphors and Ethics in Synthetic Biology', *Life Sciences, Society and Policy*, 14:1 (2018), <https://lsspjournal.biomedcentral.com/articles/10.1186/s40504-018-0077-y> [accessed 20 April 2020].

76. Claude Lormeau, Mikolaj Rybiński and Jorg Stelling, 'Multi-objective Design of Synthetic Biological Circuits' *IFAC-PapersOnLine*, 50:1 (2017), 9871–76 (p. 9871).

77. Lormeau, Rybinski and Stelling, 'Multi-objective Design', p. 9871.

important here.[78] Cybernetic machines are not deterministic; they are, amongst other things, 'stochastic' (i.e. have random probability distributions or patterns that may be analysed statistically but may not be predicted precisely).

This hints at the limits to the machine metaphor – namely a constant interaction between context and complexity:

> The engineering ideal of synthetic biology presupposes that organisms are composed of standard, interchangeable parts with a predictive behaviour. In one word, organisms are literally recognized as of a design by external agents. Biological components show massive overlapping and functional degeneracy, standard-free complexity, intrinsic variation and context dependent performances.[79]

As Carl Woese wrote in 2004: 'it is becoming increasingly clear that to understand living systems in any deep sense, we must come to see them not materialistically, as machines, but as (stable) complex, dynamic organization'.[80] These are dynamic aspects of genes, genomes, cells and organisms that are rarely talked about in the public sphere, as they are not easy to 'metaphorize'.

In the more rarefied atmosphere of, especially French, literary criticism, postmodernism and cultural studies we find however some use of the metaphor of 'bricolage' which was inspired by cybernetics. In synthetic biology there is some reflection on the notion of 'tinkering' in evolution, a notion inspired by François Jacob, which could be used to think beyond the engineering metaphors favoured in synthetic biology.[81] Both bricolage and tinkering are, unfortunately, concepts still confined to academic rather than public discourse about biology and genetics.

In current philosophy of science there is much reflection on processes and their importance in biology, as opposed to products or machines, even cybernetic machines, it is argued. Nicholson claims that servomechanisms, that is 'machines controlled by negative feedback with a certain capacity to self-regulate (e.g. thermostats) or to self-steer (e.g. homing missiles) [...] are closed, near, equilibrium systems, and consequently [...] are not capable of truly adaptive self-maintenance',[82] unlike organisms.

---

78. See Martin Döring, Imme Petersen, Anne Brüninghaus and Regine Kollek (eds), *Contextualizing Systems Biology: Presuppositions and Implications of a New Approach in Biology* (New York: Springer, 2015).

79. Manuel Porcar and Juli Peretó, 'Nature versus Design: Synthetic Biology or How to Build a Biological Non-Machine', *Integrative Biology*, 8:4 (2015), 451–5 (p. 451).

80. Christian R. Woese, 'A New Biology for a New Century', *Microbiology and Molecular Biology Reviews*, 68:2 (2004), 173–86.

81. Victor de Lorenzo, 'Evolutionary Tinkering vs. Rational Engineering in the Times of Synthetic Biology', *Life Sciences, Society and Policy*, 14:1 (2018), 18 <https://lsspjournal.biomedcentral.com/articles/10.1186/s40504-018-0086-x> [accessed 20 April 2020].

82. Nicholson, 'Is the Cell Really a Machine?', p. 117.

Cybernetics therefore can be seen as an important source of inspiration for both linguistics and molecular biology. It opened up thinking to dynamics and feedback, but perhaps not quite enough. However, even some of that thinking and some cybernetically inspired metaphors might have enabled better public discussions of genes and genomes, not only of what they are but of what they do.

Life as a signal

I shall now briefly discuss one final metaphor, that of life as a signal, which has not been taken up in popular discourse about genetics. Its use in scientific circles highlights however that cybernetics has never been far away from scientists' minds, even if they do not use that word. Remember what Chris Johnson said about cybernetics: 'In the generation of machines that informed Wiener's theorization of cybernetics, such control is effected by way of an information-bearing signal defining the actions to be performed'.[83]

In 2011 Evelyn Fox Keller captured something that was in the air for a long time, especially after the 'decipherment' of the human genome:

> I suggest that the genome that now appears before us is first and foremost an exquisitely sensitive reaction (or response) mechanism – a device for regulating the production of specific proteins in response to the constantly changing signals it receives from its environment. The signals that the genome detects come most immediately from the intra-cellular environment, but these reflect, in turn, inputs from the external environments both of the cell and of the environment.[84]

Hannah Landecker, a historian of science, quotes this passage in an article on the cybernetic legacy in the new field of epigenetics.[85]

Although not very well defined,[86] on the whole, epigenetics focuses in on various dynamic aspects of body-environment interactions, interactions shaped by cell-signalling. While in mainstream genetic discourse the focus is mainly on 'information' carried by DNA which is rather mechanistically translated into proteins via the genetic code, in epigenetics, the emphasis is on dynamic signal processing networks. Of course, these have been studied throughout the history of genetics and genomics, but had been blended out in popular discourse and popular metaphors.

---

83. Johnson, '"French" Cybernetics', p. 65.
84. Evelyn Fox Keller, 'Genes, Genomes, and Genomics', *Biological Theory*, 6:2 (2011), 132–40 (p. 139).
85. Hannah Landecker, 'The Social as Signal in the Body of Chromatin', *Sociological Review*, 64:1 (2016), 79–99.
86. See John M. Greally, 'A User's Guide to the Ambiguous Word "Epigenetics"', *Nature Reviews Molecular Cell Biology*, 19:4 (2018), 207–8.

As Paul Davies has recently said, after quoting Max Delbrück, a 1930s pioneer of molecular biology: 'A distinctive feature – perhaps the distinctive feature – of life is its ability to use [...] informational pathways for regulation and control, and to manage signals between components to progress towards a goal.'[87] This very much echoes cybernetic insights into how information works in dynamic systems (although Davies goes beyond these roots too):

> Treating information as a physical quantity with its own dynamics enables us to formulate 'laws of life' that transcend life's physical substrate. When these laws include feedback loops that make the flow of information depend on the global state of the system as well as nearby components, the main elements are in place to describe a system in which, to use the overworked phrase, the whole is greater than the sum of its parts. And so we can begin to explain notions of regulation, control and purposive behaviour that are so central to life.[88]

Life is a dynamic feedback loop, not only a code or a book! That should have been a central metaphor for talking about life, the universe and everything, despite some of the limitations pointed out by philosophers of science. But sadly, it was not, despite cybernetics offering it up at a time when the life sciences and the language sciences exploded on the scientific and on the public scene.

Metaphors such as code, book and machine (as well as programme and blueprint) still dominate biological discourse in society, making us think of life in relatively deterministic ways, whereas a focus on feedback loops may give us a glimpse of life as dynamic process, of organisms maintaining a stable internal environment while constantly adjusting to external disturbances.

It might be time to adjust the metaphorical lenses through which we see life and to no longer ask what organisms, cells, genes etc. *are*, but what they *do* and how they interact with each other and the environment. By 'we' I mean mainly us lay people, rather than scientists, who have always had a dual metaphorical vision of life as static but also dynamic and cybernetic. But to find this new vision of life, we need the help of scientists, who have to change some of the language they use when talking to and with us.

Conclusion

While the metaphors we use to talk about life have stayed static, including their deterministic connotations, scientists working to reveal the mysteries of life, have moved well beyond such static views and have become increasingly interested in the ambiguities, complexities, flexibilities and uncertainties surrounding the workings of genes and genomes. Biologists are gaining ever more understanding not only of the structure and sequence of genes and genomes but of their dynamic properties.

---

87. Paul Davies, 'What is Life?', *New Scientist*, 2 February 2019, pp. 29–31 (p. 30).
88. Davies, 'What is Life?', p. 31.

This has led some to reflect anew on 'the dual role of chance (random variation) and necessity (natural selection) in the building of a dynamic genome'.[89] Such reflections began in the early part of the twentieth century.

Scientists are likewise becoming more and more aware of the fact that to do their research properly and in order to communicate its results successfully, they and we may have to develop a different language that draws inspiration from a broader set of source domains, some old some new, such as 'cybernetics, information theory, dynamic systems theory, decision-making theory, semiotics, and many other areas'.[90]

Scientists are also becoming more attuned to the language they speak and are, on the whole, humbler and more modest when talking about the code of life, for example, than their colleagues were in the past. The 2018 Nobel prize-winner, Frances Arnold, said for example: 'The code of life is like Beethoven's Symphony – it's intricate, it's beautiful. But we do not know how to write like that.'[91]

We have to try and find a language that respects this humility, on the one hand, and the complexity and dynamics of life, on the other. We also need a language that can span the lab and the wider world. The time might be ripe for linguists, social scientists and life scientists to come together again to talk about life, language and metaphors and what role cybernetics can play in this context. A focus on complexity and dynamics might prevent the entrenchment of misunderstandings about genes, genomes and even epigenomes, both about what they are and about what they do. It might also dispel persistent myths, perpetuated by some social scientists, about how scientists understand life and what power they have over it.[92]

Some biologists have expressed the hope that by using insights from cybernetics, information theory, dynamic systems theory and, even, semiotics, they might be able to go beyond simply describing what is happening to understanding what a biological system is doing, while, at the same time, devising a new language to describe what they and the systems they are studying are doing.[93] They should be encouraged.

ORCID

Brigitte Nerlich https://orcid.org/0000-0001-6617-7827

---

89. Antonio Fontdevila, *The Dynamic Genome: A Darwinian Approach* (Oxford: Oxford University Press, 2011).

90. Mitchell, 'What are the Laws of Biology?', p. 6.

91. The Nobel Prize Twitter account, tweet of 8 December 2018: <https://twitter.com/nobelprize/status/1071398780719820800?lang=en> [accessed 15 January 2019].

92. See Jasanoff, *Can Science Make Sense of Life?*

93. See Mitchell, 'What are the Laws of Biology?', p. 6.

Nottingham French Studies 59.3 (2020): 333–349
DOI: 10.3366/nfs.2020.0294
© University of Nottingham
www.euppublishing.com/nfs

FRANÇOIS JACOB: *BRICOLAGE* AND THE POSSIBLE

JOHN MARKS

Introduction

The 'molecular revolution' in biology in the post-war era introduced a radical new conception of the living world. Bringing together genetics and biochemistry, molecular biology began to explore the relationship between three types of macromolecule: DNA, RNA and proteins. In the course of identifying the structure and function of these macromolecules, this new biology also constructed a new, informational paradigm of life. Concepts such as code and programme, taken from computer science, information theory and cybernetics, provided new ways of understanding processes that had previous been explained in terms of vital forces. François Jacob is one of the most significant figures in the small group of researchers who contributed to the emergence and development of molecular biology. His scientific career started in 1950 at the Institut Pasteur, where he worked initially with André Lwoff and Elie Wollman on lysogeny and bacterial conjugation. In the late 1950s he started working in collaboration with Jacques Monod and, in 1965, Jacob, Monod and Lwoff were awarded a Nobel Prize for their work on gene regulation. In the 1970s Jacob switched the focus of his research away from bacteria to multicellular organisms, focusing on the embryonic development of mice.

As Mark Ptashne emphasized in an obituary from 2013, Jacob's capacity to perceive links and express complex ideas in an accessible way was at the heart of his work both as a scientist and as a writer: 'If there is a secret to Jacob's power, it was his ability to see connections – analogies – where others saw only separate phenomena and then to find the underlying reality.'[1] Unsurprisingly, given this talent for concise expression, he engaged in an extended epistemological analysis of the history and practice of biology throughout this highly distinguished career as a scientist, producing a number of widely-read publications. He was, in short, a genuinely pivotal figure, both in the sense that he was able to bridge the gap between the 'two cultures',[2] and also in the way that his scientific and epistemological work operates at the historical and conceptual junction between

---

1. Mark Ptashne, 'François Jacob (1920–2013)', *Cell*, 153 (6 June 2013), 1180–2 (p. 1180).
2. Michel Morange, 'How François Jacob Bridged the Gap Between the "Two Cultures"', *Research in Microbiology*, 5 (June 2014), 391–3.

the paradigms of deterministic reductionism and emergence. This article will consider in detail the analogies, metaphors and concepts that Jacob develops in series of widely-read books: *La Logique du vivant* (1970);[3] *Le Jeu des possibles* (1981);[4] and *La Souris, la mouche et l'homme* (2000).[5] One short and highly influential paper, published in 1977, must be added to this list: 'Evolution and Tinkering'.[6] In this much-cited paper (the text of a lecture delivered at the University of California Berkeley) Jacob introduced the metaphor of DIY tinkering ('bricolage' in French), which he had adapted from Claude Lévi-Strauss, as a way of understanding evolution in the light of recent developments in biology. As this article will show, *bricolage* functions as a broader, multi-faceted metaphor for Jacob: a kind of meta-metaphor. The idea of fortuitous connections, and of contingent routes navigated through a range of possible scenarios recurs throughout his work. It encapsulates not only his distinctive understanding of evolution as an ongoing process of opportunistic solutions, but also conveys his experience of scientific practice being propelled by moments of intuitive insight and connection.

Science for Jacob is resolutely non-dialectical, in that there is no transcendental resolution of the relations between what he calls 'day' and 'night' science, reductionism and evolutionism, and the 'possible' and the 'actual'. His epistemo-logical speculations always function on two levels simultaneously, as both a reflection on the nature of living systems and also on the practice of science. As Michel Morange points out, Jacob's view of science is essentially constructivist, in the sense that scientific knowledge is the construction of a world rather than the process of revealing a world that is exterior to human consciousness.[7] It is thought that frames and directs what science can perceive, rather than the tools that are available at any particular time (*LV*, p. 345). The metaphor of *bricolage* provided Jacob with a way of conceptualizing living systems that challenged the vision of machine-like precision that characterized, for example, Monod's perspective on evolution by allowing for redundancy, useless complexity, blind alleys, and *ad hoc* arrangements. As this article will show, although Jacob recognizes the efficacy of reductionism throughout his career, he increasingly moves away from metaphors

---

3. François Jacob, *La Logique du vivant: une histoire de l'hérédité* (Paris: Gallimard, 1970). Henceforth *LV*.
4. François Jacob, *Le Jeu des possibles: essai sur la diversité du vivant* (Paris: Fayard, 1981). Henceforth *JP*.
5. François Jacob, *La Souris, la mouche et l'homme* (Paris: Odile Jacob, 2000). Henceforth *SMH*.
6. François Jacob, 'Evolution and Tinkering', *Science*, 196:4295 (10 June 1977), 1161–6. Henceforth *ET*.
7. Michel Morange, 'Introduction', in *Les Travaux scientifiques de François Jacob* (Paris: Odile Jacob, 2002), pp. 7–66 (p. 63).

drawing on code, programme and language. *Bricolage* as a concept encompasses more comfortably Jacob's dual focus on the importance of a restricted repertoire of basic building components which can be combined and recombined in new ways that depend upon historical circumstances, and which cannot be deduced from the laws governing lower levels of organization.

Jacob and Monod
François Jacob and Jacques Monod started working together in 1957 on a scientific collaboration that ultimately marked them out as key figures in the molecular biology revolution of the post-war era. As Jacob points out, much of the research carried out in the early days of molecular biology was undertaken by teams of two. Looking back on their collaboration, he suggests that it was the theoretical dimension of their work in particular that was facilitated by working as two rather than one. A scientific field in its early stages of development requires the formulation and construction of models and theories, a process that is much more productive when it emerges from dialogue and interaction: 'Car à deux, les idées jaillissent plus vite. Elles ricochent sur le partenaire. Elles se greffent les unes sur les autres comme les branches d'un arbre' (*SMH*, p. 74). Inspired by Monod's work on diauxy (the 'double growth' of bacteria in the presence of combinations of two sugars) and Jacob's work on lysogeny (the induction of viruses in bacterial hosts), they identified what they called the Operon model of gene regulation, introducing concepts such as structural genes, regulatory genes and messenger RNA that have remained highly influential. Following on from the discovery of the double-helix structure of DNA, Jacob and Monod's development of the concept of a genetic 'programme', according to which the genome contains a set of instructions for the construction of the phenotype, represents the next major landmark in the development of molecular biology. In their highly influential 1961 article on genetic regulatory mechanisms they referred explicitly to the idea of a genetic programme for the first time: 'The discovery of regulator and operator genes, and of repressive regulation of the activity of structural genes, reveals that the genome contains not only a series of blue-prints, but a co-ordinated program of protein synthesis and the means of controlling its execution.'[8] Monod's concentration on administrative work in the 1970s and his premature death in 1977 meant that he never had the chance to develop his thinking beyond *Le Hasard et la nécessité* (1970). Jacob, however, experienced and participated in the development of molecular biology from its initial concentration on single-cell organisms though to its later engagement with higher organisms.

   Despite their close scientific collaboration, Jacob and Monod also stand as iconic figures embodying distinctly different positions in the imaginative landscape

---

8.   François Jacob and Jacques Monod, 'Genetic Regulatory Mechanisms in the Synthesis of Proteins', *Journal of Molecular Biology*, 3 (1961), 318–66 (p. 354).

of this new molecular paradigm and the intellectual life of post-war France. Monod was, at heart, a Cartesian rationalist. He identified strongly with the existentialist philosophy of Camus and saw molecular biology as austerely elegant proof of a natural world that was entirely indifferent to humanity, but which functioned according to consistent and coherent scientific laws. He wholeheartedly embraced the idea that physics could act as a model for molecular biology's project to naturalize life.[9] For this reason, he favoured the use of simple models, preferring to continue to work on *E. coli* rather than moving on to more complex organisms. Directed by these preferences, and in the context of the persistence of neo-Lamarckian ideas in French biology, Monod was convinced that molecular biology helped to explain the processes of mutation and selection that were central to the Modern Synthesis. As Michel Morange neatly summarizes: 'Monod considered that all organisms obeyed simple principles of functioning that had been shaped by natural selection.'[10] There were also political and philosophical issues at stake for Monod. He articulated his determinist, mechanist perspective on molecular biology as a counterweight to Soviet agronomist Lysenko's ideological rejection of Mendelian genetics in favour of a theory of acquired characteristics that was acceptable to Stalin as an appropriately 'dialectical' conception of biological development. Published in 1970, *Le Hasard et la nécessité* is marked by Monod's experience of the 'Lysenko affair' twenty years earlier. Molecular biology shows that the genetic material is invariant as it passes from generation to generation, and this invariance is guaranteed by the clockwork, machine functioning of the cell:

> Le système tout entier, par conséquent, est totalement, intensément conservateur, fermé sur soi-même, et absolument incapable de recevoir quelque enseignement que ce soit du monde extérieur. Comme on le voit, ce système, par ses propriétés, par son fonctionnement d'horlogerie microscopique qui établit entre ADN et protéine, comme aussi entre organisme et milieu, des relations à sens unique, défie toute description 'dialectique'. Il est foncièrement cartésien et non hégélien: la cellule est bien une *machine*.[11]

In some ways Jacob's outlook was, unsurprisingly, very close to Monod's. He was also shocked by Lysenkoism, considering that it contradicted the notion that the basic units of genetic inheritance cannot 'learn' from experience for purely ideological reasons. However, Jacob saw the living world – the world of living systems – in much less rigid and mechanical terms than Monod. He explains the

---

9.   See Morange, 'Monod and the Spirit of Molecular Biology', *Comptes rendus biologies*, 338 (2015), 380–4.

10. Morange, 'Monod and the Spirit of Molecular Biology', p. 384.

11. Jacques Monod, *Le Hasard et la nécessité: essai sur la philosophie naturelle de la biologie moderne* (Paris: Éditions du Seuil), p. 125.

contrast between his perspective and Monod's by means of a surprising – and by contemporary standards ill-judged – metaphor: 'La nature, je la voyais assez bonne fille. Généreuse mais un peu sale. Un peu brouillonne. Travaillant au coup par coup. Faisant ce qu'elle pouvait avec ce qu'elle trouvait.'[12]

Science de jour, science de nuit

Jacob's conception of science and scientific practice was also marked by a recognition of the importance of contingency and lateral thinking. Although science often tends to present itself as a purely logical process, employing the hypothetico-deductive method to take to the 'voie royale' that leads from darkness to light, Jacob was convinced that a closer inspection of real scientific practice reveals a combination of 'day science' and 'night science'. Night science is the creative and unpredictable aspect of scientific work that is often nurtured by unknown scientists, working in the obscurity of a 'cellar or attic'. These scientists are feeling their way in the dark, attempting to find articulations between apparently unconnected fragments of information. Molecular biology, he suggests, provides a model for the development of original research in an unplanned manner, emerging out of the individual curiosity of a group of scientists from diverse backgrounds between the end of the 1930s and the beginning of the 1950s (*SMH*, pp. 21–7). 'Day science' is science's elegant and polished public face, the carefully edited and tidied-up version of the endeavour in which all the gears mesh. It has the formal elegance of a Bach fugue or a French garden, and it carries itself with the swagger of certainty. 'Night science', on the other hand, is full of self-doubt and anxiety, attempting to piece together some kind of coherence from a confusing array of unconnected events. There is no clear path to scientific certainty, only a labyrinth through which the mind wanders in an agitated state, looking for a route through this confusion. Rather than relying on logic, night science can only be guided by intuition and the hope that there will be a sudden flash of inspiration that will light the way. Night science is, in a metaphorical sense, a kind of scientific unconscious, restlessly shifting through potential pathways and chancing upon unexpected connections. It functions as a sort of 'atelier du possible', in which the basic building materials of scientific practice are constructed. Science is essentially, as far as Jacob is concerned, 'a world of ideas in movement', and the writing-up of scientific research in the form of published articles inevitably means that this movement is immobilized (*SMH*, pp. 181–4).

In short, science for Jacob is closely related to art. Genuinely creative scientific practice draws on the potential of night science to perform acts of imagination, to feel its way towards a zone of the 'unknown', situated just beyond what logic and experience allows to be knowable at any given time in order to invent a fragment of a 'possible' world (*JP*, p. 28). These tropes of unconscious

---

12. François Jacob, *La Statue intérieure* (Paris: Gallimard, 1990), p. 356.

knowledge and radical reorientations of perspective are clearly influenced by Jacob's close reading of Michel Foucault's *Les Mots et les choses* (1966).[13] Jacob suggests, for example, that the orientations of art and science in a particular episteme may mirror each other. In the same way that the plays of Shakespeare, Molière, Racine and Calderon, in what Foucault calls the 'classical' age, construct a taxonomy of behaviours conveyed in the language and action of characters, so the natural sciences attempt to classify living beings according to their visible, surface characteristics. In both cases, analysis is focused on external appearance. However, at the end of the eighteenth century a significant shift occurs in both natural science and art. Poetry and the novel displace theatre as the most important literary forms, and they shift focus to the interior psychological world of the author and the characters that they portray. At the same time, the natural sciences are now interested in the common properties of interior organization that lie below the surface differences between living beings. In this context, the issue of life and what separates it from death emerges as a central question (*SMH*, pp. 190–1). The next epistemic revolution, which occurs at the end of the nineteenth century, shifts focus to the enigmatic and potentially vertiginous nature of internal structures. Again, there are parallels between the preoccupations of art and science: just as literature explores the idea that the attempt to represent interior states is always undermined by the impersonal and self-referential qualities of language, so science encounters phenomena of instability and contingency (*SMH*, p. 191–3). Although each episteme effectively sets the rules for what can be thought and perceived in a particular era, Jacob insists that they are by no means entirely coherent and homogeneous systems of thought. Instead, he suggests that it is precisely because of the instability and contingency of a given episteme as a regime of knowledge that the components of the network can be rearranged or reshuffled to reveal new possibilities.

As Jacob acknowledges, there are clear differences between art and science. Whereas the fact that science is inextricably linked to notions of progress means that the work of scientists is always consigned to history, however powerful and influential their theories and discoveries may be, a great work of art is not subject to the same historical judgement. Beethoven does not in some way surpass Bach in the same way that Einstein's work surpasses Newton's (*SMH*, pp. 195–6). Similarly, whereas a work of art is an imaginative invention, a new object that is created by the human mind, scientists discover phenomena that already exist in the real world. In short, only Flaubert could write *Madame Bovary*, but scientists are interchangeable. It is not surprising, then, that scientists rarely think of their work as creative but, Jacob insists, scientific work amounts to more than simply recording facts. Since our sensory and cerebral functions filter and organize the information that, along

---

13. Michel Foucault, *Les Mots et les choses: une archéologie des sciences humaines* (Paris: Gallimard, 1966).

with flows of matter and energy, constitutes our relationship with the world, it is clear that scientists undertake a process of selection and composition that is similar to the work of the artist. As Jacob puts it, the physicist's description of the atom is not simply a fixed representation of reality, but rather an abstract model developed over centuries: it is as much a creation as a discovery (*SMH*, p. 200). In this sense, science is a question of *style* just as much as art: a way of questioning the world and formulating a narrative. Jacob is strikingly effusive and expansive in his admiring description of Pasteur's 'style': his Napoleonic capacity to think strategically and intuitively, and to move rapidly from one scientific field to another in the manner of the cavalry charge (*SMH*, p. 201). By means of such acts of intellectual and imaginative audacity, science constructs the world rather than discovering it, and significant breakthroughs often occur unexpectedly in moments of distraction, when the mind is absorbed in banal daily activities. It is as if the unconscious mind has carried out the work of 'night science', sorting through cognitive components and suddenly landing upon a novel configuration that provides a new way of proceeding. In this way, the imaginative, creative impulse that motivates science is also a *technological* act, constructing the world around us: 'Nous vivons dans un monde créé par notre cerveau, avec de continuelles allées et venues entre le réel et l'imaginaire' (*SMH*, p. 210).

Programme and language

In *La Logique du vivant*, Jacob's first major published work, he frames his explanation of molecular biology in terms of the metaphor of a genetic 'programme'. The egg, made up from the chromosomes of each parent, contains the 'instructions' for the development and the form of the living being that will emerge. This message is written in code using sequences of four chemical radicals (A, C, G, T), which constitute the architectural plans for the future organism. The programme metaphor retains the persistent biological themes of memory and design but strips them of any connotations of agency or vitalism. The programme contained in the genetic inheritance is kind of memory, but it is not a memory of what the organism has learnt from experience (*LV*, p. 11). It is handed down untouched, as it were, apart from random mutations that occur in the process of copying the instructions from one generation to the next. These purely contingent modifications may confer an advantage on an organism in the sense that it is adapted to survival and therefore successful reproduction. Mutations of this kind are, Jacob suggests, like the minor errors that a copyist or a printer inadvertently introduces into text: although this process of random modification and reproductive sorting may, viewed on the grand scale of evolution, look like it is driven by some kind of agency of conscious design, in fact it is simply a function of the relentless pressure of natural selection. The genetic message in the organism is like a text without an author, which has been refined and improved over two billion years by an anonymous proof-reader, with the effect that reproductive failures have been eliminated in favour of a collection of 'successes' (*LV*, pp. 307–8).

In 1974, four years after the publication of *La Logique du vivant*, Jacob published a short piece in which he revisited and revised his thinking on the 'linguistic model' in biology.[14] The article is informed by Jacob's ongoing dialogue with Roman Jakobson, who suggested that the isomorphism of the genetic and linguistic codes was evidence of underlying structural principles of 'communication' in living beings.[15] Jacob, in contrast, had come to the conclusion that there was nothing more than an analogous relationship between the two systems. Whereas the linearity of language is a function of the physical structure of the human vocal and auditory apparatus, the linear sequencing of the genetic message allows for the precise reproduction of complex spatial structures. In short, the two systems employ linearity for different reasons.[16] The linguistic model was useful for biology, but it did not provide a theoretical explanation of heredity, and the analogous relationship between the genetic code and language should not be mistaken for a fundamental identity.[17] Although he does not say it directly, Jacob suggests that, if there is a universal principle underpinning mechanisms of life and communication, it is the shuffling of a limited repertoire of basic elements that are empty of significance in isolation in different combinations in order to create 'meaning'. Jacob refers to this as 'la combinatoire':

> La combinatoire d'éléments ne se limite pas au langage et à l'hérédité. C'est le principe qui nous paraît opérer dans la nature chaque fois qu'il s'agit d'engendrer une grande diversité de structures avec un nombre restreint de matériaux. Cela s'applique, par exemple, à la série des atomes qui se forment par les combinaisons de quelques particules élémentaires, dont on ne sait pas encore si elles ne résultent pas elles-mêmes de la combinatoire d'unités encore plus élémentaires.[18]

He draws attention in this respect to the way in which the genetic code resembles the symbolic system described in the ancient Chinese text the *I Ching*. As is well known, this system is built around the fundamental relationship between the two opposing elements of Yin and Yang. 'Old' and 'young' versions of these two elements provide four basic structures that are in turn combined in groups of three in order to form sixty-four hexagrams, with each one representing a fundamental aspect of life. Jacob notes that Jesuit missionaries apparently showed the *I Ching* to

---

14. François Jacob, 'Le Modèle linguistique en biologie', *Critique*, 30:322 (March 1974), 197–205.
15. See François Jacob, Roman Jakobson, Claude Lévi-Strauss, Pierre L'Héritier, Michel Tréguer, 'Vivre et Parler', *Les Lettres françaises*, no. 1221 (1968), 1–7 (p. 6).
16. Jacob, 'Le Modèle linguistique en biologie', p. 203.
17. Jacob, 'Le Modèle linguistique en biologie', p. 204.
18. Jacob, 'Le Modèle linguistique en biologie', p. 201.

Leibniz, who was struck by the similarity with the binary numbering system that he had invented. Similarly, Jacob suggests that the *I Ching* system corresponds closely to the contemporary understanding of the genetic 'code':

> Car si l'on assimile convenablement chacun des quatre diagrammes chinois à l'une des quatre paires de radicaux chimiques composant l'ADN, chaque hexagramme équivaut à l'une des triplets génétiques. La structure de l'ordre 'naturel' décrit dans *I Ching* se trouve alors correspondre point par point à celle du code génétique.[19]

The integron

Although, as discussed above, Jacob focuses at some length on the significance of molecular biology, *La Logique du vivant* is, unlike Monod's *Le Hasard et la nécessité*, in large part a detailed history of biology, which is marked by the influence of Kuhn's *The Structure of Scientific Revolutions* (1962)[20] and Michel Foucault's *Les Mots et les choses*. Jacob draws on Kuhn's framework of successive scientific paradigms and Foucault's concept of the episteme in tracing the history of biology not as the linear overturning of previous errors, but rather as a series of epochs, each one of which limits the field of what it is possible to perceive as an object and to analyse (*LV*, pp. 19–20). Jacob identifies four such biological epochs, each of which corresponds to a level of organization: the arrangement of visible surfaces in the Renaissance; a focus on internal structures – organs and cells – which begins in the second half of the eighteenth century; genes and chromosomes at the end of the nineteenth century; and finally DNA and molecular biology in the second half of the twentieth century. To these four levels of spatial organization he adds a fifth temporal dimension of evolution.

In the final chapter of *La Logique du vivant* Jacob undertakes a characteristic act of theoretical bridge-building, analysing the organization of the organism – a living 'system' – in a way that resonates with the historical schema of linked but discrete historical epochs that he has set out previously in the book. He formulates the concept of the 'integron' to describe the way in which living systems are organized like a series of 'parcels', in which units of relatively well-defined size and practically identical structure function together to form a unit in the higher level of organization, and so on. Each of these units formed from sub-units is an 'integron': 'Un intégron se forme par l'assemblage d'intégrons de niveau inférieur; il participe à la construction d'un intégron de niveau supérieur' (*LV*, p. 323). The articulation between these integrons depends upon, and stimulates, systems of communication, regulation and memory: the 'algorithms' of living systems (*LV*, p. 321). According to this logic of living systems, both limitations *and* new properties emerge at each higher new level of organization. Viewed from this perspective, although biological

---

19. Jacob, 'Le Modèle linguistique en biologie', p. 205.
20. Thomas Kuhn, *The Structure of Scientific Revolutions* (University of Chicago Press, 1962).

phenomena could not exist without the physics of atoms and molecules, biology cannot be reduced to physics: 'La biologie ne peut, ni se réduire à la physique, ni se passer d'elle' (*LV*, p. 328). In this way, Jacob's thinking was already pointing forward to an epistemological view of living systems that is closer to what is now known as *complexity*. The concept of the integron corresponds closely to the contemporary understanding of a complex system as the articulation of non-autonomous hierarchical levels by means of multiple ascending and descending pathways.[21]

Adding another metaphorical dimension to *La Logique du vivant*, Jacob uses the image of Russian dolls to build connections between the logic of the integron and the historical development of scientific knowledge. As he puts it, biology, like other natural sciences, no longer searches for 'truth'. Instead, it constructs an architecture of living systems by negotiating a route through successive levels of organization, which are encased within each other. Each new level reveals new principles of organization that encompass and incorporate the principles of the previous level. The discovery of each new Russian doll does not result from an accumulation of observations and experiments, but rather entails a radically new way of understanding and conceptualizing the living world (*LV*, pp. 24–5). He closes the book with this metaphor, acknowledging that the paradigm of messages, codes and information that at that point defined and explained living systems would at some point in the future be superseded as a new level of organization inevitably appeared: 'Quelle dissection demain disloquera nos objets pour les recomposer en un espace neuf? Quelle nouvelle poupée russe en émergera?'

After the Operon

In *La Logique du vivant* Jacob draws a clear distinction what he calls an integrationist, evolutionist approach to biology and a reductionist perspective (*LV*, pp. 14–18). The reductionist approach explains the organism as a whole solely in terms of its parts. In this sense molecular biology constitutes a triumph for reductionism: the organism as a living system can be explained in terms of the chemical interaction of its physical components. The integrationist approach, in contrast, views the organism as an element in a higher order system, such as a species or a population. As indicated already, Jacob remained attached to the efficacy of the reductionist approach throughout his career, but he was always conscious of the fact that the evolutionist perspective was not entirely compatible with reductionism. Although the programme is impervious to external modification, it cannot set out in exhaustive detail the future development of the organism. Instead, Jacob emphasizes, as the programme unfolds in the course of the development of the organism, it interacts with its environment and is brought into

---

21. Rémy Lestienne, 'Chance, Progress and Complexity in Biological Evolution', *SubStance*, 29:1 (2000), 39–55 (pp. 52–3).

contact with new sources of information (*LV*, pp. 17–18). In the later part of his career Jacob's writing on biology focuses increasingly on this evolutionist perspective.

In *La Souris, la mouche et l'homme* Jacob emphasizes that the optimism associated with post-war molecular biology had begun to dissipate by the early 1970s. Techniques that had worked so spectacularly well with single-cell organisms were not equally well-suited to higher organisms, and it seemed that molecular biology had reached a limit beyond which it could not progress. It was only with the development of genetic engineering in the 1970s that new, exciting possibilities were opened up. These new techniques held out the promise of analysing molecules in detail, including those of higher organisms, a prospect which radically transformed the conception of the living world that molecular biology had painstakingly constructed up until the 1970s (*SMH*, pp. 127–8). Up until this point, molecular biology had focused on the functioning of genes within single-cell organisms such as bacteria, and the basic molecular machinery of living organisms was thought to function in a linear way, rather like a car production line. It was generally assumed that there was a perfect collinearity between the genetic code and protein structures, and that this held for higher organisms as well as bacteria.[22] Chromosomes were thought to be precisely engineered structures that contained just enough genetic material to provide information for the development and functioning of the organism (*JP*, p. 74). It now appeared that, at the molecular level, the functioning of higher organisms was not quite as straightforward as had been previously assumed. Morange, drawing on the metaphor of DNA as text, suggests that a 'text' that was at one time thought of as clearly and concisely written, with precise use of punctuation, now appeared confused and prolix, with many redundancies.[23] From this point on, genes and proteins can no longer be thought of as the unique objects of particular species. They are rather mosaics, made from a store of 'motifs' derived from a small number of, as Jacob puts it, 'ancient modules' (*SMH*, pp. 131–2). Genetic engineering also facilitated scientific work which revealed that basic developmental genes were common to a wide range of organisms (*SMH*, p. 136). In summary, new molecular techniques revealed an unexpected underlying unity concerning the basic components of the living world. Not only are all living organisms composed of more or less identical molecules, but also, from yeast through to humans, groups of closely related molecules carry out universal life functions (*SMH*, p. 10).

Advances in genetic engineering also meant that the faith in the absolute power of natural selection that had come to predominate with the Modern Synthesis was challenged from the 1970s onwards. As Jacob indicated in *La Logique du vivant*, it

---

22. See Morange, *Histoire de la biologie moléculaire* (Paris: La Découverte, 2003), chap. 17, pp. 266–77.

23. Morange, *Histoire de la biologie moléculaire*, p. 270.

had been assumed that evolution was a broadly linear process whereby genetic
mutations altered the forms of proteins, and that natural selection selected between
the different organisms that resulted from these mutations. The structure of the
living world no longer appeared to be linear and continuous, but rather non-linear
and discontinuous (*SMH*, pp. 115–16). Gould and Eldredge's theory of 'punctuated
equilibria', for example, directly challenged the idea that new genes were added in a
linear fashion (*SMH*, p. 123). All that is needed for evolution to take place is genetic
variation in a population, which can occur suddenly or over a long period. There are
a number of factors which can work alongside natural selection: genetic 'drift',
random gene fixation, and the differential growth of organs (*JP*, p. 43). Jacob also
emphasizes that, if the theory of evolution had once implied a relentlessly creative
power to modify living organisms, it was now necessary to acknowledge limits to
this creativity. The capacity to photosynthesize would, for example, free human
beings from the need to spend large amounts of time feeding themselves. However,
the basic bodily structure of a species places a limit upon possible evolutionary
developments (*JP*, pp. 42–3).

Bricolage: evolution as 'tinkering'

Jacob's short essay on evolutionary 'tinkering' in 1977 played a highly significant
role in establishing a radically new understanding of the process of evolution. Jacob
adapts the idea of *bricolage* from Lévi-Strauss's *La Pensée sauvage* (1962).[24]
Whereas the engineer works with custom-made components that have been
designed for a specific project, the *bricoleur* is a spontaneous and inventive tinkerer,
who works on any number of tasks using whatever tools and materials are at hand in
a limited stock. These resources have not been accumulated with any particular
project in mind, but simply on the grounds that they 'might be useful'. In short, they
can be used in different ways at different times.[25] Jacob suggests that it is at the
molecular level that the clearest evidence can be seen of evolutionary *bricolage*.
Molecular biology has revealed the unity of the underlying molecular structure and
function across the entire spectrum of the living world. Jacob argues that the basic
repertoire of molecules, the building blocks from which life is constructed, must
have appeared at a very early point in the history of life, since large segments of
DNA are homologous among different organisms (*ET*, p. 1164). Subsequently,
any new molecular structures have been variations on these basic molecular
themes. What distinguishes species is not the fact that they have radically different
molecular components, but rather that these components are organized and
distributed in different ways. The diversification of organisms has not been
generated by 'biochemical novelties', but rather by changes in the way that the basic

---

24. Claude Lévi-Strauss, *La Pensée sauvage* (Paris: Plon, 1962).
25. Lévi-Strauss, *La Pensée sauvage*, p. 27.

chemical constituents of life are deployed: evolution results from changes in regulation rather than in basic structure. Genes are either configured in new regulatory networks or reassembled from existing components: 'It is always a matter of using the same elements, of adjusting them, of altering here or there, of arranging various combinations to produce new objects of increasing complexity. It is always a matter of tinkering' (*ET*, p. 1165). He also sees plenty of evidence of evolutionary tinkering at the level of morphology. Taking inspiration from Darwin's emphasis on structural and functional imperfections in the natural world, and also acknowledging the influence of Lévi-Strauss, Jacob highlights the opportunistic nature of the evolutionary process:

> Often, without any well-defined long-term project, the tinkerer gives his materials unexpected functions to produce a new object. From an old bicycle wheel, he makes a roulette; from a broken chair the cabinet of a radio. Similarly evolution makes a wing from a leg or a part of an ear from a piece of jaw. Naturally, this takes a long time. Evolution behaves like a tinkerer who, during eons upon eons, would slowly modify his work, unceasingly retouching it, cutting it here, lengthening there, seizing the opportunities to adapt it progressively to its new use. (*ET*, p. 1164)

An example of evolutionary tinkering of this kind is the vertebrate lung that evolution 'builds' from a piece of the oesophagus of fresh-water fish. Fish living in stagnant pools with low oxygen levels would have swallowed air and absorbed oxygen through the walls of the oesophagus. Consequently, an oesophagus with a larger surface area would offer a selective advantage. Over time, this selective pressure leads to the development of lungs. Although the process appears to be remarkably similar to a Lamarckian conception of acquired characteristics, it is in fact the interplay of genetic mutation, the reproductive reshuffling of genetic programmes, and of adaptation and selection under environmental pressure that lead to evolution. Evolutionary tinkering also results in superposed structures within an organism, as illustrated by example of the human brain, in which the neocortex has been 'bolted onto' the old structure of the rhinencephalon. The older structure has been relegated in humans to emotional and visceral activities, whereas the newer structure deals with intellectual and cognitive activity. It is, Jacob suggests, 'like adding a jet engine to an old horse cart' (*ET*, p. 1164). Living organisms in this sense are marked by historical contingency. They constitute an accumulation, a 'patchwork' of components put together as and when opportunities arise. Similarly, the existence of an area of the brain responsible for pleasure – the centre of autostimulation – is expedient in encouraging individuals to have sex and reproduce. Living organisms are not methodically sculpted creations, but rather creations of history:

> They represent, not a perfect product of engineering, but a patchwork of odd sets pieced together when and where the opportunities arose. For the opportunism

of natural selection is not simply a matter of indifference to the structure and operation of its products. It reflects the very nature of a historical process full of contingency.[26]

Significantly, Jacob frames his conceptualization of *bricolage* in the context of a set of broader reflections on the issue of reductionism. Although he does not explicitly signal that these remarks constitute a shift in his thinking, he does point to important deficiencies in a rigidly reductionist perspective. Reductionism provides a way of bridging the gaps between scientific fields that analyse different objects with different concepts. There is a route through physics, chemistry, biology and sociology that analyses each more complex set of objects by referring back to the basic components of the simpler level. However, Jacob emphasizes that, although it is necessary to understand the simple in order to understand the more complex, it is not sufficient. Epistemological reductionism in its purest form would lead to the absurd claim that democracy can be explained in terms of the elementary particles of physics (*ET*, p. 1162). Reductionism is not sufficient because the dimension of time – 'history' as Jacob puts it – introduces an element of contingency, particularly as far as the production of complex objects is concerned (*ET*, p. 1163).

In *La Souris, la mouche et l'homme* Jacob goes on to refine the idea of evolutionary tinkering. It seemed that the huge diversity of forms and behaviours in the living world was underpinned by molecular structures that had persisted practically unchanged from the Cambrian era through five hundred million years of evolution (*SMH*, pp. 122–3). One of the key discoveries was the fact that genes in higher organisms are broken up into coding (exons) and non-coding sequences (introns). The discovery of so-called 'split genes' ('gènes mosaïques' in French) constituted, according to Morange, a 'mini-revolution' in molecular biology: evolution tinkers with molecules. At the molecular level, biochemical evolution, as a process 'bricolage moléculaire' operates in two ways (*SMH*, pp. 118–20). In the history of life, the first genes were formed from short sequences of thirty or forty nucleotides, and these segments have subsequently been either joined up with other sequences or doubled one or several times. The second method for the production of genes is the 're-shuffling' ['le réassortiment'] of existing fragments to form split genes. It seems that the process of evolution depends less upon spontaneous mutations and more upon the duplication of genes and the recombination of gene fragments. A picture emerges of a series genetic 'fixed points' around which other fragments of DNA are exchanged in a sort of molecular 'ballet'. Living organisms share the same 'structures de base', which are deployed

---

26. Lévi-Strauss, *La Pensée sauvage*, p. 166.

and articulated in different contexts, just as Meccano pieces can put together in innumerable different ways:

> Le monde vivant ressemble à une sorte de Meccano. Il est le produit d'un vaste combinatoire où des éléments à peu près fixes, segments de gènes ou blocs de gènes déterminant des modules d'opérations complexes, sont agencés selon des arrangements varies. La complexité apportée par l'évolution provient de réassortissements de ces éléments préexistants. (*SMH*, 123–4)

The combinatorial and biotechnology

Writing in *Le Nouvel observateur* in 1981, Claude Lévi-Strauss discussed at some length the philosophical significance of *bricolage* and the idea of what he called the 'la combinatoire' in Jacob's book, *Le Jeu des possibles*.[27] He is struck by the philosophical significance of Jacob's vision of the historical evolution of the biological world as the limited actualization of a small number of the vast range of theoretical combinations which exist in a virtual, possible realm. This Leibnizian metaphysics has, he emphasizes, long been overshadowed by the Cartesian dualism that characterized Monod's thinking.[28] Nature is not Cartesian; it does not function according to a principle of sufficient reason, but rather operates in an *ad hoc* manner – 'travaillant de bric et de broc' – between the poles of logic and experience.[29] Lévi-Strauss also expresses his admiration for Jacob's capacity to move with ease between science and art, highlighting the analysis of the fears aroused by biotechnology in *Le Jeu des possibles*. Here, Jacob suggests that these fears focus on the perception that it is now possible to take genes from one organism and insert them into another. This scenario evokes a fundamental, mythic fear of unnatural, monstrous hybrids, such as those that feature in Hieronymus Bosch's depictions of Hell (*JP*, pp. 84–5). The dangerous material consequences of scientific discovery are, Jacob suggests, often unintended and unpredictable, and the fear of biotechnology stems at least in part from the fact that it throws into relief the contingent, opportunistic aspects of biological evolution.

Claude Debru has also developed this philosophical reflection on the possible in relation to biology, and in particular to biotechnology, drawing in particular on Jacob's concept of *bricolage*. As Debru indicates, the close relationship between the possible and the actual is a well-established theme in philosophy.[30] According to this strand of ontological speculation – he points to Wittgenstein and

---

27. Claude Lévi-Strauss, 'La Biologie, science exemplaire', reprinted in *Le Nouvel Observateur*, 74 (November–December 2009), 48–51.

28. Lévi-Strauss, 'La Biologie, science exemplaire', p. 49.

29. Lévi-Strauss, 'La Biologie, science exemplaire', p. 50.

30. Claude Debru, 'François Jacob et la notion du possible', in *Une nouvelle connaissance du vivant: François Jacob, André Lwoff et Jacques Monod*, ed. by Claude Debru, Michel Morange and Frédéric Worms (Paris: Éditions Rue d'Ulm, 2012), pp. 99–106.

Schrödinger – the real cannot be separated from the 'shadow' of the possible. In this way, the relation between the actual and the possible provides an alternative to Monod's description of chance and necessity as absolute categories, according to which pure chance is captured 'on the wing' and transformed into necessity.[31] Emphasizing the proximity of the real and the possible, Debru argues that the natural world is characterized by a 'conditional necessity', in the sense that an unpredictable future state unfolds in a context of relative structural stability. This is the scenario described by what is now known as 'complexity', according to which complex systems maintain a certain degree of stability whilst functioning as open systems that are 'far from equilibrium'. The stability of complex systems is derived from their internal variations and dynamic interactions with the environment.[32] Viewed in this light, contingency is not a matter of random chance, but rather a recognition of the fact that the existing world could, quite simply, be a 'little different'.[33] Debru goes on to argue that biotechnology draws on the insights of evolutionary *bricolage* in order to engage in a form of 'directed' evolution. Put simply, biotechnology mimics the evolutionary dynamic of rearranging existing genetic components to make something new:

> La perception du possible et celle du réel sont profondément solidaires. Le possible se découvre au fur et à mesure que le réel se découvre. L'un découle de l'autre. Les sciences de la vie donnent à cette solidarité un relief particulièrement saisissant. Les biotechnologies imposent donc, philosophiquement, une vision très réaliste du possible.[34]

Conclusion

In purely scientific terms, Jacob's concept of *bricolage* has been highly influential, and is today an important concept in thinking on evolution.[35] A number of biologists have argued that subsequent research has tended to confirm the prescience of Jacob's insight.[36] At the point that Jacob published his 1977 paper, experimental evidence was only just coming to light that molecular systems were

---

31. Claude Debru, 'Le Possible, le réel et les sciences de la vie', *Revue de métaphysique et de morale*, 43 (2004), 381–97 (p. 383).
32. Claude Debru (avec la collaboration de Pascal Nouvel), *Le Possible et les biotechnologies: essai de philosophie dans les sciences* (Paris: Presses universitaires de France, 2003), p. 97.
33. Claude Debru, 'Le Possible, le réel et les sciences de la vie', p. 381.
34. Claude Debru, 'Le Possible, le réel et les sciences de la vie', p. 397.
35. Manfed D. Laublicher, 'Tinkering: a conceptual and historical evaluation', in *Tinkering: The Microevolution of Development*, ed. by Gregory Bock and Jamie Goode (Chichester: Wiley, 2007), pp. 20–34 (p. 21).
36. See Denis Duboule and Adam S. Wilkins, 'The Evolution of "Bricolage"', *TIG*, 14:2 (February 1998), pp. 54–9 and Bock and Goode (eds), *Tinkering: The Microevolution of Development*.

underpinned by remarkable genetic continuities. However, the observation that multicellular organisms share the same basic stock of gene products has been borne out in subsequent research.[37] The motor of evolutionary change does not come from new genes, but rather from already-existing genes deployed in new ways. In this way, Jacob's concept of evolutionary tinkering fed directly into the emergence of evolutionary developmental biology. The reductionist approach of molecular biology has been challenged by the complexity of gene action that has been revealed in the era of genetic engineering. It is no longer possible to explain complex structures and functions with reference to the molecular structure of genes. Instead, it is now necessary to think in terms of the complex pathways and networks of genes and gene products that operate in different ways in different organisms. We are now, as far as Morange is concerned, in a 'post-genomic' era. The complexity of higher organisms such as humans cannot be explained simply by looking at the macromolecular components of these organisms; it is rather a question of understanding how properties emerge from these complex networks.[38] It now appears that all living beings share much more in common at the molecular level than was previously thought to be the case. Genes and proteins can no longer be thought of as being the property of a particular species. What is more, a molecular structure that has a particular role in one organism might appear in the same organism with a different function. At the same time, very similar structures can be located in different organisms.[39]

In a more general sense, the concept of *bricolage* has a central role in Jacob's work, bringing together his thinking on evolution and science in general. The ordered vision of the world that science produces can only ever be provisional and local. At the same time, the insights of science can provide a means of technological interaction with the living world, as is the case with biotechnology. The centrality of *bricolage* for Jacob positions him philosophically in many ways in the opposing camp to the Cartesian tradition, which was at the core of Monod's vision of science in the world.

ORCID
John Marks ⓘ https://orcid.org/0000-0002-4959-5776

---

37. Duboule and Wilkins, 'The Evolution of "Bricolage"', p. 54.

38. Michel Morange, 'Post-Genomics, Between Reduction and Emergence', *Synthese*, 151:3 (2006), 355–60.

39. Jacob, 'François Jacob: éloge du darwinisme', *Magazine littéraire*, no. 374 (1999), 18–23 (p. 20).

Nottingham French Studies 59.3 (2020): 350–367
DOI: 10.3366/nfs.2020.0295
© University of Nottingham
www.euppublishing.com/nfs

THE 'TECTONIC SENSIBILITY' IN ARCHITECTURE: FROM THE PRE-HUMAN TO THE POST-HUMAN

JONATHAN HALE (iD)

Introduction

One of the problems that haunts any discussion of tectonics in architecture (typically defined as the raising of construction to an art form) is that it can often seem like a fallacy is being committed, broadly of the *pars pro toto* variety. If we become too fixated on the fabric of the building as the very raw material of architecture, then it can soon seem – as David Leatherbarrow once claimed in a conference on this very subject – that tectonics is a 'very small glass into which we are trying to pour an awful lot of wine'.[1]

Leatherbarrow may indeed be right, especially if we consider (as the standard definition above suggests) that tectonics simply aims at some sort of symbiotic union between technology and aesthetics. In which case, it clearly only addresses the second and third of the famous Vitruvian triad of architectural characteristics, 'firmness' and 'delight', while ignoring the equally important quality of functionality or 'commodity'. If this is in fact the case, and tectonic expression is *merely* the aestheticization of construction, then it could easily be dismissed as an optional extra, something added on to an otherwise already technically adequate architectural solution. If constructional richness and articulation is thus seen as a luxury – and therefore mainly the province of high-end projects for wealthy private clients – then where does that leave the majority of what we might call 'everyday architecture'? Is there another role or perhaps a deeper significance buried away within the definition of tectonic expression, beyond the simple sensory pleasures of hand-based craftsmanship and expensive materials?

Many of these ideas were initially formulated in discussions with members of the interdisciplinary Science, Technology and Culture research group (STC) at the University of Nottingham, from 2003 onwards. I am especially indebted to Chris Johnson for his inspirational leadership of the group. Some of this material is also discussed in more detail in my book *Merleau-Ponty for Architects* Thinkers for Architects (Abingdon: Routledge, 2017).

1. Unpublished comment from a panel discussion at the international symposium *Towards an Ecology of Tectonics*, at the Royal Danish Academy of Fine Arts (KADK), Copenhagen, Denmark, 1 November 2012.

I would like to suggest that tectonics does indeed have a broader relevance in architecture, beyond the particular attractions of 'aestheticized technology', whether we prefer a stripped-back, bare-bones Brutalism, or the current digital revival of surface ornamentation, with its connotations of playfulness and excess. If we think instead of a kind of 'meta tectonics' – or what I prefer to call a *tectonic sensibility* – then we might also be able to draw some broader lessons from the familiar narrow focus on materials and construction details that tectonic expression typically sets out to celebrate. My suggestion is that the kind of bodily sensitivity towards the qualities and opportunities that emerge while working 'hands-on' with a physical material might also be transferable into the realm of spatial and functional possibilities, offering a way of incorporating that missing third Vitruvian term, commodity, within a new and broader definition of *tectonic architecture*.

By way of background, I should first point out that this notion of a bodily sensibility towards the 'way things are' and the 'way they want to be' is based on the idea of a material continuity between buildings and human bodies. Rather than suggesting some kind of mystical pan-psychism that tries to humanise 'dead' matter, I want to suggest instead that there is something fundamentally human at the heart of the technological – in other words, that the human and the technological are deeply co-constitutive. As one of the key ideas behind this article, it is important briefly to unpack this statement, not least because I believe it also has a number of useful corollaries.

Firstly, to be human – and hence to be embodied – is to be already extended into what Maurice Merleau-Ponty labeled 'the flesh of the world', a liminal realm where it is impossible to make a definitive distinction between what belongs to the self and what belongs to the environment.[2] Merleau-Ponty's notion of an *intertwining* between the body and its perceptual field also implies that we perceive the world only through the medium of the experiencing body. Hence, our experience of the objects around us is more accurately described as an experience of the body itself in the act of experiencing. As Taylor Carmen has usefully explained: 'Flesh is the *identity* of perception and perceptibility, even below the threshold of conscious awareness. As bodily perceivers we are necessarily part of the perceptible world we perceive; we are not just *in* the world, but *of* it.'[3] While recalling the Biblical notion of the body's organic continuity with the physical world ('for dust thou art and unto dust shalt thou return') this statement also questions the everyday assumption of a fixed and stable boundary between the self and its surrounding environment. A further illustration of this shifting zone of interchange that crosses the body-world boundary is provided by Merleau-Ponty in one of his earlier essays on the painter Paul Cézanne: 'Le peintre "apporte son corps", dit Valéry. Et, en effet, on ne voit

---

2.   Maurice Merleau-Ponty, 'L'Entrelacs – Le Chiasme', in *Le Visible et l'invisible* (Paris: Gallimard, 1968), pp. 170–201.

3.   Taylor Carmen, *Merleau-Ponty* (London: Routledge, 2008), p. 133.

pas comment un Esprit pourrait peindre. C'est en prêtant son corps au monde que le peintre change le monde en peinture.'[4]

Extending this idea of a continuum linking mind, body and world also makes it possible to question another commonly accepted distinction: the division between nature and society, which – as both Bruno Latour[5] and Félix Guattari have suggested – should be seen as an artificial and highly misleading convention. As a way of subverting this restrictive binary logic Guattari posited a new ontological category to capture the merging of the organic and the mechanical that he labeled the 'machinic phylum'.[6] Partly based on a claim by the anthropologist André Leroi-Gourhan that the technical object only exists in the context 'technical ensemble' to which it belongs,[7] Guattari's ensemble also includes the social, cultural and material networks within which individual technologies are embedded. The idea of the human 'becoming machine' and the machine 'becoming human' had of course also been suggested by Deleuze and Guattari in their famous example of the symbiotic engagements between wasps and orchids.[8]

What Latour described as a general tendency of technology to 'mix humans and non-humans' together often involves delegating acts of human agency to new technical devices – for instance where the top-hatted corporate concierge is replaced by the humble hydraulic door-closer.[9] While the industrial revolution has spawned countless examples of mechanical devices replicating ever more complex human activities, this process could also be seen as a continuation of a longer evolutionary trajectory characterized by the desire to extend the body's ability to act on the world through the medium of ever more sophisticated tools. We could therefore conclude that all technologies might usefully be seen in terms of their prosthetic relationship with the body, but at the same time, and even more fundamentally, we might also concur with Bernard Stiegler's suggestion that: 'La pro-thèse n'est pas un simple prolongement du corps humain, elle est la constitution de ce corps en tant qu'"humain".'[10] Despite the strength of Stiegler's argument, it is clear that it runs counter to much of the twentieth-century discourse on the prosthetic dimension of technology, which has generally been haunted by its apparent threat to our

---

4. Maurice Merleau-Ponty, *L'Œil et l'Esprit* (Paris: Gaillmard, 1964), p. 16.

5. Bruno Latour, *We Have Never Been Modern*, transl. by Catherine Porter (New York and London: Harvester Wheatsheaf, 1993).

6. Felix Guattari, *Chaosmose* (Paris: Gallimard, 1992) pp. 53–84.

7. Ibid., pp. 56–57.

8. Gilles Deleuze and Felix Guattari, *Mille Plateaux: capitalisme et schizophrénie, 2* (Paris: Minuit, 1980), p. 17.

9. Bruno Latour, 'Mixing Humans and Nonhumans Together: The Sociology of a Door Closer', *Social Problems*, 35 (1988), 298–310.

10. Bernard Stiegler, *La Technique et le temps, I: la faute d'Épiméthée* (Paris: Galilée, 1994), p. 162.

'true nature' as human beings. As one important recent collection has recalled,[11] Sigmund Freud saw it as one of the major sources of a curiously modern malaise:

> With every tool man is perfecting his own organs, whether motor or sensory, or is removing the limits to their functioning. [...] Man has, as it were, become a kind of prosthetic God. When he puts on all his auxiliary organs, he is truly magnificent; but these organs have not grown on to him, and they still give him trouble at times. [...] Present day man does not feel happy in his Godlike character.[12]

Writing on the same theme in the 1960s, Marshall McLuhan struck a more celebratory tone, treating technological devices as if they were simply external organs of the human body and, likewise, communication media as 'the extensions of man'.[13] Later, in *The Medium is the Massage* – a surprisingly postmodern collection of graphic images, aphorisms and typographical games – he went on to claim that: 'All media are extensions of some human faculty – psychic or physical.'[14] By way of illustration, he described the wheel as an extension of the human foot; clothing, of the skin; radio, of the ear; and print of the eye. Ultimately, perhaps even electronic circuitry should be seen as 'an extension of the central nervous system'.[15] This final reference clearly betrays one of the darker elements of McLuhan's prognosis, as already hinted at in *Understanding Media*. One of the body's instinctive responses to this kind of technological enhancement of one of its sensory channels might involve a damping down or recalibration of the other senses in a compensatory act of suppression. McLuhan coined the term 'auto-amputation' to express the negative consequences of this process of suppression, as the nervous system tries to protect itself against the risks of overstimulation. Ultimately, the consequences of this gradual technological invasion of the biological body were summed up in a memorable passage entitled 'The Gadget Lover'. Here he reversed the traditional hierarchy between the body and technology – as suggested by Freud's statement referred to above – while also anticipating Deleuze and Guattari's discussion of the uncanny symbiosis between wasps and orchids:

> By continuously embracing technologies, we relate ourselves to them as servome-chanisms. That is why we must, to use them at all, serve these objects, these extensions of ourselves, as gods or minor religions. [...] Physiologically, man in the

11. Marquard Smith and Joanne Morra (eds), *The Prosthetic Impulse: From a Posthuman Present to a Biocultural Future* (Cambridge, MA: MIT Press, 2006).

12. Sigmund Freud, *Civilization and Its Discontents*, transl. by James Strachey (New York: W. W. Norton, 1961), pp. 43–4.

13. Marshall McLuhan, *Understanding Media: The Extensions of Man* (New York: McGraw-Hill, 1964).

14. Marshall McLuhan and Quentin Fiore, *The Medium is the Massage: An Inventory of Effects* (New York: Random House, 1967), p. 26.

15. McLuhan and Fiore, *The Medium is the Massage*, p. 40.

normal use of technology (or his variously extended body) is perpetually modified by it and in turn finds ever new ways of modifying his technology. Man becomes as it were, the sex organs of the machine world, as the bee of the plant world, enabling it to fecundate and to evolve ever new forms.[16]

From the extended body to the extended mind

Before returning to address some of the architectural implications of this apparently apocalyptic scenario, it is perhaps worth considering in more measured terms some of the underlying forces at work over a broader historical trajectory. To better understand the principle of technological embodiment, it is useful to recall examples of the simplest hand-operated tools. Heidegger referred to the experience of using a hammer, describing how, when skilfully handled, it effectively 'disappears' or withdraws from the user's awareness.[17] Perception shifts from the immediate physical contact between the hand and the shaft of the hammer, out towards the metal surface which is touching the head of the nail. Conscious awareness is instead dominated by the task rather than the tool, which, with a little practice, quickly becomes absorbed into an extended 'body schema'. This process is perhaps more easily observed in the use of tools that directly enhance sensory awareness, such as wearing glasses to improve vision or, in Merleau-Ponty's most memorable example, a blind person walking with the aid of a white cane.[18] In these cases it becomes easier to see the technology not as a barrier placed between the body and the world but rather as a means to bring the world even closer. As Merleau-Ponty's concept of 'flesh' implies, in its suggestion of an intertwining between the body and the world, its 'thickness' is not an obstacle but rather a means of communication: 'C'est que l'épaisseur de la chair entre le voyant et la chose est constitutive de sa visibilité à elle comme de sa corporéité à lui; ce n'est pas un obstacle entre lui et elle, c'est leur moyen de communication.'[19]

The idea of the body being prosthetically extended through the use of various tools and technologies is also echoed in the writings of the American pragmatist philosopher John Dewey. While highlighting a similar organic continuity between the body and the 'outside' world, he also hints at an ethical element in the dependent relationship between an organism and its environment:

> The epidermis is only in the most superficial way an indication of where an organism ends and its environment begins. There are things inside the body that are foreign to it, and there are things outside of it that belong to it *de jure* if not *de facto*; that must, that

16. McLuhan, *Understanding Media*, p. 46.

17. Martin Heidegger, *Being and Time*, transl. by John Macquarrie and Edward Robinson (New York: Harper Collins, 1962), pp. 98–107.

18. Maurice Merleau-Ponty, *La Phénoménologie de la perception* (Paris: Gallimard, 1945), p. 179.

19. Merleau-Ponty, 'L'Entrelacs – Le Chiasme', p. 176.

is, be taken possession of if life is to continue. On the lower scale, air and food materials are such things; on the higher, tools, whether the pen of the writer or the anvil of the blacksmith, utensils and furnishings, property, friends and institutions – all the supports and sustenances without which a civilised life cannot be. The need that is manifest in the urgent impulsions that demand completion through what the environment – and it alone – can supply, is a dynamic acknowledgment of this dependence of the self for wholeness upon its surroundings.[20]

Dewey's words should also act as a timely reminder of just how important it is to find a more equitable and sustainable relationship with the world's finite natural resources, as much as it shows how our sense of self identity is likewise dependent on a whole network of external elements that support both our physical and intellectual functions. Like our clothing and our cars, these objects soon become integral to our personality and our social standing, part of the definition and representation of who we are and what we can do. From notepads to photograph albums, these external memory-aids act like computer hard-drives or online file-stores into which we upload important data to be retrieved at the vital moment, a form of what the cognitive scientist and philosopher Andy Clark has recently described as our 'intellectual scaffolding'.[21] Clark's important work also suggests that the hybrid human-machine 'cyborg' entity feared by Freud and others is hardly a new phenomenon. In fact, ever since the first random rock was used by an ape to smash a nut, bodies have been merging temporarily with simple technologies in carrying out even the most basic technical tasks.

This idea of an externalized and distributed intelligence suggested by the simple act of recording a thought in a notebook also invites a further consideration of the potential evolutionary consequences of so-called 'primitive' technical activities. By way of analogy, we could imagine an archaeologist 'reading' a set of ancient tool fragments as a store of valuable information about the material culture of a lost society. But, by the same token, we could also argue that early humans derived a double benefit from the use of tools: these external objects extended their bodily abilities while also acting as carriers of technical knowledge. While ethologists and paleo-anthropologists might argue over the exact chronology of innovations in early human culture, one likely scenario is that tool-use in fact came before verbal language. The ability to plan and execute a specific sequence of actions in the making of simple stone tools could perhaps form the basis of the core skills necessary for communication through ordered sounds. This conclusion is also supported by accumulating evidence from brain imaging research, which has revealed overlapping areas of specialization for both language and manual skill – a correspondence also previously noted by the French

---

20. John Dewey, *Art as Experience* (New York: Perigee Books, 1934), p. 59.

21. Andy Clark, *Natural-born Cyborgs: Why Minds and Technologies are Made to Merge* (New York: Oxford University Press, 2003), pp. 6–11.

anthropologist André Leroi-Gourhan in the 1960s.[22] Clusters of neurons in the left cerebral hemisphere which deal specifically with language comprehension (such as the so-called Broca's area) also turn out to be involved in the control of the facial and vocal muscles. These areas are also implicated in the recently discovered 'mirror-neuron' system, neural circuits which are used in both perceiving and executing goal-directed manual activities.[23] These recent findings go some way to escape the problem of speculating upon scant archaeological evidence, a dilemma of which Leroi-Gourhan was all too aware:

> À partir de là, peut-être, une paléontologie du langage pourrait être tentée, paléontologie toute squelettique d'ailleurs, car il n'y a guère d'espoir de retrouver jamais la chair des langages fossiles. Un point essentiel peut toutefois être dégagé: il y a la possibilité de langage à partir du moment où la préhistoire livre des outils, puisque outil et langage sont liés neurologiquement et puisque l'un et l'autre sont indissociables dans la structure sociale de l'humanité.[24]

This scenario has been further extended more recently by the cognitive psychologist Michael Corballis in the book *From Hand to Mouth* (2002), which provides a convincing, if still somewhat controversial, account of the origins of spoken language.[25] Ranging back over two million years of prehistory to consider the first appearance of the genus *homo* following the divergence of ape and human species, Corballis describes the gradual emergence of a bodily language of visual signs and gestures. From the archaeological evidence of tool-use among early hominin species Corballis infers that increasing levels of manual skill would have begun to facilitate more articulate forms of visual communication, even in the period prior to the final anatomical changes necessary for the production of articulate speech. The development of a gestural proto-language might thereby have established a kind of generalized 'linguistic competence', the ideal conditions needed to create a selective evolutionary pressure capable of driving the development of other more sophisticated forms of verbal communication. It therefore seems reasonable to conclude that an embodied language of manual gestures assisted by secondary emotional vocalizations would later have been superseded by the more precise articulations of spoken language. This development would also have begun to free the hands for the subsequent development of more intense forms of technical and

---

22. André Leroi–Gourhan, *Le Geste et la parole, I: technique et langage* (Paris: Albin Michel, 1964), pp. 123–8.

23. Giacomo Rizzolatti and Corrado Sinigaglia, *Mirrors in the Brain: How Our Minds Share Actions and Emotions*, transl. by Frances Anderson (Oxford: Oxford University Press, 2008), pp. 118–23.

24. Leroi-Gourhan, *Le Geste et la parole, I: technique et langage*, p. 163.

25. Michael Corballis, *From Hand to Mouth: The Origins of Language* (Princeton, NJ: Princeton University Press, 2002).

artistic innovation. Corballis concludes that this is only likely to have happened among so-called 'anatomically modern' humans, beginning around a hundred thousand years ago with the appearance in the fossil record of the species *Homo Sapiens*. Evidence for what has been labelled a 'big bang' of cultural and cognitive evolution begins to emerge in the cave paintings of the upper-paleolithic period (around 30,000–40,000 years ago) which shows clear signs of sophisticated social and ritual behavior, as claimed by a number of other respected sources.[26]

An often-debated question regarding the potential primacy in human development of technical, social or linguistic intelligence[27] actually overlooks the fact that language itself involves a fundamentally technical dimension.[28] By offering another means to reach out beyond the body and make things happen in the wider world, language also echoes the embodied origins of technology in the effort to extend our physical capacities. As the anthropologist Marcel Mauss also suggested, technology could be seen to have originated in the development of 'techniques of the body': 'Le corps est le premier et le plus naturel instrument de l'homme. Ou plus exactement, sans parler d'instrument, le premier et le plus naturel objet technique, et en même temps moyen technique.'[29] This notion also recalls Aristotle's description of the hand as the 'tool of tools', which was, likewise, to the nineteenth-century anatomist Sir Charles Bell, 'the consummation of all perfection as an instrument'.[30] More recently, Raymond Tallis in a book entitled *The Hand: A Philosophical Enquiry into Human Being*, also described how the emergence of the earliest technologies might even have been the catalyst for the slow dawning of human self-consciousness.[31] Perhaps it was the growing realization of the instrumentality of the hand as the counterpart of early stone tools that acted as the stimulus for the emergence of a vital cognitive feedback-loop. As bodily techniques became gradually solidified in the form of durable material artifacts, these external deposits of human agency began to function as what Levi-Strauss called 'tools to think'. This curious dialectical process by which the human is both 'inventor of'

26. Richard Klein and Blake Edgar, *The Dawn of Human Culture* (New York: John Wiley and Sons, 2002); David Lewis Williams, *The Mind in the Cave: Consciousness and the Origins of Art* (London: Thames & Hudson, 2004); Steven Mithen, *The Prehistory of the Mind: A Search for the Origins of Art, Religion and Science* (London: Phoenix Books, 1998).

27. Mithen, *The Prehistory of the Mind*, pp. 31–64.

28. Tim Ingold, 'Tool-use, Sociality and Intelligence', in *Tools, Language, and Cognition in Human Evolution*, ed. by Kathleen Gibson and Tim Ingold (Cambridge: Cambridge University Press, 1993), pp. 429–45.

29. Marcel Mauss, *Sociologie et anthropologie* (Paris: Presses universitaires de France, 1950), p. 372.

30. Sir Charles Bell, *The Hand: Its Mechanism and Vital Endowments as Evincing Design* [1834] (Whitefish, MT: Kessinger Publishing, 2008), p. 231.

31. Raymond Tallis, *The Hand: A Philosophical Inquiry into Human Being* (Edinburgh: Edinburgh University Press, 2003), pp. 273–95.

and 'invented by' technology was also earlier referred to in Friedrich Engels's discussion of the evolutionary function of manual work: 'Thus the hand is not only the organ of labour, it is also the product of labour.'[32] This notion of a mutual reinforcement created by the co-development of technology and human consciousness, has also been employed by Jacques Derrida – again with reference to Leroi-Gourhan[33] – in his analysis of the archaic impulse of mark-making as a form of externalized human memory, and perhaps even the ultimate source of an enduring sense of self:

> Si l'on acceptait l'expression risquée par A. Leroi-Gourhan, on pourrait parler d'une 'liberation de la mémoire', d'une extériorisation toujours déjà commencée mais toujours plus grande de la trace qui, depuis les programmes élémentaires des comportements dits 'instinctifs' jusqu'à la constitution des fichiers électroniques et des machines à lire, élargit la différance et la possibilité de la mise en réserve: celle-ci constitue et efface en même temps, dans le même mouvement, la subjectivité dite consciente, son logos et ses attributs théologiques. .[34]

So, to turn the more familiar idea of technology-as-prosthesis on its head: instead of thinking of technology simply as an 'extension of the body', it might be more enlightening to claim that the body is in fact an 'extension of technology'. In other words, that the process of becoming self-aware – aware of 'having' a body and a choice as to what to do with it – may ultimately be seen as a consequence of the extension of the body through technology.

'Since feeling is first'[35]

Having set out a case for understanding 'the human' and 'the technological' as mutually co-constitutive, I now turn back to the basic principles of tectonic expression in architecture and towards what the Dutch architect and theorist Lars Spuybroek has called *The Sympathy of Things*.[36] This capacity consists of an intuitive, bodily 'feel' for the constraints and possibilities of tectonic elements, arising from the embodied experience of working directly with building materials. This sensibility can be gained either from direct personal experience (the architect as 'self-builder' for example) or from close observation and dialogue with tradesmen and craftspeople such as stonemasons, carpenters, joiners and,

---

32. Frederick Engels, *Dialectics of Nature*, transl. by Clemens Dutt (London: Lawrence and Wishart, 1940), p. 281.

33. I am indebted to Chris Johnson for pointing out this connection.

34. Jacques Derrida, *De la grammatologie* (Paris: Minuit, 1967), pp. 125–6.

35. E. E. Cummings, *Selected Poems*, ed. by Richard S. Kennedy (New York: Liveright, 1994), p. 99.

36. Lars Spuybroek, *The Sympathy of Things: Ruskin and the Ecology of Design* (London: Bloomsbury Academic, 2016).

increasingly, factory workers involved in the processes of prefabrication and assembly. This kind of embodied empathy for the qualities and capacities of particular materials is based on learning how they respond to various processes of transformation; for example, chiselling stone, sawing wood, moulding clay, pressing steel, etc. As these qualities emerge during the process of construction, the challenge is how best to preserve them within the finished building – how to retain distinctive surface textures that 'tell a story' about how the materials have been worked.

The other important ingredient of tectonics in architecture relates to the joining together of different materials, a process that is embedded in the etymology of the word itself. The ancient Greek term *techne*, referring broadly to the 'art of making' or craftsmanship, is based on a Proto-Indo-European word *tec*, meaning 'to make'. The related Greek word *tikto*, referring to a form of production involving a bringing together of distinct elements – as in biological reproduction[37] – relates it in turn to the origins of 'articulate,' meaning 'jointed'. This goes some way to explain the recent tectonic emphasis on the expressive elaboration of details, such as connections between structural members, or junctions between different materials. Typical examples would include key buildings from the British 'high-tech' tradition such as Richard Rogers's Lloyd's Building (1986) and Norman Foster's Hong Kong and Shanghai Bank headquarters (1985).

This second aspect of the definition of tectonics helps us to widen the scope of the discussion by moving beyond the simple enjoyment of surface textures and sensory qualities of individual materials towards a consideration of those emergent qualities and characteristics of more complex assemblies of components. Any individual piece of natural, organic material – a block of stone or a plank of wood, for example – has its own unique properties which give it a distinctive 'personality'. This is even more the case when it comes to complex combinations of materials – whether 'natural' or 'synthetic' – whose behaviour becomes more difficult to predict because of their multiple levels of interaction, both between the components themselves and between the components and their surroundings.

Bruno Latour, the French philosopher and sociologist of technology, has built his career around the study of these complex technical assemblies, developing the conceptual framework known as 'actor-network theory' (ANT) to help explain them. One of the strengths of the actor-network approach is its avoidance of the traditional ontological distinction between human and non-human actors. A degree of agency is ascribed to all components of a system, as well as to the larger configurations into which these components are arranged. One of Latour's particular interests is the behaviour of larger technical systems such as the national

---

37. David Farrell Krell, *Architecture: Ecstasies of Space, Time, and the Human Body* (Albany, NY: State University of New York Press, 1997), pp. 16–17.

networks of electrical power, susceptible as they are to unpredictable failures. Famously, this happened in North America in August 2003 when a small-scale local fault cascaded into widespread power blackouts across several states in the USA and Canada.

One of Latour's broader objectives is to question the possibility of the human domination of nature that modern science appears to offer us, and he uses the example of craft construction to illustrate his argument:

> The scientist makes the fact, but whenever we make something *we* are not in command, we are slightly *overtaken* by the action: every builder knows that. Thus the paradox of constructivism is that it uses a vocabulary of *mastery* that no architect, mason, city planner, or carpenter would ever use. [...] I never *act*; I am always slightly surprised by what I do. That which acts through me is also surprised by what I do, by the chance to mutate, to change, to bifurcate, the chance that I and the circumstances surrounding me offer to that which has been invited.[38]

The last line of the quotation contains a reference to the French historian François Jullien, specifically his work on the Chinese concept of *Shi*. This summary of his findings by the political theorist Jane Bennett nicely captures both the origin and potential of the term:

> *Shi* is the style, energy, propensity, trajectory, or élan inherent to a specific arrangement of things. Originally a word used in military strategy, *shi* emerged in the description of a good general who must be able to read and then ride the *shi* of a configuration of moods, winds, historical trends, and armaments: *shi* names the dynamic force emanating from a spatio-temporal configuration rather than from any particular element within it.[39]

This idea suggests that good military strategy is based – perhaps counterintuitively – on an ability to work with the given conditions, rather than trying to reconfigure everything again from the beginning. The best route to a successful outcome might therefore involve a more subtle 'steering' of the direction of events, beginning by identifying how a situation is already tending to unfold. I would argue that the sensibility required to do this is exactly analogous to the skill of the craftsman: an ability to work with the natural grain of the material, or as Louis Kahn famously said, to listen to what the brick itself 'wants to be'.

The key thing to note here is the way in which embodied processes inevitably generate innovations. Even in cases where repetition might be desirable, such as in

---

38. Bruno Latour, *Pandora's Hope: Essays on the Reality of Science Studies* (Cambridge, MA: Harvard University Press, 1999), p. 281.

39. Jane Bennett, *Vibrant Matter: A Political Ecology of Things* (Durham, NC: Duke University Press, 2010), p. 35.

the mass-production of components like clay bricks, stone blocks or natural timber window-frames, there is always some unpredictability in the outcome and each one has its own unique character. This is one source of the kind of creativity evident in traditional vernacular architecture, where skilful builders were able to adapt their work to suit the individual characteristics of the given material.

Materiality in the design process
Innovation also occurs during the process of designing, due to the effects of the chosen drawing technique, where the materiality of the medium can suggest unexpected opportunities for the designer. One could think of a drawing being rather like a scientist's experimental apparatus: what begins as a means of testing a hypothesis often turns out to reveal something else – often very different from what the investigator originally intended. What appears within the design drawing as the 'surprise' of the designer's action can often be a direct consequence of the equipment involved. The architectural theorist Marco Frascari has written about the creativity inherent in the use of traditional drawing instruments and has also described the effects of different kinds of paper typically used at different stages of the design process. This included a student exercise with Carlo Scarpa where the whole project was developed and presented on a single panel of white-painted wood.[40] An interesting recent example of the influence of the drawing technique on the development of the design appears in Peter Zumthor's early sketches of the thermal baths at Vals. Using the side of a stick of pastel to create what he later called 'block drawings,' the idea for the distinctive subterranean atmosphere of the interior space began to emerge. The 'slabs' of colour in these early sketches evolved into a bold composition of free-standing stone blocks, with narrow slots in the roof allowing daylight to illuminate the spaces between them.[41]

Other design approaches also have their own distinctive 'materiality'. I am thinking, for example, of Peter Eisenman's use of geometry as a starting point for formal exploration. By subjecting simple Platonic diagrams to a process of step-by-step transformation, even these abstract generic shapes can produce unexpectedly complex effects. This same combination of constraints and opportunities also emerges with the use of digital design tools, where the specific affordances offered by different software packages can also have a direct impact on the final outcome. Buildings that have been modelled in Rhino,

40. Marco Frascari, 'A Reflection on Paper and its Virtues Within the Material and Invisible *Factures* of Architecture', in *From Models to Drawings*, ed. by Marco Frascari, Jonathan Hale and Bradley Starkey (Abingdon: Routledge, 2007), pp. 23–33.

41. Matthew Mindrup, 'The Resistance of Factures in Drawing-out Architectural Constructions', in *The Material Imagination: Reveries on Architecture and Matter*, ed. by Matthew Mindrup (Farnham: Ashgate, 2015), pp. 61–4.

as opposed to Sketchup, are often quite easy to distinguish, due to the two applications' very different abilities to deal with complex double-curved surfaces.

Each of these examples suggests the potential for embodied material processes to generate novel solutions. They do this partly by escaping the constraints of imposed, top-down intellectual frameworks. Instead of adopting pre-conceived models or readymade solutions, many architects work instead from the 'bottom up', following what the anthropologist Tim Ingold has called the 'lines of flight' suggested by the chosen materials of their design or construction process.[42] Whether these materials are physical (i.e. constructional), typological, geometrical, or even conceptual, they all exert some influence on the outcome of the design process. By pushing against their distinctive material resistances, new design opportunities are inevitably generated. This might happen, for example, in the modelling workshop, as with architects like Frank Gehry who work directly on physical maquettes. And likewise with self-builders and *bricoleurs* improvising on site with recycled materials or re-purposed components. This last example serves as a reminder of the creativity inherent in the embodied knowledge of the skilled builder, something that is typically suppressed by today's legal and contractual relationships that attempt to enforce an absolute split between the processes of design and construction. Historically, by contrast, it was common for the architect's construction drawings to convey only the basic outlines of the completed design and for the building contractor to 'fill in the gaps' from their own embodied knowledge. Builders would therefore creatively contribute to the outcome of the project by drawing on their personal experience of local contextual factors such as climate, ground conditions, and local building materials.

Re-use and reinterpretation

I began this article with the familiar definition of tectonic expression based on the way that the building's visible surfaces carry traces of the original construction process. I also want to suggest that this is a key characteristic of spaces that invite the occupation of the user, with the result that they become further animated with the traces of life lived within the building – for example, bronze door handles or stone steps polished by the hands and feet of previous users. These accumulated records of previous patterns of use can also help to subvert a building's dominant 'meaning' by suggesting other possible uses beyond its official designation (as home, school or office, for example). This idea also echoes Roland Barthes's famous concept of the *punctum* which emerged from his analysis of photographic images first published in 1980. This idea suggests the power of the personal detail, which might be overlooked or partially concealed within a photograph and which

---

42. Tim Ingold, *Making: Anthropology, Archaeology, Art and Architecture* (Abingdon: Routledge, 2013), p. 102.

retains the power to disrupt the manifest content and suggest alternative interpretations of the overall image.[43]

This idea of a 'historical tectonics' – traces of former functions which also suggest new possibilities – introduces a critical dimension to tectonic expression that I will return to in the final section of this article. I also believe that this idea can shed some light on the enduring appeal of historic buildings that have been adapted to fulfil new functions. I am thinking especially of the recent tendency to convert former industrial buildings into art museums, as well as the preference among many contemporary artists for both producing and presenting their work in so-called 'found spaces'. One reason for this could be the kind of visual disjunctions that typically emerge in 'adaptive re-use', where the original relationship between form and function has often been displaced. For example, if the traces of former uses are still visible alongside the new insertions, this can produce a space with a heightened potential for creative re-appropriation. There is also another kind of opening up that often happens with adapted buildings, such as when walls or floors are removed and new views are created between previously isolated spaces. This has also been described by Fred Scott, in his book *On Altering Architecture*, in terms of the excitement and the sense of transgression that often results from interventions in redundant buildings:

> For the occupants, the new circulation of the altered interior may be like a journey through ruins, taking previously impossible routes, and having new, almost aberrant viewpoints as a result. An altered building explains itself; it is in this way an inhabited ruin. [...] The altered condition may have qualities of exposure that previously one thought of as confined to drawings, such as sectional perspectives.[44]

Scott also makes reference here to the power of drawing as a tool for exploration and discovery, suggesting a connection to what Maurice Merleau-Ponty once noticed in a slow-motion film of Henri Matisse: seeing the artist hesitating in front of a drawing while deciding which of the faint outlines to select, he was seemingly aware that each offered a different opportunity for new significations and meanings to emerge.

The performance theorist Carrie Noland also draws on Merleau-Ponty's ideas in making a similar interpretation of the work of American video artist Bill Viola.[45] In a time-lapse video work from 2000 entitled *The Quintet of the Astonished*, Viola shows five actors' faces performing the five classic emotional expressions: fear, anger, sorrow, pain, and joy. By shooting the video at a faster-than-normal speed

---

43. Roland Barthes, *La Chambre claire: notes sur la photographie* (Paris: Éditions de l'Étoile/Gallimard/Le Seuil, 1980), pp. 47–9.

44. Fred Scott, *On Altering Architecture* (Abingdon: Routledge, 2008), p. 171.

45. Carrie Noland, *Agency and Embodiment: Performing Gestures/Producing Culture* (Cambridge, MA: Harvard University Press, 2009), pp. 66–72.

(384 frames per second instead of the typical 24), but showing it at standard speed, one minute of live action creates 16 minutes of viewing time. The effect is to allow the actors' previously unnoticeable facial movements to suddenly become highly visible, and this has the effect of blurring the normal distinctions between one emotional expression and another. The viewer is therefore able to witness the previously unseen transitions between them, and this offers a range of new expressions ready to be assigned to new meanings.

One lesson I would like to take from this, as with the other examples referred to above, is that all materials – and tectonic systems – will always be beyond our complete control. And at same time it is this unruly, uncontainable 'excess' that ensures that we will always be surprised by what they can do. Likewise, in the broader realm of personal and political freedom, it is our own bodily materiality that helps us resist the top-down imposition of political power, contrary to what many critics have concluded from reading the later work of Michel Foucault. A similar point has also been made by Kenneth Frampton in his important work on critical regionalism, where he also emphasizes the role of materiality and bodily experience in the process of political resistance:

> Two independent channels of resistance proffer themselves against the ubiquity of the Megalopolis and the exclusivity of sight. They presuppose a mediation of the mind/body split in Western thought. They may be regarded as archaic agents with which to counter the potential universality of rootless civilization. The first of these is the tactile resilience of the place-form; the second is the sensorium of the body. These two are posited here as interdependent, because each is contingent on the other. The place-form is inaccessible to sight alone just as simulacra [images or virtual 'simulations'] exclude the tactile capacity of the body.[46]

While Frampton's definition of critical regionalism has often been over-simplified in recent years, it could also be argued that 'traditional' regional architectures are also, in a sense, inherently critical. By this I mean that new ideas – new materials, new techniques, even new forms and new ways of living – are in fact an inevitable outcome of bottom-up processes of material exploration. This is an important consequence of the way in which vernacular traditions were passed on through so-called 'experiential learning', where both design and construction practices were learnt by attempting to imitate (inevitably imperfectly) the behavioural routines of already skilled practitioners.[47] This direct 'body to body' learning process contrasts with the conceptual model that is generally prevalent today, where architectural knowledge is communicated through textbooks in a formal academic setting.

---

46. Kenneth Frampton, 'Intimations of Tactility: Excerpts from a Fragmentary Polemic', in *Architecture and Body*, ed. by Scott Marble (New York: Rizzoli, 1988), unpaginated.
47. Jean Lave and Etienne Wenger, *Situated Learning: Legitimate Peripheral Participation* (Cambridge: Cambridge University Press, 1991), pp. 34–7.

This process tends to freeze knowledge in a systematic and rigid form, binding practices to fixed principles that are often unable – or very slow – to adapt to changing requirements. By contrast, when techniques are passed on directly through some form of material embodiment, the inherent looseness and ambiguity of these processes acts as a kind of 'engine' of innovation. I would argue that this process is inherently more responsive to social and cultural changes, as well as offering some resistance to the top-down imposition of written rules and regulations that are often out of touch with everyday reality.

Frampton has also described this kind of process as a way of maintaining local distinctiveness when so much of global culture is becoming more homogenous. He did this by celebrating three characteristics that all buildings should try to maintain – the *tactile*, the *tectonic* and *telluric* – and which all, in some way, refer to the quality of uniqueness.[48] The *telluric* involves a connection between the building and the site, which involves both its material and its historical character. The *tectonic*, as we have seen already, refers to the history of the building's construction, while the *tactile* dimension includes and encourages the bodily engagement of the user.

Merleau-Ponty also saw embodiment as a means to resist the generalizing effect of philosophical reflection – the tendency of 'high-altitude' thought to 'bask in its acquisitions'[49] and thereby lose its initial connection with experience. As he said, in his late essay 'Sur la phénoménologie du langage', it is the nature of 'expressive language' to be constantly renewing itself – or at least always striving to restore its unstable grasp on the world it is referring to:

> Chaque acte d'expression littéraire ou philosophique contribue à accomplir le vœu de récupération du monde qui s'est prononcé avec l'apparition d'une langue, c'est-à-dire d'un système fini de signes qui se prétendait capable en principe de capter tout être qui se présenterait. Il réalise pour sa part une partie de ce projet et proroge de plus le pacte qui vient de venir à échéance en ouvrant un nouveau champ de vérités. Cela n'est possible que par la même "transgression intentionnelle" qui donne autrui, et, comme elle, le phénomène de la verité, théoriquement impossible, ne se connaît que par le praxis qui la *fait*.[50]

Critical phenomenology

Much of the foregoing may seem like a strange reorientation of tectonic thinking, into what would normally be considered an *immaterial* realm. Nonetheless, I would

---

48. Kenneth Frampton, 'Towards a Critical Regionalism: Six Points for an Architecture of Resistance', *The Anti-aesthetic: Essays on Postmodern Culture*, ed. by Hal Foster (Port Townsend, WA: Bay Press, 1983), pp. 16–30.

49. Maurice Merleau-Ponty, *La Phénoménologie de la perception* (Paris: Gallimard, 1945), p. 446.

50. Maurice Merleau-Ponty, *Signes* (Paris: Gallimard, 1960) pp. 119–20.

argue that this is precisely what emerges from thinking about a building (as philosophers of technology like Bruno Latour and others typically do), less as a fixed object and more as a set of tools: spaces that offer the user a structured field of possibilities for action. What I am suggesting is that spatial and functional organisation – just like the processes of design – have a materiality and a tectonic dimension all of their own. It is this very sensibility towards a kind of 'immaterial materiality' that might actually be honed and refined by our hands-on experience of working with materials.

This idea is partly drawn from the work of two historical figures, the French phenomenologist Merleau-Ponty and the American psychologist James J. Gibson (1904–79). Gibson developed his 'theory of affordances'[51] to describe those opportunities offered to a living organism by the various features of its surrounding environment. In the case of buildings, the most obvious examples would be things like windows, doorways and staircases, features that either afford views or bodily movement between what would otherwise be disconnected spaces. Other technologies, like tools or even musical instruments, also remind us that these affordances vary according to the bodily abilities of the individual user to exploit them – as we have seen already in the case of a skilled craftsman adapting the working process to suit the opportunities afforded by the material.

Likewise, Gibson suggested that our perception of the environment is grounded in a sense of its possibilities for bodily interaction, an idea that also echoes an earlier analysis in Merleau-Ponty's *Phenomenology of Perception*. For Merleau-Ponty, perception begins with what he variously named 'motor intentionality' or 'motor cognition', meaning a primary bodily reaction to what he called the solicitations of the world around us. Just as built spaces offer affordances for particular kinds of behaviour, for Merleau-Ponty language could also be said to offer affordances for activities such as thinking, reasoning and communication. Most importantly for Merleau-Ponty, language is not simply a tool for 'representing' pre-conceived ideas, rather it acts as a mechanism for constituting thoughts as such. As he wrote in an especially memorable line from 'Sur la phénoménologie du langage': 'Il y a une signification "langagière" du langage qui accomplit la médiation entre mon intention encore muette et les mots, de telle sorte que mes paroles me surprennent moi-même et m'enseignent ma pensée.'[52] The same sense of discovery and creativity inherent in all material practices was also highlighted by Bruno Latour in his notion of 'the slight surprise of action'[53] developed as a critique of the assumption of mastery inherent in the conventional definition of top-down design.

---

51. James J. Gibson, *The Ecological Approach to Visual Perception* (Hillsdale, NJ: Lawrence Erlbaum Associates, 1986), pp. 127–43.

52. Merleau-Ponty, *Signes*, p. 111.

53. Latour, *Pandora's Hope*, pp. 280–3.

In conclusion, as I have suggested above, the tectonic sensibility involves thinking of spatial and functional possibilities as affordances for bodily action, but always within the relational framework set out in Gibson's work. Rather than rigidly imposing programmatic functions in a top-down deterministic manner, spaces could instead be designed to offer more loosely structured fields for creative appropriation – in other words, to solicit the unpredictable creativity of the future building user. Features designed for one purpose can then also be turned to other uses, as Merleau-Ponty suggested in the case of language: words are – often unwittingly – 'coherently deformed' in order to invoke and express new layers of meaning.[54] By extending this kind of sensitivity towards material affordances into the realm of spatial and even conceptual configurations, it could perhaps then be argued that 'tectonic architecture' is after all, simply *architecture as such*.

ORCID

Jonathan Hale https://orcid.org/0000-0002-4929-0497

---

54. Merleau-Ponty, *Signes*, p. 114.

Nottingham French Studies 59.3 (2020): 368–383
DOI: 10.3366/nfs.2020.0296
© University of Nottingham
www.euppublishing.com/nfs

LIVING AS WE DREAM: AUTOMATISM AND AUTOMATION FROM SURREALISM TO STIEGLER

MADELEINE CHALMERS

À quand les logiciens, les philosophes dormants?

André Breton[1]

As a species, we have been doing a lot of sleepwalking of late. If thinkpieces are to be believed, the twenty-first century has produced a generation of technological somnambulists unconsciously wandering into 'automated obscurity', 'artificial intimacy' and ultimately 'human disaster'.[2] The automatic behaviour of sleepwalking is metaphorically applied to our own attitude towards the increasing automation of the workplace and the increasing imbrication of artificial intelligence into our lives, to suggest indifference or lack of agency faced with a situation of existential threat. Even in our dreams, we can yield control to a device which 'wakes up the wearer not at a prearranged hour but at the point near that hour when, according to the device's measurements, the wearer is in a state of light rather than deep

---

My warmest thanks to Prof. Nikolaj Lübecker and Dr. Martin Crowley for their generous readings – and to Dr. John Marks for the invitation.

1. André Breton, 'Manifeste du surréalisme' in *Œuvres complètes*, ed. by Marguerite Bonnet and others, Bibliothèque de La Pléiade, 4 vols (Paris: Gallimard, 1998–2008), I, pp. 309–46 (p. 317). Hereafter, this and other volumes cited in-text by relevant Roman numeral followed by page number.

2. David Edwards, 'American Workers Sleepwalking into Automated Obscurity, Says New Report', *Robotics and Automation News*, <https://roboticsandautomationnews.com/2017/ 07/18/american-workers-sleepwalking-into-automated-obscurity-says-new-report/13355/> [accessed 12 March 2019]; Todd Essig, 'Sleepwalking Towards Artificial Intimacy: How Psychotherapy Is Failing The Future', *Forbes*, <https://www.forbes.com/sites/ toddessig/2018/06/07/sleepwalking-towards-artificial-intimacy-how-psychotherapy-is-failing-the-future/> [accessed 12 March 2019]; 'Society Is "Sleepwalking into a Human Disaster" of Uncontrolled and Unaccountable AI Technology Development, the Founders of Institute for Ethical AI in Education Warn', *UCL Educate*, 2018 <https://educate. london/society-is-sleepwalking-into-a-human-disaster-of-uncontrolled-and-unaccountable-ai-technology-development-in-schools-the-founders-of-institute-for-ethical-ai-in-education-warn/> [accessed 12 March 2019].

sleep'.[3] This mutual linguistic and conceptual contagion of automatism, understood as non-conscious behaviour, and automation – the performance of human tasks by machines – is particularly pronounced in the French 'automatisme' and 'automatisation' (which can refer both to psychological automatism and industrial automation). For the *encyclopédistes* Diderot and D'Alembert, 'automatisme' was a 'mot […] pour exprimer la qualité d'automate dans l'animal, c'est-à-dire, le système des mouvemens [*sic*] qui dépendent uniquement de l'organisme du corps animé, sans que la volonté y ait aucune part'.[4] As early as the eighteenth century, machines were retrofitted to the organic creature which created them, in order to explain what was most primal about the human being. French thought and culture took up Diderot and D'Alembert's definition with alacrity, forming the automatic lineage which this article explores in the company of a surrealist (André Breton), an anthropologist (André Leroi-Gourhan) and a philosopher (Bernard Stiegler).

While Stiegler has drawn on Leroi-Gourhan's technological anthropology from the outset of his philosophical career and Leroi-Gourhan was a lifelong admirer of Breton,[5] no attempt has been made to draw a technocritical genealogy from Breton to Stiegler. However, in modern and contemporary French culture, 'automatisme' in a literary context has one primordial association: the much-maligned automatic writing of surrealism. In modern and contemporary Anglo-American technological thought and the public imagination, automation means the replacement of human workers by machines and computer systems. On the surface, the two meanings would seem opposed: automatic writing is about unfurling human subjectivity and automation about eliminating it from the workplace. Yet when Bernard Stiegler published the first volume of *La Société automatique*, entitled *L'Avenir du travail*, in 2015, his understanding of work and automation extended far beyond using machines to replace human workers and focused on the automation of every aspect of human life. In particular, his third chapter is devoted to dreams – the mother lode of Bretonian surrealism.

This article therefore argues that this genealogy offers us the chance to make sense of the uniquely French approach to our automated age which Stiegler continues to spearhead, and to understand how our mainstream discourse has simultaneously projected human automatism onto automation and incorporated automation back into human behaviour. I begin by setting out the three thinkers' understanding of automatism and its relationship to recording technology, with a

---

3. Jan Van den Bulck, 'Sleep Apps and the Quantified Self: Blessing or Curse?', *Journal of Sleep Research*, 24:2 (2015), 121–3 (p. 121).

4. Denis Diderot and Jean le Rond d'Alembert, *Nouveau Dictionnaire, pour servir de supplément aux dictionnaires des sciences, des arts et des métiers* (Paris: Panckouke, 1776), I, p. 756.

5. André Leroi-Gourhan and Claude-Henri Rocquet, *Les Racines du monde: entretiens avec Claude-Henri Rocquet* (Paris: Pierre Belfond, 1982), p. 77.

focus on Breton's major statements on automatism ('Entrée des médiums', the two *Manifestes du surréalisme* and 'Le Message automatique'), Leroi-Gourhan's two-volume *Le Geste et la parole* and Stiegler's *L'Avenir du travail*. A second section unpacks the relationship of surrealism's automatic language to art and technics, before my final section returns to Breton's seminal statements on dreams in *Les Vases communicants* and our contemporary hypnagogic state, to ask how our attitudes to automatism and automation might interact positively, to generate a new form of lucid sleepwalking.

Automatic recording: writing, reading, mediating
An 'automatisme psychique qui correspond assez bien à l'état de rêve, état qu'il est aujourd'hui fort difficile de délimiter' – it is thus that André Breton tentatively defines that twilight state in which the first surrealist phrases appeared to him in 1919.[6] Fully-formed, striking in their unexpected imagery, they appear without any conscious effort on his part, in the strange borderland between waking and sleep. In this 1922 definition of surrealism in 'Entrée des médiums', automatism does not emerge with the glint of sleek machines but in a series of false starts. As he attempts to unearth the source of these phrases, Breton constantly gets in his own way. The automatic voice of subjectivity speaks in broken whispers – access is dependent on total abstraction of the world and the conscious subject, constantly stymied by 'l'incursion dans ce domaine d'éléments conscients le plaçant sous une volonté humaine, littéraire' (I, p. 275), notably through the effort of memory required to record dreams and half-remembered phrases. At first, Breton tells us, René Crevel's initiation of the nascent surrealist circle into mediumistic seances and induced sleep seemed to provide an answer, culminating in the surrealist speaking sessions of Robert Desnos, in which Desnos would speak aloud while in a trance: a kind of automatic speaking. However, as Aragon recorded in 1924, these sessions had to be suspended as subjects sank into a contagious and dangerous addiction: 'ils s'endorment à voir dormir un autre, [...] ils se querellent, et parfois il faut leur arracher les couteaux des mains'.[7] The automatic voice is pure experience, yet there is also a need to conserve it, to hold onto this automatic subjectivity in order to explore and deploy it but also to preserve oneself from it, to retain an anchor in the everyday world. There can be no trace of this automatic subjectivity without some form of technically mediated recording. Ultimately, Breton returns to pen and paper and the pitfalls of conscious recording, while seeking to minimize consciousness as much as possible.

    The *Manifeste* which followed in 1924 reframes these experiments as theory, in a legitimizing foundation myth which rehabilitates the paradox of automatic writing. The purely internal focus of automatism in 'Entrée des médiums' is converted into a

---

6.   André Breton, 'Entrée des médiums' in *Œuvres complètes*, I, pp. 273–79 (p. 274).
7.   Louis Aragon, *Une vague de rêves* (Paris: Hachette, 1964), pp. 22–3.

'résolution [...] de ces deux états, en apparence si contradictoires, que sont le rêve et la réalité, en une sorte de réalité absolue, de *surréalité*' (I, p. 319). The evolution can be seen in Breton's new definition of surrealism:

> automatisme psychique pur par lequel on se propose d'exprimer, soit verbalement, soit par écrit, soit de toute autre manière, le fonctionnement réel de la pensée. Dictée de la pensée, en l'absence de tout contrôle exercé par la raison, en dehors de toute préoccupation esthétique ou morale. (I, p. 328)

Automatism is no longer simply the passive 'état' of 'Entrée des médiums' but the active expression of a subject's inner thought. Now, assimilating thought to speech (and to its technical prostheses), Breton argues that 'la vitesse de la pensée n'est pas supérieure à celle de la parole, et [...] ne défie pas forcément la langue, ni même la plume qui court' (I, p. 326). This opens up the possibility of a form of real-time recording, with no temporal gap between the inner voice of automatism and its technological mediation in writing, thereby resolving the intrusion of conscious thought and active memory evoked in 'Entrée des médiums'. Here, the subject's unfettered thought alone is the guide, as a 'dictée de la pensée' demanding recording.

This rehabilitation of writing by minimizing its mediatory quality culminates in the image of the automatic subject as recording machine: 'les sourds réceptacles de tant d'échos, les modestes *appareils enregistreurs* qui ne s'hypnotisent pas sur le dessin qu'ils tracent' (I, p. 330, original emphasis). The automatic writing subject becomes a recording technology which creates a faithful written trace, an unconscious medium who barely mediates. As Friedrich Kittler puts it, 'whereas (according to Derrida) it is characteristic of so-called Man and his consciousness to hear himself speak and see himself write, media dissolve such feedback loops'.[8] However, Breton's image is underpinned by a paradox: the recording machine can record 'le fonctionnement réel de la pensée' because it is without thought or consciousness – yet the very thought it records is, impossibly, its own. This is made explicit by Aragon, who compares the surrealists to 'cet homme qui assembla le premier de petites plaques sensibles, des charbons et des fils de cuivre, croyant parvenir à enregistrer les vibrations de la voix, et qui, la machine montée, entendit sans erreur le son de la voix humaine'.[9] The movement from the 'vibrations de la voix' to the voice itself is key. The trace of the automatic voice recorded by the surrealist's roving hand *is* the voice itself. However, where the phonograph-maker assembles heterogeneous components to construct a machine that is external to himself, Aragon's surrealists construct the phonograph, become the phonograph

---

8.   Friedrich A. Kittler, *Gramophone, Film, Typewriter*, transl. by Geoffrey Winthrop-Young and Michael Wutz (Stanford: Stanford University Press, 1999), pp. 22–3.
9.   Aragon, *Une vague de rêves*, p. 15.

and produce what the phonograph records, thereby collapsing distinctions between subject, experience and recording.

When previous scholarship on surrealism has sought to extend the concept of automatism by exploring its etymological links with the concept of automation, it has done so without committing to the radical implications of Breton's understanding of automatism. David Lomas – theorizing predominantly with Bataille rather than Breton – suggests that André Masson's automatic drawings employed the same formal tools as proponents of the machine aesthetic in 'an oppositional practice' designed to *counter* the recording device rather than incorporate it.[10] Similarly, Hal Foster's analysis of the surrealist preoccupation with machines and automata as an experience of the Freudian uncanny draws primarily on Hans Bellmer, who sits on the very fringes of Bretonian surrealism.[11] What we see here, in Breton and Aragon's early texts, is a thought process, the endpoint of which is that automatic subjectivity *is* automatic writing; experience *is* experience-exteriorized in language; to be human *is* to give oneself over to that 'qualité d'automate', to be one's own medium.[12]

The full ramifications of the Bretonian model of automatism and language are thrown into relief by comparison with that laid out by Leroi-Gourhan in his work *La Technique et le langage*. Here, Leroi-Gourhan offers a tripartite understanding of human functioning, suggesting that we operate at three levels of consciousness: automatic, mechanical and lucid. At the core of human function are those biologically automated behaviours which unfold without our conscious participation. When in good health, we rarely give a second thought to our inhalations and exhalations, to the diastole and systole of our heartbeat, the peristalsis of our guts. Whatever our differences, these automatisms are the core of our human functioning – but are also biological behaviours that we share with other species. On this foundation accretes the 'comportement machinal qui intéresse des chaînes opératoires acquises par l'expérience et l'éducation'.[13] Unfolding in a 'pénombre' of consciousness, in which light pierces through but only dimly, these mechanical gestures involve a combination of actions, linked together in a *chaîne opératoire* which gets us from one situation to another. We are aware of

---

10. David Lomas, *The Haunted Self: Surrealism, Psychoanalysis, Subjectivity* (New Haven: Yale University Press, 2000), p. 28.

11. Hal Foster, *Compulsive Beauty* (Cambridge, MA and London: MIT Press, 2003), p. 129.

12. Alan Clinton assimilates automation and automatism terms suggesting that as a recording technology, the human being becomes a machine with 'no subjectivity to make it concerned with one outcome over another'. Clinton equates conscious, rational thought with subjectivity, yet Bretonian automatism is about suspending the former in order to explore the latter: there is no automatism without subjectivity. See *Mechanical Occult: Automatism, Modernism, and the Specter of Politics* (New York: Peter Lang, 2004), p. 13.

13. André Leroi-Gourhan, *Le Geste et la parole, I: technique et langage* (Paris: Albin Michel, 1964), p. 26. Hereafter cited in-text as *TL*.

what we are doing when we are eating, writing and moving, to reprise Leroi-Gourhan's examples – but in good health we do not necessarily need to concentrate with every ounce of mental energy on the movement of fork to mouth, or of putting one foot in front of the other (*TL*, p. 29). While we might have automatic behaviours in common with other species, it is the mechanical behaviours which we learn from parents and peers which allow us to become identifiably human, part of social and ethnic groups, woven into deep-rooted collective memory and tradition.

This is the very opposite of Aragon's declaration that surrealist automatism is a means by which 'l'esprit se déprend un peu de la mécanique humaine'.[14] For Aragon, the automatic and the mechanical are not synonymous; the former is a space of freedom, constrained by the latter. Aragon's differentiating juxtaposition of the automatic and the mechanical, moves us *away* from the human as commonly understood, by undoing our habitual processes, particularly those related to memory: 'alors je ne suis plus la bicyclette de mes sens, la meule à aiguiser les souvenirs et les rencontres'.[15] This surrealist automatism devalues *some* automatic behaviours (the involuntary sensory processing of the external world) and the conscious act of memory and its role in social 'rencontres'. It lifts us beyond the human to a point at which 'je me dépasse'.[16] The automatic – that which lies at the core of our being – is also what pushes us to surpass ourselves; a wellspring of raw experience on which we overlay a humanistic veneer. There is more to the human being than the 'human'.

Where Aragon and Breton celebrate the automatic – and incorporate language and thought into the category of the automatic – for Leroi-Gourhan, language and thought are elements which only begin to come into play in mechanical behaviours which are inherited through collective memory and its exteriorizations and which involve 'chaînes opératoires' (*TL*, p. 27). For Leroi-Gourhan, 'language is […] co-emergent with technical intelligence'.[17] They reach their apogee in what Leroi-Gourhan terms our 'comportement lucide' in which 'le langage intervient de manière prépondérante, soit qu'il conduise à réparer une rupture accidentelle dans le déroulement de l'opération, soit qu'il conduise à créer des chaînes opératoires nouvelles' (*TL*, p. 27). Our lucid behaviours are our human problem-solving abilities, our ability to innovate. Lucidity is a moment of abstraction, pulling us out of the immanence of the 'vécu' into a state of being where we are able to 'fixer la pensée dans des symboles matériels' which allow us not only to make decisions but

---

14. Aragon, *Une vague de rêves*, p. 9.
15. Ibid.
16. Ibid.
17. Christopher Johnson, 'Leroi-Gourhan and the Limits of the Human', *French Studies*, 65:4 (2011), 471–87 (p. 477).

to inscribe them in collective memory (*TL*, p. 261). Surrealism accesses life through language, but for Leroi-Gourhan, language moves us away from language: it is 'l'instrument de la libération par rapport au vécu'.[18] Leroi-Gourhan describes this as if it were a kind of encephelogram: 'la lucidité suit une sinusoïde dont les creux correspondent aux séries machinales alors que les sommets marquent les ajustements des séries aux circonstances de l'opération' (*TL*, p. 31).[19] Where surrealism seeks a 'nuit des éclairs', Leroi-Gourhan shows us existing on a continuum of consciousness from darkness to daylight.

Leroi-Gourhan's descriptions reprise and invert the language of surrealist automatism: the curve or trace and the alternation of waking and sleeping from dusk to dawn. Indeed, Lomas has discussed Breton's image with reference to the technological devices of Étienne-Jules Marey, which create a visible graphical trace of the human pulse.[20] Aragon describes how 'dans l'expérience surréaliste [...] tout se passe comme si la courbe d'un mobile, duquel nous ne savons rien, s'inscrivait. [...] Ses hauts, ses bas, ses interruptions valent par ce qu'ils expriment d'inconnu'.[21] However, there is also a hint at common ground. In the *Manifeste*, Breton imagines the day when 'on parviendra à nous rendre compte du rêve dans son intégrité (et cela suppose une discipline de la mémoire qui porte sur des générations [...]), où sa courbe se développera' (I, p. 319). The automatic recording machine contributes to collective memory and ultimately to a later interpretation; automatism is a phenomenon to be experienced first but also examined and understood. Breton begins to make his peace with exteriorization. Indeed, as Christopher Johnson concisely summarizes, in Leroi-Gourhan's account of human evolution 'the neurological continuity of the control of hand and face means that in evolutionary terms the technique of writing is as "natural" an extension of the human mind as speech'.[22] While the western philosophical tradition from Plato onwards has posited a metaphysical opposition between speech and writing, Derrida draws on Leroi-Gourhan to argue that speech both implies and depends upon writing. As a form of recording, writing 'supplements'

---

18. André Leroi-Gourhan, *Le Geste et la parole, II: la mémoire et les rythmes* (Paris: Albin Michel, 1965), p. 21. Hereafter cited in-text as *MR*.

19. The first electroencephalograms were produced in 1924, the same year as the *Manifeste*. See L. F. Haas, 'Hans Berger (1873–1941), Richard Caton (1842–1926), and Electroencephalography', *Journal of Neurology, Neurosurgery and Psychiatry*, 74:1 (2003), 9.

20. David Lomas, '"Modest Recording Instruments": Science, Surrealism and Visuality', *Art History*, 27:4 (2004), 627–50; 'Becoming Machine: Surrealist Automatism and Some Contemporary Instances', *Tate Papers*, <http://www.tate.org.uk/research/publications/tate-papers/18/becoming-machine-surrealist-automatism-and-some-contemporary-instances> [accessed 7 June 2017].

21. Louis Aragon, *Traité du style* (Paris: Gallimard, 1928), p. 195.

22. Johnson, 'Leroi-Gourhan and the Limits of the Human', p. 477.

speech's inevitable transience and by leaving a permanent trace thereby renders further speech possible.[23]

Bernard Stiegler's own conception of technics – set out in the seminal *La Faute d'Épiméthée* (1994) – is explicitly founded both on Leroi-Gourhan's statement of the coevolution of technics and language and on writing's status as the Derridean 'supplément d'origine'.[24] In this first volume of *La Technique et le temps*, Stiegler applies this relationship of supplementarity to the imbrication of temporality into technics. Human beings have limited lifespans and capacity for the storage of memories which Stiegler terms '*finitude rétentionnelle*' (original emphasis).[25] Technical exteriorization marks these finite boundaries while transcending them. For Stiegler, technical exteriorization, such as writing, is a form of memory which supplements our retentional finitude. It allows for the posthumous transmission of knowledge acquired by individuals during their lives, thus also creating an anticipation of mortality. Technics is the ground from which human beings emerge and crystallize, and to which they return. As Stiegler terms it, 'la vie [...] est inscription dans le non-vivant, espacement, temporalisation, différenciation et différement par, de et dans le non-vivant, dans le mort'.[26] We are only aware of life as life because it emerges within the mortality-defining temporal framework of epiphylogenetic 'before us' and anticipatory 'after us' made available to us by technics. According to Stiegler's framework, the technological mediation of writing gives Breton access to subjectivity but, precisely because it is a form of mediation, it bars complete access to the originary moment of that subjectivity.

Exteriorization is the prism for Stiegler's approach to automation in our contemporary society. For Stiegler, our era commenced with the advent of industrialization and large-scale automation, coinciding with a change in our modes of exteriorization: 'la grammatisation des gestes par les premiers automatismes industriels'.[27] *Grammatisation* – which Stiegler has deployed in the context of imperialist colonization to describe the imposition of the colonizer's language on the indigenous population – is a framing of exteriorization by power, which changes our relationship to language in order to achieve a 'contrôle de la conscience, des corps et de l'inconscient'.[28] What we choose to remember shapes our understanding of the past and, following Stiegler's understanding of technics

---

23. Jacques Derrida, *De la grammatologie* (Paris: Éditions de Minuit, 2015), p. 422.

24. Ibid.

25. Bernard Stiegler, *La Technique et le temps I: la faute d'Épiméthée* (Paris: Galilée, 1994), p. 31.

26. Ibid., p. 150.

27. Bernard Stiegler, *La Société automatique I: l'avenir du travail* (Paris: Fayard, 2015), p. 25. Hereafter cited in-text with abbreviation *AT*.

28. Bernard Stiegler, *De la misère symbolique I: l'époque hyperindustrielle* (Paris: Galilée, 2004), pp. 117–18.

and mortality, our present and future. To control methods of exteriorization is to control consciousness, suppressing critical reflection and individuals' desire and ability to act to shape the future. In the twenty-first century, *grammatisation* takes the form of large-scale data gathering, its deployment in algorithms, producing an automated existence: not only in the workplace but in every aspect of our lives.

> Les technologies numériques de la traçabilité constituent le stade le plus avancé d'un processus de grammatisation [...] à partir duquel l'humanité apprend à discrétiser et à reproduire selon divers types de traces les flux qui la traversent et qu'elle engendre: images mentales (inscriptions rupestres), discours (écritures), gestes (automatisation de la production), fréquences sonores et lumineuses (technologies analogiques d'enregistrement) et à présent comportements individuels, relations sociales et processus de transindividuation (algorithmes de l'écriture réticulaire). (*AT*, p. 42)

In this genealogy of our contemporary digital technologies, Stiegler traces his way through the metaphors and focal points of the surrealists and Leroi-Gourhan the prehistoric anthropologist. Surrealism borrows automatism not only because it refers to something deep in the psyche; technical images of automatic recording are also used *because* they bypass critical reflection. For Leroi-Gourhan, automatism is buried deep in the psyche; technics is a source of critical reflection because of our interaction with it. But for Stiegler, technics – while indispensable for critical reflection through exteriorization – when pushed to extremes of automation diminishes our capacity for critical reflection, as our psychic automatisms become automated. In the twenty-first century, the automation of autism is effected through the mediating force not of a pen but of an algorithm, which does not simply record but analyses, processes and feedbacks information. Aragon's more-than-human 'je me dépasse' coexists uneasily with a 'je suis dépassé' filtered through the nonhuman agent of the algorithm.

Short circuits: voice, verb, visuals
A recurrent motif in Stiegler's narrative of automation is that of the short circuit. This is also one of surrealism's most prominent leitmotifs of liberation – the happy fault, the felicitous break in the chain. In the *Second manifeste du surréalisme*, automatic writing becomes a 'court-circuit [...] entre une idée donnée et sa répondante' (I, p. 809). Operating between the poles of an idea within the machine of consciousness, the lifting of constraints on the current of ideas through a 'conducteur de résistance nulle ou trop faible' yields the spark of inspiration (I, p. 809). This short circuit appears in the context of a manifesto well-known for its denigration and expulsion of almost every surrealist ally – including those present at its very inception, particularly Desnos, the original surrealist sleeper.

Breton's dogmatism is visible in his final explicit theorization of automatic writing, 'Le Message automatique' (1933), which also represents the culmination of this move of the rehabilitation of technics into automatic writing.

In a contradiction of his statement in the *Manifeste* that surrealist phrases can be accompanied by a 'faible représentation visuelle' (I, p. 325), here he emphasizes that 'aucune représentation visuelle' accompanies the surrealist phrases he perceives, reaffirming automatism as virtually synonymous with automatic *writing* (II, p. 377).[29] Breton asserts that automatic speech presents no advantages over automatic writing and advocates filtering out visual images that are 'désorganisantes du murmure' (II, pp. 387–8). Breton retains the recording machine's inscription of sound but the clear conscious filtration of perceptions effaces its previous machinic quality, rooted in the absence of conscious thought. The contrast between the earlier analogy of recording machines and this process of filtration seems paradoxical. In her analysis of this text, Rosalind Krauss depicts Breton as a self-hating Platonist, who affirms that in automatic writing 'thought is not a representation but is [...] untainted by the distance and exteriority of signs' – a statement which Krauss claims to be wholly disingenuous, a case of Breton having his cake and eating it.[30] However, as we have seen, this is less a conceptual sleight of hand on Breton's part than a clear evolution, visible in the trajectory of his texts. The recording machine analogy of the *Manifeste* was deployed to suggest that automatic writing uncovers a pre-existing form of consciousness and to incorporate mediation through technical exteriorization into the very experience of automatism as pure thought. The filtration process of 'Le Message automatique' simply extends the purview of that integrated mediation by stressing that the automatic voice is fraught with interference.

Krauss also rejects Breton's extension of automatism to the visual arts as an aggressive annexation, since 'when it is transferred to the domain of visual practice, as in the work of André Masson, automatism is no less understood as a kind of writing'.[31] Yet in the text on Masson which she examines, Breton does *not* occlude the differences between production in the visual arts and automatic writing. Quite the opposite: he actually *loosens* the definition of automatism, suggesting that it need be present only '*sous roche*' and can coexist with 'certaines intentions préméditées' in visual production (IV, p. 432). In this 1941 text, automatism moves away from a purely internal focus, as the hand as exteriorizing organ becomes an organ of liberation, taking wing together with 'lui', the painter as intellectual entity. Body and psychic activity work as one. Breton's description of Masson skirts away

29. For a detailed reading of surrealism's relationship to visuality, see Kim Grant, *Surrealism and the Visual Arts: Theory and Reception* (Cambridge: Cambridge University Press, 2005).

30. Rosalind Krauss, 'The Photographic Conditions of Surrealism', in *The Originality of the Avant-Garde and Other Modernist Myths* (Cambridge, MA and London: MIT Press, 1986), pp. 87–118 (p. 96).

31. Ibid., p. 94.

from representation as Krauss suggests, but it does so only to propose an alternative understanding of how the visual arts can relate to the external world:

> La main du peintre *s'aile* véritablement avec lui: elle n'est plus celle qui calque les formes des objets mais bien celle qui, éprise de son mouvement propre et de lui seul, décrit les figures involontaires dans lesquelles l'expérience montre que ces formes sont appelées à se réincorporer. (IV, p. 428)

Masson's hand is not hypnotized by what it draws – it is 'éprise' of its own motion. That loving gesture traces 'figures involontaires' in which the forms of external objects are irrevocably destined to 'se réincorporer'. The painter mediates forms, which are then folded back into external reality. The dynamic is one of cyclic reciprocity, rather than the unidirectionality of artistic representation as traditionally understood. Automatism becomes an artistic embrace, an '*unité rythmique*' of seamless, synchronized motion of hand and thought (IV, p. 432, original emphasis).

Krauss's issues with Breton stem from a particular understanding of what a graphic language is and what it means to be representational. They rest on the assumption that languages are made up of words, which are oral and verbal entities, while visual arts are a separate category of expression. However, Leroi-Gourhan argues that 'l'art figuratif est, à son origine, directement lié au langage et beaucoup plus près de l'écriture [...]. Il est transposition symbolique et non calque de la réalité' (*TL*, p. 266). Prehistoric art records the *experience* of the real – the push and pull, ebb and flow – rather than the *content* of the real, offering us first 'des rythmes et non des formes' (*TL*, pp. 265–6). The coexistence in humanity's earliest days of two forms of language – the sounds produced by human beings and graphic traces – creates a cognitive and experiential landscape of great richness. They both fulfil different needs: 'le symbolisme graphique [...] exprime dans les trois dimensions de l'espace ce que le langage phonétique exprime dans l'unique dimension du temps' (*TL*, p. 270). Faced with an image, I can read *into* and *around* it (mediation); it sparks off new ideas, new *chaînes opératoires*: 'déclencher le processus verbal', which Leroi-Gourhan imagines as a ceaseless source of myths, told once and forgotten but forever open to reinvention and reconfiguration as each new subject comes face to face with the graphic trace (*TL*, pp. 270–2). We need only think of the sleep speech of Desnos, as he riffs on Marcel Duchamp's crossdressing alter ego Rrose Sélavy to understand how Leroi-Gourhan is able to make an explicit connection with surrealism, as a mode of engagement with the world which is 'relativement proche de celle du Paléolithique' (*MR*, p. 252). Unspooling from one punning name comes writing which demands speech for its sense: 'Rr'ose, essaie là, vit. [...] Rosée c'est la vie. [...] Rose, est-ce, hélas, vie? [...] Rrose est-ce aile, est-ce elle? | est celle | AVIS'.[32] Desnos's radiant trace ends with an affirmation of opinion and freedom of choice. His 'avis' both is and is not the last word as the

---

32.   Robert Desnos, *Corps et biens* (Paris: Gallimard, 2005), p. 110.

decomposition and recomposition of syllables can continue to unfurl indefinitely in the reader's mind.

In contrast to our contemporary linearity, paleolithic – and surrealist – language is 'rayonnante comme le corps de l'oursin ou de l'astérie' (*TL*, p. 292), like the starfish of Man Ray's *Étoile de* mer (1928) – featuring Desnos – or Dalí's sea urchins, in *Un Chien andalou* (1929) and on canvas. The marine creatures which populate surrealist film are often connected or juxtaposed with the human hands which are so key to Leroi-Gourhan's anthropology.[33] Indeed, when Deleuze and Guattari evoke Leroi-Gourhan's 'pôles hétérogènes [...]: le couple voix-audition, et main-graphie', it is tempting to see these two poles as interacting in a form of short circuit, sparking off those images of radiance.[34] The sense of loss that our homogenized form of language, with its 'appauvrissement des moyens d'expression irrationnelle', has wrought is palpable in Leroi-Gourhan's work; it represents a loss of contact with 'la totalité du réel' (*TL*, p. 293) – or what Breton would term 'surréalité'.

For Stiegler, 'le phonogramme est *d'abord et massivement* l'une des conditions de possibilité de [...] la misère symbolique' (original emphasis).[35] This symbolic poverty is a '*perte de participation esthétique*, celle-ci étant elle-même induite par le processus de *perte d'individuation*'.[36] Stiegler borrows a number of concepts here. He derives individuation from Gilbert Simondon: an ever-unfolding becoming in which individual is folded around this core of pre-individual potentiality, sensitive to fluctuations in its *milieu*. This 'individu-milieu' contains at its core 'une certaine incompatibilité par rapport à lui-même' – a permanent tension which suffuses the individual with change.[37] Stiegler also draws on Deleuze and Guattari's notion that all things, from the human body to social institutions, are 'machines désirantes', connected in processes of production and interruption of flows of desire.[38] Within a healthy libidinal economy, these flows of desire are sublimated into socially productive forms of amateurism, which in its etymological sense means love: 'l'*amour du savoir* [...], amour de la science et amour de l'art'.[39]

---

33. P. Adams Sitney, *Visionary Film: The American Avant-Garde, 1943–2000*, 3rd edn (Oxford: Oxford University Press, 2002), p. 15.

34. Gilles Deleuze and Félix Guattari, *Capitalisme et schizophrénie I: l'anti-Œdipe* (Paris: Éditions de Minuit, 1972), pp. 226–7.

35. Bernard Stiegler, *De la misère symbolique II: la catastrophè du sensible* (Paris: Galilée, 2005), p. 50.

36. Ibid.

37. Gilbert Simondon, *L'Individuation à la lumière des notions de forme et d'information* (Paris: Éditions Jérôme Millon, 2013), p. 25.

38. Deleuze and Guattari, *Capitalisme et schizophrénie I*, p. 13.

39. Bernard Stiegler and Ars Industrialis, *Réenchanter le monde: la valeur esprit contre le populisme industriel* (Paris: Flammarion, 2006), p. 61.

Yet for Stiegler in the twenty-first century, capitalism blocks this process, because it blocks desire in a series of 'déformations et détournements industriels de l'attention court-circuitant ces processus' (*AT*, p. 44). The twenty-first century data economy seeks to:

> contrôler par des automatismes fondés sur les réseaux sociaux ces pulsions déliées tout en les fonctionnalisant, c'est-à-dire en les mettant au service d'une stimulation 'personalisée' de la pulsion consumériste à travers des mécanismes mimétiques qui ne font cependant que rendre ces pulsions plus incontrôlables, contagieuses et menaçantes que jamais. (AT, p. 51)

Our drives and desires – our 'automatismes' – are recorded by automatic processes, in order to build up an automatic, computational and algorithmic portrait of us, which then loops back to promote that desiring behaviour, until ultimately even our desires are not our own any more. More than any primitive feedback loop, this is a commercially driven system by which those elements of ourselves that are the core of our (human) being are exteriorized and *not* fully interiorized. Surrealist automatic writing incorporates mediation and exteriorization into its process and is about bringing the automatic to consciousness in order to make use of it. Automation as Stiegler describes it here involves mediating non-conscious impulses and making use of them but crucially, making sure that they remain non-conscious. As Mark Hansen has argued, 'the data made available to consciousness by today's microsensors capture experiences that not only were not but *can never be*, lived by consciousness'.[40] The temporal gap which Breton effaces with the metaphor of the automatic recording device is effaced today in the digital profiles of ourselves which are constantly self-updating in real time but the ability to read oneself back is elided. In this automatic society, the loving hand of Masson does not embrace the world; it is subsumed in its own movement, until it becomes mimetic, representational, locked into the stale repetition of a version of itself. What Breton moved away from with the passing years, as he constantly redefined automatism, is now our reality: a short circuit in which the path of least resistance involves eliding the human conductor. There is no spark, no radiance, no change – love is lost.

Creative superconductors: the art of the dream
Across the century, Breton speaks to Stiegler: 'que pour commencer il défasse [...] l'autre homme, celui à qui toute intériorisation est interdite, le passant pressé dans le brouillard' (II, p. 202). In *Les Vases communicants*, Breton resurrects the *récit de rêve* rejected in 'Entrée des médiums', as he moves beyond objective recording of dream content to its active interpretation in the service of social transformation and

---

40. Mark Hansen, *Feed-Forward: On the Future of Twenty-First-Century Media* (Chicago: Chicago University Press, 2015), p. 53.

the 'balaiement du monde capitaliste' (II, p. 187). Within this libidinal economy of the dream, it falls to the poet to institute a new relationship between dream and waking life, between dream and action: 'Le poète à venir surmontera l'idée déprimante du divorce irréparable de l'action et du rêve. Il tendra le fruit magnifique de l'arbre aux racines enchevêtrées et saura persuader ceux qui le goûtent qu'il n'a rien d'amer' (II, p. 208). This rewrite of the Edenic Tree of Knowledge seems to ancitipate Stiegler's amateurism and promotion of *savoir*. As a communicating vessel, the poet must institute a new relationship between dream and waking life, between dream and action: 'il maintiendra coûte que coûte en présence les deux termes du rapport humain [...]: la conscience objective des réalités et leur développement interne' (II, p. 208). To be human is to be a conductor. In communicating vessels, hydrostatic pressure maintains an equal level of one liquid in each of the connected vessels. In Breton's usage, the poet maintains at a continuous level the liquid which runs through our waking contact with concrete, material reality; and our processing of that reality in the dream state. The poet thus becomes the technological object which facilitates relationships between subjects and between subjects and society; the human as the 'médiateur par excellence' working in, with and through language (II, p. 202).

For Leroi-Gourhan, language – whether verbal, graphic, or oral – is 'l'échappée libératrice, celle de l'artiste ou celle du consommateur, dans le confort d'une parfaite insertion dans la pensée collective ou dans la contradiction et le rêve' (*MR*, p. 208). As Johnson has argued, 'the externalization of body functions has reached a point where one can envisage their ultimate subsumption in machine systems, rendering the body itself redundant. The atrophy of [...] the hand, is for Leroi-Gourhan the atrophy of thought'.[41] The loss of practical skills and knowledge identified by Leroi-Gourhan – 'la libération de l'art culinaire dans la conserve' (*MR*, p. 203) – aligns with Stiegler's concept of *misère symbolique*. One of the consequences of our symbolic poverty and the ensuing proletarization – the loss of knowledge and special skills to automation – is a 'bêtise systémique' (*AT*, p. 61). This stems from the blocking of what Stiegler terms a 'double redoublement épokhal', the process by which 'un choc commence par détruire des circuits de transindividuation établis, issus d'un choc précédent, puis donne lieu à la génération de nouveaux circuits de transindividuation, qui constituent les nouveaux savoirs' (*AT*, p. 29). Proletarization does not deliver this latter shock (*AT*, p. 57). In Leroi-Gourhan's terms, we might say that it blocks our lucid ability to adapt our *chaînes opératoires*; it does not give us the opportunity to think and react.

For Stiegler, 'c'est le *pouvoir de rêver* qui est à l'origine de toute *pensée*' and *tekhnè* is the '*pouvoir de réaliser ses rêves*' (*AT*, p. 132). However, this is not a

---

41. Johnson, 'Leroi-Gourhan and the Limits of the Human', p. 485.

unidirectional process. Dreams are transindividual processes – in Simondon's terms, a transindividual relationship is one a relationship that does not exist *between* entities, but instead *moves through* them in waves of 'affectivité'.[42] The transindividual processes through which dream creates a new reality are also subject to the *double redoublement épokhal*, as they in turn become 'automatismes [...] jusqu'à ce qu'une nouvelle intermittence les ranime, c'est-à-dire y retrouve le pouvoir de rêver en les désautomatisant' (*AT*, p. 137). Sleep and waking exist in a relation of Derridean supplementarity: 'l'intermittence est ce qui ménage les possibilités de l'existence' (*AT*, p. 142). As Stiegler summarizes:

> Le rêve serait ainsi ce qui articule une *époque faite d'automatismes* hérités, formant un fonds préindividuel [...] où se produisent les tournants, changements d'époque et bifurcations issus de la logique quasi causale qui commande le désir, c'est-à-dire l'inconscient. (*AT*, pp. 145–6)

The resonances of the notion of dream as a cyclical process of de- and re-*automatisation* with *Les Vases communicants* are undeniable. Breton's dreams expose a '*tissu capillaire*' between the subject and the external world, a space of 'interpénétration continue' between the sleeping and waking states, between desire and its realization (II, p. 202). Breton's declaration that 'l'amour humain est à réédifier' finds its echo in Stiegler's call for a renovation of the libidinal economy, which has artist-dreamers at its heart. For Stiegler, artists generate those moments of dreamlike intermittence in which the shock of the new can be processed: 'ils trans-forment ainsi les ondes de choc plus ou moins proches ou lointaines en bifurcations inaugurales de nouveaux circuits de transindividuation' (*AT*, p. 144), thereby producing new modes of knowledge for new amateurs.

For Stiegler, the dream-artists for our contemporary era are the surrealists and Marcel Duchamp (*AT*, p. 143).[43] Breton appropriated Rrose Sélavy/Duchamp's *readymades* – which predate the theorization of surrealism itself – as one of the earliest forms of surrealist object. In his major essay on Duchamp, 'Phare de *La Mariée*' (1934), Breton states emphatically that '*il est inadmissible que le dessin, la peinture en soient encore aujourd'hui où en était l'écriture avant Gutenberg*' (IV, p. 457, original emphasis). Art must not remain mired in a pre-industrial, pre-mechanical, pre-mass (re)production period, a 'glorification stupide de la *main*' (IV, p. 455). Breton rejects the material nuts and bolts of artistic technique, in favour of the encounter between the artist's mind and the material, technologically mass-produced object. Defining readymades as 'objets manufacturés promus à la dignité d'objets d'art par le choix de l'artiste' (IV, p. 454),

---

42.   Simondon, *L'Individuation*, p. 160.

43.   See also Stephen Barker, 'Unwork and the Duchampian Contemporary', *boundary 2*, 44:1 (2017), 53–78.

Breton emphasizes how choice – embodied in Duchamp's signature of urinals or snow-shovels – transcends the material object to reveal the artist-subject: 'une lumière intense, fascinante, se répand grâce à elle, non plus sur l'objet étroit […] mais sur toute une opération de la vie mentale' (IV, pp. 453–4). As Stiegler puts it, 'chez lui [Duchamp], c'est la vie qui devient œuvre d'art' (*AT*, p. 364). For all three thinkers, the artist-dreamer is a superconductor – a mediating force which integrates subjectivity and society in a charged circuit.

Surrealist automatic writing expresses subjectivity and reflects it back to itself in order to endow the subject with the power to effect change. With the algorithms decried by Stiegler, we are expressed back to ourselves – mediated by profit-driven technologies – in ways which block our agency, block our capacity to change ourselves and the world. The artful dreaming of surrealism resurfaces as a Stieglerian solution, which recreates a space for freedom in an automated age – it puts the automatism back in automation. In a 1982 interview, Leroi-Gourhan recalled a notorious incident involving a middle-aged Breton and a mammoth. Visiting the prehistoric caves of Pech-Merle in 1953, Breton – sceptical of the age of a drawing of a mammoth – leaned over to test its authenticity by rubbing it with his finger, with the result that 'le noir lui est resté au bout du doigt'.[44] The resulting fistfight with his tour guide culminated in a court case and a fine.[45] Leroi-Gourhan points out that cave paintings can take millennia to fully calcify. If, as Leroi-Gourhan puts it, we must investigate 'formes de pensée qui nous sont devenues étrangères alors qu'elles restent sous-jacentes à […] nos comportements' (*TL*, p. 273), then it is vital to understand that Stiegler's automatic society and his project for re-enchantment are not new. We can still replicate Breton's gesture, interrogating a form of thought which seems far removed from our twenty-first-century data economy, and finding that it is still fresh to the touch. When we see ourselves not as sleepwalking through an impending technological nightmare but as lucid dreamers operating in an individuating landscape suffused with change and possibility, then we are empowered to act, to circumvent calcification and – perhaps – to change the world.

---

44. Leroi-Gourhan and Rocquet, *Les Racines du monde*, p. 77.
45. 'Séance du 26 novembre 1953', *Bulletin de la Société préhistorique de France*, 50:11–12 (1953), 565–93.

Nottingham French Studies 59.3 (2020): 384–398
DOI: 10.3366/nfs.2020.0297
© University of Nottingham
www.euppublishing.com/nfs

WHAT LIES CONCEALED IN THE ROOTS OF CYBERNETICS: THE RENEWAL OF EARLY GREEK THINKING OF BEING AS *PHYSIS* IN MARTIN HEIDEGGER AND EDGAR MORIN[1]

HENRY DICKS ⓘ

Introduction

Martin Heidegger and Edgar Morin are rarely discussed in the same breath. This is in large part due to the quite different intellectual traditions in which their thought originated. Whereas Heidegger's principal philosophical influence was phenomenology, Morin's thinking is indebted above all to cybernetics and systems theory. But these traditions are not just different; they are also quite separate and even opposed to each other in their general orientation. Phenomenology has tended to focus on analysing the way things appear in the 'lifeworld' (Husserl) or in their 'average everydayness' (Heidegger). Cybernetics and systems theory, by contrast, are concerned with the scientific study of the dynamic organization of complex systems.

Further, while in *Mes philosophes*, Morin explicitly recognizes Heidegger as one of 'his' philosophers and talks of how he made the journey to visit Heidegger in

---

1. The present volume is dedicated to the memory of Christopher Johnson. In addition to participating in this collective dedication, I would also like to add a personal message of thanks. Chris was a pioneer in French studies in his recognition that this field does not need to be limited to the arts and humanities, and that French thinking about science and technology may be included in French studies. As a doctoral student, interested in both science and technology, I thus turned to Chris as an external examiner for my D.Phil, which looked at the ecological aspects of the relation between Heidegger and contemporary French philosophy. But Chris did much more for me than just read and examine my doctoral thesis; he also invited me to numerous conferences and seminars on science and technology, included me in Nottingham's science and technology reading group, offered generous intellectual and institutional support for a number of research proposals, and, most importantly in the present context, introduced me to cybernetics. Through these and other kind actions, much of my subsequent thinking about science and technology, and cybernetics in particular, is indebted to Chris, and it is thus with great pleasure – and great sadness too – that I dedicate the present article to his memory.

his cabin at Todtnauberg, he also remarks that he does not enter into 'the core [*fond*] of his philosophy'.[2] Morin goes on to explicate this remark as follows:

> La différence de l'Être et de l'étant ne me parle guère, la philosophie du '*Dasein*' m'a intéressé sans m'illuminer. Ce sont les dimensions multiples, multidimensionnelles, contradictoires, génératives et auto-génératrices de l'existence qui me paraissent essentielles, au-delà du fait même de l'existence.[3]

Heidegger, on this reading, is above all a thinker of the facticity of existence, and of being (*l'Être*) in contradistinction to beings (*l'étant*). Morin, by contrast, sees himself as a thinker of the complex *generation* of existence. So, whereas in *Being and Time* Heidegger undertakes an analysis of existence (the 'existential analytic'), but without considering its genesis (for *Dasein* is simply 'thrown into the world'), Morin is concerned rather with how existence – and not only the existence of *Dasein* – is generated.

The basic insight underlying the present article is that Heidegger's thinking of being and existence is in many respects much closer to Morin's than the latter seems to realize. In particular, there are strong parallels between Heidegger and Morin's thinking of being and existence as it unfolds with respect to three topics. First, both philosophers put forward a critique of cybernetics, arguing that it obscures the thinking of being and existence. Second, they both advance a conception of being as self-production. Third, they both affirm that the thinking of being as self-production involves a renewal of the early Greek conception of being as *physis*. But merely to establish parallels between Heidegger and Morin does not in itself lead anywhere. These parallels only become productive once it is realized that Heidegger and Morin's quite different approaches to these topics are, taken on their own, insufficient and incomplete, and that it is only through their articulation that there may emerge a new thinking of being capable of giving rise to the 'new beginning' to which they both aspire.

The ontological critique of cybernetics

Cybernetics emerged in the immediate post-war period in the work of Norbert Wiener and others. An important trait of cybernetics emphasized by Wiener in his first major work, *Cybernetics*,[4] was that it applies to both natural systems and to the breakthrough control and communication technologies of the time. Further, in Wiener's second major work, *The Human Use of Human Beings*,[5] the scope of

---

2. Edgar Morin, *Mes philosophes* (Paris: Germina, 2011), p. 114, my translation.
3. Ibid., p. 114, my translation.
4. Norbert Wiener, *Cybernetics: Or Control and Communication in the Animal and the Machine* (New York: Technology Press, 1948).
5. Norbert Wiener, *The Human Use of Human Beings: Cybernetics and Society* (Boston: Da Capo, 1954).

cybernetics was extended beyond biology and engineering into the human and social sciences, the result being that cybernetics could come to appear as a foundational, transdisciplinary science capable, as such, of grounding and unifying all the others.

The ambition of cybernetics to establish itself as a foundational, trans-disciplinary science goes some way to explaining why Heidegger claimed it had become a 'replacement for philosophy'.[6] Prior to cybernetics, the individual sciences could still be understood as 'regional ontologies', the common foundation of which lay in philosophy, understood as the study of being itself. So, whereas physics was concerned with physical beings, biology with living beings, and anthropology with human beings, philosophy was concerned rather with the common foundation underlying each and every being: being itself. With the advent of cybernetics, however, there was apparently no longer any need for philosophy to hold the sciences together, for this role had been appropriated by cybernetics. And in replacing philosophy as the unifying foundation of the sciences, cybernetics also replaced the basic concepts of philosophy (being, existing, becoming, appearing, etc.) with those of cybernetics (information, communication, control, feedback, etc.).

But cybernetics, Heidegger thought, did not only underlie the totality of the natural and the human sciences, for, in keeping with Wiener's initial analysis, it also underlay modern technology. The truth of this view has become ever more evident as the information and communication technologies theorized by cybernetics and information theory[7] have increasingly come to monopolize the contemporary understanding of technology. The 'technology' sections of today's newspapers, for example, only ever deal with information and communication technologies – computing, software, smartphones, the internet, social networks, etc. – and not older mechanical technologies like cars or washing machines, let alone such non-mechanical technologies as hand tools, furniture, or kitchen-ware. The reason for this is not difficult to discern. According to Heidegger, nature, in the age of modern technology, presents itself as a vast 'standing reserve' of material and energy resources to be 'ordered' by human beings.[8] And the conceptual foundations of this ordering are provided by cybernetics. If the shelves of our supermarkets are stocked with produce from the four corners of the planet,

---

6. Martin Heidegger, *Four Seminars*, transl. by Andrew Mitchell and François Raffoul (Indianapolis: Indiana University Press, 2003), p. 63.

7. As a first approximation, the difference between cybernetics and information theory is that whereas the latter is concerned with the transmission of information, the former is concerned with the transmission of information for purposes of communication, control and regulation.

8. Martin Heidegger, 'The Question Concerning Technology', transl. by William Lovitt, in *Basic Writings*, ed. by David Farrell Krell (Oxford: Routledge, 1993), pp. 311–41.

if the planes and trains arrive on time, if video conferences may be organized across multiple time zones, it is thanks to the use of information for the purposes of control and communication theorized by cybernetics.

It is well known that Heidegger saw modern technology as the 'supreme danger'. And yet he also thought that it harboured within itself what he called the 'saving power'. This saving power, which he thought was blocked (*verstellt*) by the essence of technology (the *Gestell*) and thus also by the activity of ordering (*bestellen*) the standing reserve (*Bestand*), was none other than what the Greeks called *poiēsis*, which, Heidegger tells us, means both producing (*herstellen*) and presenting (*darstellen*). *Poiēsis*, Heidegger further notes, was present in the thought of the ancient Greeks in two main contexts, which they differentiated as follows: first, in *physis*, which was understood as '*poiēsis en heautōi*', that which produces and presents itself; and second, in *technē*, which was understood as '*poiēsis en allōi*', that which is produced and presented by something other, namely humans. So, whereas modern thinking about technology interprets technology primarily as an instrument manipulated by humans, Heidegger sees the essence of technology (in the sense of *technē*) as lying in the production or bringing forth of things other than the self. Further, while he does not discuss *physis* in detail in 'The Question Concerning Technology', there can be little doubt that he saw its essence as lying in self-producing and self-presenting (*poiēsis en heautōi*) and, furthermore, that he also identified it with 'being itself'.[9]

To summarize, it would seem that Heidegger holds the following views: first, cybernetics has established itself as the foundational transdisciplinary science, and, as such, has replaced philosophy and therewith also the thinking of being; second, modern technology, which is grounded in cybernetics, is the supreme danger, though it also harbours within its roots the saving power, *poiēsis*; third, *poiēsis* is present in the ancient Greek concepts of *technē* (*poiēsis en allōi*) and *physis* (*poiēsis en heautōi*); and fourth, *physis* is being itself. From these four views, it is possible to deduce the following conclusion: cybernetics, which, as a replacement for philosophy, conceals being, also harbours within its roots the possibility of a renewed thinking of being, understood as *physis* (*poiēsis en heautōi*).

Essentially the same conclusion as this was arrived at quite independently by Morin. At the outset of the first volume of his *magnum opus*, *La Méthode*, Morin tells us that he had originally sought to pursue his inquiry using the theoretical and conceptual frameworks of cybernetics and systems theory.[10] Over time, however, he came to realize that these transdisciplinary sciences were inadequate, for, as he puts

---

9.   See, for example, Martin Heidegger, *Introduction to Metaphysics*, transl. by Gregory Fried and Richard Polt (New Haven: Yale University Press, 2000), p. 15.

10.   Edgar Morin, *La Méthode: tome 1, la nature de la nature* (Paris: Éditions du Seuil, 1977), p. 27.

it, they 'evacuate' being and existence.[11] But why and how exactly do they do that? To answer this question, it is instructive to consider the origin of the word and concept of cybernetics. The word 'cybernetics' was coined by Wiener via his reading of Plato's discussion of the *kybernetes* (steersman) in the *Gorgias*. The role of the *kybernetes* is to detect and correct deviations from his chosen trajectory; and much the same phenomenon, Wiener tells us, is present also in animals and machines. Just as a predator will constantly adjust their trajectory when tracking a moving prey, so the same is true of cybernetic anti-aircraft missiles. Wherever in nature, technology, or human society, there is some sort of *telos*, this *telos* is achieved by feedback mechanisms capable of correcting deviations away from it (negative feedback) and amplifying positive steps taken towards it (positive feedback). These twin feedback processes may be grouped together within the central cybernetic concept of self-regulation. For cybernetics, not just cybernetic machines, but also ecosystems, living beings, social systems, and so on, may all be characterized as self-regulating systems: they regulate themselves by means of both negative and positive feedback in order to achieve whatever *telos* or *teloi* it is that characterizes them (stability, reproduction, growth, constant output, etc).

According to Morin, the key element missing from cybernetics is a theory of where the various systems it theorizes come from. Cybernetics theorizes only how these systems function, not how they come into existence. But, when one seeks to answer this latter question, the unified theoretical approach to nature and technology characteristic of cybernetics collapses, for, as Morin points out, whereas the technological artefacts theorized by cybernetics are produced by something other than themselves, namely humans, natural beings produce themselves.[12] In saying this, Morin was undoubtedly heavily influenced by Maturana and Varela, who also put forward a direct critique of cybernetics, including its key concepts of code, information, and teleonomy, while at the same time proposing 'autopoiesis' (self-production, self-bringing forth) as the essence of the living.[13] One important way in which Morin goes beyond Maturana and Varela, however, is in his extension of the concept of what he calls simply 'self-production' beyond the realm of biology. For Morin, many purely physical beings, such as atoms, vortices, and stars, but also living beings, ecosystems, human beings, and even human societies come into existence by *producing themselves*. In this way, then, the concept of self-production, which lay concealed under the central cybernetic concept of self-regulation, may account for how it is that natural beings come into existence: they produce themselves. Further, identifying self-production

---

11. Ibid., p. 214.
12. Ibid., p. 170.
13. Humberto Maturana and Francisco Varela, *Autopoiesis and Cognition: The Realization of the Living* (Dordrecht: D. Reidel, 1980).

with the ancient Greek concept of *physis*, which Morin takes to be the 'nature of nature', he argues that this concept could take on the role of basic unifying concept for the individual sciences.[14]

Self-production as unifying ontological concept

In keeping with the claim common to both Heidegger and Morin that cybernetics conceals being and existence, the concept of *physis* is identified by both thinkers with being. There is, however, an important difference in how these two thinkers apprehend the concept of *physis*. Whereas Morin focuses on the systems-theoretical dimension of *physis*, which leads him to emphasize *poiēsis* in the sense of generation, Heidegger focuses on its phenomenological dimension, which leads him to emphasize *poiēsis* in the sense of bringing forth or bringing to presence. Further, while Morin is aware of various connections between *physis* on the one hand, and being and existence on the other, the concept of *physis* has a number of significant ontological implications of which he is not aware and which only become apparent in the light of Heidegger's project – largely ignored by Morin – of deconstructing Western metaphysics. With this in mind, the present section will first provide a preliminary understanding of the concept of *physis* as self-production, and second show how the articulation of Heidegger and Morin's thinking about this concept makes it possible to overcome the problematic ontological divisions that Heidegger thought were introduced into Western thinking by metaphysics.

According to Morin, the basic meaning of production is 'bringing into being and/or existence'.[15] To produce a table, for example, is to bring a table into existence. But in the case of *physis*, as opposed to *technē*, production is not of the other but of the self. A being that self-produces, it follows, is a being that *brings itself into existence*. But what does that mean? The image chosen for the front cover of the first tome of *La Méthode*, M. C. Escher's *Drawing Hands*, may shed some light on this question (Figure 1).

What this image depicts are two hands drawing each other and at the same time also a work of art drawing itself. This is of course an illusion. The hands did not draw each other and the work of art did not draw itself. Both the hands and the work of art were drawn by the artist. Like all works of art, Escher's *Drawing Hands* is an instance of *technē*, not of *physis*. And yet, as we have already seen, there are beings that do produce themselves. Indeed, the basic trait common to beings that are in the way of *physis* is self-production.

---

14. Edgar Morin, *Introduction à la pensée complexe* (Paris: Éditions du Seuil, 2005), p. 68.
15. Morin, *La Méthode*, p. 157. As I read Morin, the meaning of the words 'being' and 'existence' are identical in this context. The point of the 'and/or' is simply to show that we can talk of both or either 'bringing into existence' and 'bringing into being'.

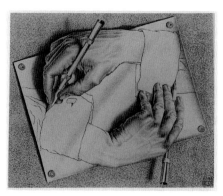

Figure 1. M.C. Escher, *Drawing Hands*. All M.C. Escher works © 2020 The M.C. Escher Company – the Netherlands. All rights reserved. Used by permission. www.mcescher.com.

But how might we characterize more precisely the concept of self-production? One aspect of the concept underlined by Morin is the idea of the *circular production* of the different parts of an entity. In Escher's artwork, for example, the hands manifestly draw each other in a circular manner. Simply to affirm, however, that whenever circular production is present, a being produces itself or brings itself into existence would be mistaken. To see why, it is instructive to consider the etymological sense of the word 'existence', namely, 'standing out' (ek-sistence). A being that brings itself into existence is a being that brings itself to stand out (ek-sist) with respect to its environment. So, just as paintings are clearly delimited from their environment thanks to their rectangular form and sometimes also the presence of a frame, so what Heidegger sometimes calls '*physei*-beings' create their own limit with respect to what thereby becomes their environment. Examples from the realm of biology include cell membranes or the skin of mammals. Returning to Escher's *Drawing Hands*, this allows us to see that the hands do not only draw each other but also the limit – provided in this instance by the rectangular piece of paper – within which, but also from out of which, their own activity takes place. This chimes with Heidegger's claim that self-delimitation is what differentiates genuine beings from non-beings, and, as such, is none other than the 'being of beings':

> The *peras* [limit] is not something that accrues to a being from outside. Much less is it some deficiency in the sense of a detrimental restriction. Instead, the self-restraining hold that comes from a limit, the having-of-itself wherein the constant holds itself, is the being of beings; it is what first makes a being be a being as opposed to a nonbeing. For something to take such a stand therefore means for it to attain its limit, to de-limit itself.[16]

---

16.   Heidegger, *Introduction to Metaphysics*, p. 63.

Bringing these insights of Morin and Heidegger together, we may say that beings that self-produce are beings whose parts produce each other in a circular manner and which, in so doing, also produce a limit (*peras*) that delimits them from what thereby becomes their environment.

Now that we have obtained a clearer understanding of the concept of *physis*, understood as self-production, let us turn our attention to the way in which this concept makes it possible to overcome three of the basic divisions that, according to Heidegger, were introduced into ontology by metaphysics. The first of these is the division between being and becoming.[17] According to metaphysics, being means remaining ever the same. Becoming, by contrast, means changing, being altered, and thus made different. But self-producing beings are constantly changing, while at the same time remaining the beings that they are. Living beings may serve as an example here. There can be little doubt that living beings undergo processes of becoming. Over the course of their lives they may become bigger or smaller, adults or parents, and they may even undergo processes of metamorphosis, as when larvae become butterflies. But throughout all these processes of becoming they continue producing themselves. Indeed, it is only at the moment of their death that they stop producing themselves, at which point their way of being (i.e., self-producing) fails and their existence come to an end.

The second metaphysical division that the concept of self-production makes it possible to overcome is the division between being and appearing.[18] Metaphysics makes a radical distinction between being and appearing, claiming that on the side of being are the 'things in themselves' and on the side of appearing the 'things as they appear to us'. The classic statement of this is the philosophy of Kant, which affirms a radical and insurmountable gap between the two, in which case, he thinks, the study of the nature of things (ontology) must be replaced by the study of the conditions of possibility of their appearance to us (the transcendental analytic).[19] In the case of *physis*, however, appearing is a necessary consequence of being. To see why, it is important to consider again the basic difference between Heidegger and Morin's interpretations of the concept of *poiēsis*. Whereas Morin interprets *poiēsis* simply as producing, Heidegger interprets *poiēsis* as producing *and presenting*. A being that produces itself is at the same time also a being that brings itself into appearance. The concept of *physis* thus makes it possible to overcome the metaphysical distinction between being and appearing, between things in themselves and things as they appear to us. A *physei-being* is neither a Kantian thing in itself, for it appears, and yet neither is it a Kantian appearance, for it brings

---

17. Ibid., pp. 100–103.

18. Ibid., pp. 103–122.

19. Immanuel Kant, *Critique of Judgement*, transl. by James Meredith (Oxford: Oxford University Press, 2007), p. 256.

itself forth, and, as such, is by definition not produced or brought forth by the human mind in the way that Kant thinks all phenomena ultimately are.[20]

The third and final division I would like to discuss is the division between being and existence.[21] This division hinges on the identification of being with ideas first put forward by Plato. The being of beings, Plato thinks, are the ideas. But the ideas are also the true beings, those that genuinely exist. The beings we perceive in the world around us, by contrast, are but 'shadows' of these beings, and, as such, lack both genuine being and genuine existence. But when, in later incarnations of idealism, the ideas were brought down from the otherworldly realm they inhabited in Plato and transposed into the human mind, beings were only considered to exist if their idea was instantiated in a reality external to the human mind. The being or essence (*essentia*) of beings, their 'whatness', thus became the idea or concept of the being, whereas their existence (*existentia*), their 'thatness', became their realization in the external world. This in turn led being to be identified with possibility and existence with actuality. One may have an idea or concept of something and yet be unsure as to whether that thing exists. To have an idea of something tells us only that the thing is possible, not that it is actual. There is thus, on this account, a logical abyss between being and existence; one cannot get from the former to the latter (using pure reason).

The concept of *physis* makes it possible to bridge the metaphysical division between being and existence. The being of *physei*-beings is self-production. And by virtue of nothing but the meaning of the expression 'self-production', beings that self-produce also bring themselves into existence. A *physei*-being could not be what it is, self-producing, without existing; *physei*-beings self-produce, therefore they are. There is, in other words, something in the event[22] of self-production that implies the existence of a being. This is not to say, however, that one can deduce the

---

20. It is important to note that Kant does discuss the concept of self-production, understood as the circular production of causes and effects, in the context of his discussion of organized nature. But while Kantian organized nature may *produce* itself, it does not *present* itself, for what brings self-producing beings forth, Kant thinks, is not the beings themselves but rather the teleological judgements of the human mind. See Kant, *Critique of Judgment*, p. 199.

21. See Martin Heidegger, 'Metaphysics as History of Being', transl. by Joan Stambaugh (London: Harper & Row, 1973), pp. 1–54.

22. I use the word 'event' here, rather than such obvious alternatives as 'process' or 'phenomenon', because in its etymological sense of 'coming out' (ex-venire) it implies both coming into being and coming to appear. The word 'process', by contrast, has purely ontological connotations that obscure and obstruct the sense of *poiēsis* as bringing into appearance, and the word 'phenomenon' has phenomenological connotations that obscure and obstruct the sense of *poiēsis* as bringing into existence. Nevertheless, it is important to realize that the 'event' in question must be understood not as something momentary or fleeting but rather as something enduring. In the case of biology, for example, self-production is an event that characterizes the enduring existence of a living being and not just the fleeting moment of its birth.

existence of a self-producing being from the idea or concept of a self-producing being (in a comparable way to how the so-called ontological argument attempts to deduce the existence of God from the mere idea of God). But this is to be expected, for self-production is precisely not an idea, but an event. We may, of course, also have an idea of this event, namely, the idea of self-production, but being is located in the event of self-production not in the idea of this event. In the case of *physis*, then, the necessary relation between being and existence does not allow us to derive the existence of a self-producing being from the mere idea of such a being, but rather to affirm that where self-production occurs a being necessarily exists. Whether self-production does indeed occur is an affair of judgement, but if we have reason to believe that it does occur, then, by virtue of the very meaning of the concept of self-production, we also have reason to believe that a being exists, that what we see in front of us is a being, not a non-being.

In view of this, the key implication of the logical bridge that the concept of *physis* builds between being and existence is not that it allows us to affirm the existence of some beings as necessarily following from the idea of that being, but rather that it allows us to distinguish the genuine beings, those that bring themselves into existence, from those that are not genuine in the sense that they have in one way or another been produced or constructed by humans. The concept of *physis*, it follows, does not only hark back to the ancient Greeks in that its meaning is the same, *poiēsis en heautōi*, but also in the ontological role it plays: to use critical judgement to distinguish the genuine beings from the others. This brings us to a third commonality between Heidegger and Morin: their belief in the need for a 'new beginning' based on the renewal of early Greek thinking of being as *physis*.

Renewing early Greek thinking of being as physis

Morin explicitly takes up Heidegger's idea of a new or other beginning.[23] But his thinking of this other beginning shares with Heidegger much more than just the abstract idea of starting again, for, like Heidegger, he thinks that the first beginning occurred with the early Greeks and their inceptive thinking of being as *physis* and that it is this thinking that must, as he puts it, be 'resuscitated'[24] if we are to begin anew.

There is, however, a significant obstacle to drawing on the first beginning to think the other beginning: it is far from clear that the early Greeks developed an *explicit* understanding of being as *physis* in the sense of self-producing and self-presenting. Our knowledge of the early Greeks is of course restricted by the fact that we only possess fragments of their writings. But nothing in these fragments allows us to conclude that any of the major early Greek thinkers – Anaximander, Anaximenes, Heraclitus, etc. – developed an explicit theory of being as *physis* in

---

23. Morin, *Mes philosophes*, p. 115.
24. Morin, *La Méthode*, p. 27.

the sense of self-producing and self-presenting. The lack of an explicit theory of *physis* as self-producing and self-presenting is, however, to be expected. If the early Greeks had developed such a theory then to renew their thinking would simply be a matter of digging out and repeating what had already been said a long time ago. And this would go against Heidegger's idea that the new beginning will be both 'entirely other and nevertheless the same'[25] as the first beginning.

But if the early Greeks did not explicitly think of *physis* as self-production, then in what way exactly are they relevant to thinking the new beginning? The answer, I suggest, is that the thinking of *physis* as self-production, though not explicit, was nevertheless implicit in early Greek thinking. With this in mind, it is instructive to note that when Heidegger's analyses of the early Greeks get closest to the idea of *physis* as self-production is not when he analyses the extant fragments of this or that thinker, but rather when he analyses the meaning of the word '*physis*' itself, including its etymology, cognate terms, and so on[26] – as if even the early Greeks could only think *physis* under the guise of something other (water, air, fire, etc.) and not as itself. Likewise, in Morin, there is the suggestion that implicit in the thinking of the early Greeks, and the Ionians especially, is the idea that beings first arose by primitive processes of self-production (e.g., vortices). So, while Heidegger may again emphasize the more phenomenological sense of *physis* as self-bringing forth, and Morin the more systems-theoretical sense of *physis* as self-generating, in both cases there is an attempt to make explicit something that remained implicit in early Greek thinking of *physis*.

Indirect support for the claim that the thinking of *physis* as self-production and self-presentation was present in the early Greeks, but only implicitly, may also be found in the subsequent 'fall' away from this thinking. Heidegger locates this fall with Socrates and Plato, and more specifically the passage from the thinking of being as 'enduring' (*wesen*, *währen*) to the thinking of being as 'permanent enduring' (*fortwähren*).[27] So, whereas *physei*-beings do indeed endure, but only as long as they produce themselves, Plato's ideas endure *permanently*. All sensible beings could come to an end, but the ideas would still endure. But the transition from enduring to permanent enduring did not arise first with Plato, but with Parmenides. For Parmenides, to be is to endure permanently, in which case all belief in both coming to be (*genesis*) and destruction (*phthora*) is but mortal opinion (*doxa*), not the way of truth (*aletheia*). This, then, is why the word '*physis*' is not present in the first part of Parmenides's poem, the way of truth, but only in the

25. Martin Heidegger, *Basic Questions of Philosophy: Selected 'Problems' of 'Logic'*, transl. by Richard Rojcewicz and André Schuwer (Indianapolis: Indiana University Press, 1994), p. 39.

26. See, for example, Martin Heidegger, *Basic Problems of Phenomenology*, transl. by Albert Hofstadter (Indianapolis: Indiana University Press, 1988), p. 107.

27. Heidegger, 'The Question Concerning Technology', pp. 335–6.

second part, on mortal opinions[28]; in identifying being with permanent enduring, *physis* was dismissed from the way of truth (*aletheia*) and sent over to mortal opinion (*doxa*).

It is of great significance that the conception of being as permanent enduring introduced by Parmenides did not only underlie the idealism of Plato but also the atomism of Democritus.[29] On the standard interpretation of Western philosophy as 'footnotes to Plato',[30] Democritean atomism is problematically lumped together with the thinking of the Ionians and the Eleatics as Pre-Socratic or Pre-Platonic; but Democritus was a contemporary of Socrates and Plato, and, while his thought may not lie at the origin of Western philosophy, this is not because it is more primitive, but rather because it lies at the origin of something equally momentous, Western science, which, even in its contemporary conception of physical reality as composed of elementary particles (leptons, quarks, gauge bosons, the Higgs boson…), remains essentially atomistic (in the Democritean sense). The Parmenidean origin of this fundamental bifurcation between idealism and materialism, between philosophy and science, may be explained as follows. In rejecting the early Greek identification of being with *physis* and instead identifying being with permanent enduring, Parmenides paved the way for future attempts to identify those beings that do endure permanently and which, as such, are radically divided from becoming and seeming, both of which concern only the changing beings perceived by the senses. In Plato, these permanently enduring beings are the ideas; and in Democritus, they are the atoms.

If, however, we are to disclose and unfold the thinking of being as *physis* that occurred prior to the introduction of metaphysics by Parmenides, we also need to show that this thinking of being as *physis* can, once unfolded and made explicit, provide a response to Parmenides's objections to his predecessors. After all, if Parmenides's ontology of permanent enduring was taken up by both Plato and Democritus, thus initiating the subsequent unfolding of all Western thinking (philosophy and science), was this not because of some fundamental problem in the early Greek conception of being as *physis*? Parmenides's key argument against the identification of being with *physis*, and thus also both coming to be and perishing, is advanced in fragment B8, where he claims that being (and beings) cannot come from nothing, or, conversely, that nothing cannot produce being (and beings). This is true. Things cannot come from nothing; they cannot be produced by nothing. But it does not follow from this that being is permanent enduring and coming to be and passing away but mortal opinion. For the truth is rather that beings produce

---

28. Alexander Mourelatos, *The Route of Parmenides* (Las Vegas: Parmenides Publishing, 2008), p. 62.

29. Patricia Curd, *The Legacy of Parmenides* (Las Vegas: Parmenides Publishing, 2004).

30. Alfred North Whitehead, *Process and Reality: An Essay in Cosmology* (New York: Free Press, 1978), p. 39.

themselves, that they come from themselves, that self-production is their way of being in the double sense of being both their *manner* of being (they are self-producing) and their *path* into being (they bring themselves into existence). But while the thinking of being as *physis* can provide a response to Parmenides, the nature of this response also confirms the claim that the thinking of *physis* as self-production or self-presentation was not *explicit* in Parmenides's predecessors, for, if it had been, Parmenides dissociation of being from *physis* would have lacked the credibility necessary for it to have been taken over by his illustrious successors.

One important objection that could be made to the idea that beings bring themselves into existence is the following: that such self-producing beings are composed ultimately of pre-existing material elements, in which case their existence is due at least in part to these material elements. So, to speak in Aristotelian terms, while self-production may be the efficient cause of *physei*-beings (that *through* which they are), their formal cause (that *as* which they are), and perhaps even their final cause (that *for* which they are), it is not their material cause (that *of* which they are). Further, in keeping with this objection, it is worth noting Morin's claim that it is quite 'trivial' to say that everything is at base physical in the sense of being composed of fundamental material elements.[31]

As I earlier affirmed, however, Morin's conception of self-production, which derives from his initial decision to focus on the organization of *physis*, is insufficient and incomplete, and, as such, requires articulation with Heidegger's phenomenological conception of *physis* as self-bringing forth. And it is this articulation that allows us to respond to the objection under discussion. Recall that there are two basic types of being: those that produce themselves (*physis*) and those produced by humans (*technē*). Now, as we have already seen, those that produce themselves do so through the circular production of their parts and through their self-delimitation as wholes. Democritean atoms, it follows, are not self-producing. The word 'atom' means that which cannot be cut (from '*a-*', not, and '*tomos*', cutting), but a being that cannot be cut by definition has no parts and no limit that holds it together. It follows that if atoms 'exist' in the sense of 'standing out', it is not because they produce themselves and in so doing delimit themselves from their environment, but rather because the human process of cutting has not been able to go any further, because it has reached a point beyond which it cannot go: the a-tom. Foucault once remarked that 'knowledge is not made for understanding; it is made for cutting'.[32] While, as we will see presently, he was mistaken to see knowledge *in general* in this manner, cutting is nevertheless the basic purpose of science, which, as both its etymology tells us (from the PIE root, *skie*, to 'cut' or to 'split') and its origin in Democritean a-tomism clearly imply, is in essence a technique for cutting

---

31. Morin, *La Méthode*, p. 27.
32. Michel Foucault, 'Nietzsche, la généalogie, l'histoire', *Hommage à Jean Hyppolite* (Paris: Presses universitaires de France, 1971), pp. 145–72 (p. 160, my translation).

and thus producing and delimiting beings *artificially*. It is we humans who cut out and thus bring forth the atoms, not the atoms themselves. Science, it follows, is a mode of *technē*, not in the sense that it forms artificial entities from raw materials, but in the sense that it brings its objects forth by isolating them – whether physically or only in thought – from what thereby becomes their environment.

To return, then, to the objection that *physei*-beings are produced from basic material elements, it turns out that the reverse is true; these material elements are produced by science, that is to say, by cutting them out from self-producing beings. The *physei*-beings, by contrast, are not produced and delimited by us, but by themselves; they cut themselves out, as it were, from what thereby becomes their environment. This, then, is why not all knowledge is for cutting; philosophical knowledge is knowledge of being, of what produces and delimits itself, not of what is produced and delimited by us.

Conclusion

By way of conclusion, I would like to return to the idea that modern technology, in its obstruction of *poiēsis* and thus also *physis* (*poiēsis en heautōi*), is the 'supreme danger'.

We have already seen that cybernetics, as the transdisciplinary science underlying modern technology, has become a replacement for philosophy and, as such, has come to prevent and obscure the thinking of being. So is the danger simply that being, and *a fortiori* being itself as *physis*, will remain concealed by cybernetics and modern technology, and that we will thus remain inattentive to the truth of being? The danger, I think, is much greater than that, for the danger is not simply that being, understood as self-production, will remain *concealed*, but also that it will remain *obstructed*, that it will not be able to be. There is, from this perspective, no intentional effort in modern technology to destroy nature (in the sense of *physis*), to prevent it from being. And yet, when the destiny of humankind becomes nothing but to order the standing reserve, self-production is nevertheless obstructed and beings are not allowed to be, that is, to self-produce. It is above all in this *existential* sense, then, that being, understood as self-production, and therewith also beings, as particular instances of self-production, are in danger.

This existential danger to being is unprecedented in Western thinking. The early Greeks experienced only wonder in the face of self-bringing-forth, not a sense that it is radically obstructed, that it is in danger. And ever since Parmenides, the danger experienced by philosophers has never been an existential danger to being, but only an epistemological danger to humans. Parmenides himself worried that our thinking would mix together being and not-being, thus failing to know being in all its purity. Plato worried that we would take the sensible beings for reality, thus failing to see the ideas. Descartes worried that we may be mistaken in everything we hitherto believed, that we may not know anything at all. And even Heidegger seemed predominantly concerned that philosophy would die out, that we would no longer seek knowledge of being, let alone of being itself. Indeed, perhaps the only significant exception to this rule occurred in the Christian Middle Ages, when the principal danger was not that the beings that endured permanently – the immortal souls – would not be known, but rather that they would end up in hell rather than heaven. For us today, however, the danger lies not in where our immortal souls might go after we die, and nor is it solely that we may fail to understand the being of beings, and thus find ourselves lacking in true knowledge of being. The danger is rather that modern technology is preventing being (i.e., *physis*) from being (i.e., self-producing), that beings produced by us are preventing beings from producing themselves. And while, as the organizer of the standing reserve, and in that respect different from other beings, we may believe ourselves to be exempt from this fate, inasmuch as we too are also *physei*-beings we would be wise to think again.

ORCID

Henry Dicks https://orcid.org/0000-0002-9534-0299

Nottingham French Studies 59.3 (2020): 399–400
DOI: 10.3366/nfs.2020.0298
© University of Nottingham
www.euppublishing.com/nfs

NOTES ON CONTRIBUTORS

MADELEINE CHALMERS is Stipendiary Lecturer in French at Wadham College, University of Oxford, where she specializes in modern literature and contemporary thought. Her doctoral thesis on 'Unruly Technics in the French Literary Avant-Garde' explores how avant-garde French literature of the late nineteenth and early twentieth centuries negotiate the increasingly tight imbrication of technology into human life, and the challenge it poses to how we think about ourselves, our relationship to others and to our world. It seeks to place these texts of the past in dialogue with current philosophical reflections on technology, to explore how this encounter can help us to think about our technological present, and future. Her work has appeared or is forthcoming in *Dix-Neuf* and *French Studies*.

HENRY DICKS specializes in twentieth-century French and German philosophy, particularly as it relates to science, technology, and the environment. His publications have appeared in numerous journals, including *Philosophy and Technology*, *Europeana*, *Environmental Ethics*, *Journal of Agricultural and Environmental Ethics*, *Environment and Planning D*, and *Environmental Philosophy*. His current research project is on the philosophy of biomimicry. He is Associate Lecturer in the Department of Politics, Philosophy and Religion at Lancaster University. He is a member of the Science, Technology and Culture research group at the University of Nottingham.

YVES GILONNE is Assistant Professor in French and Francophone Studies in the Department of Modern Languages and Cultures at the University of Nottingham. His main research interests are in post-war French thought, society and culture, focusing in particular on Maurice Blanchot and his contemporaries, French thought and literature on prehistory and technology, and discourses and representations of the atomic era. His major publications include *La Rhétorique du sublime dans l'œuvre de Maurice Blanchot* (2008) and *« L'apocalypse déçoit »: Blanchot, Derrida, Levinas: penser le désastre à l'ère atomique* (2020). He is member of the Science, Technology and Culture research group at the University of Nottingham.

JONATHAN HALE is an architect and Professor of Architectural Theory in the Department of Architecture and Built Environment at the University of Nottingham, where he is Head of the Architecture, Culture and Tectonics research group (ACT). His research interests include architectural theory and criticism; phenomenology and the philosophy of technology; the relationship between architecture and the body; museums and architectural exhibitions. He is founder and current steering group member of the international subject network: Architectural Humanities Research Association (AHRA), and a member of the Science, Technology and Culture research group at the University of Nottingham. Recent publications include *The Future of Museum and Gallery Design*, co-edited with Suzanne MacLeod, Tricia Austin and Oscar Ho (Routledge, 2018), and a book for the Routledge series *Thinkers for Architects* on the philosopher Maurice Merleau-Ponty, published in 2017.

CHRIS JOHNSON (1958–2017) was Professor of French Studies in the Department of French at the University of Nottingham. His major publications included *System and Writing in the Philosophy of Jacques Derrida* (1993) and *Claude Lévi-Strauss: the Formative Years* (2003). He also published numerous articles in journals such as *French Studies* and *Paragraph*. His later research concerned history of technology, focusing in particular on cybernetics and the work of the French prehistorian André Leroi-Gourhan. He was editor of the journal *Paragraph* from 1987 to 2010 and founded the Science, Technology and Culture research group at the University of Nottingham.

JOHN MARKS is Associate Professor in French and Francophone Studies in the Department of Modern Languages and Cultures at the University of Nottingham. His main areas of research interest are social theory, critical theory and the history of ideas. He is a member of the Science, Technology and Culture research group at the University of Nottingham. He has published articles in various journals, including *French Cultural Studies*, *Modern and Contemporary France* and *Contemporary French Civilization*. He is the editor of a special issue of *Paragraph* entitled *Deleuze and Science* (2006). His current research is focused on work and social theory in France.

BRIGITTE NERLICH is Emeritus Professor of Science, Language and Society at the Institute for Science and Society, School of Sociology and Social Policy, University of Nottingham. She studied French and philosophy in Germany. After her DPhil in French linguistics she went to Oxford as a Junior Research Fellow in General Linguistics. She then moved to Nottingham, where her research has focused on the cultural and political contexts in which metaphors and other framing devices are used in the public, policy and scientific debates about biotechnology, infectious diseases and climate change. She has written books and articles on the history of linguistics, semantic change, metaphor, metonymy, polysemy and more recently the social study of science and technology. In 2011 the University of Nottingham awarded her a DLitt. She is a Fellow of the Academy of Social Sciences. She is a member of the Science, Technology and Culture research group at the University of Nottingham.

Vient de paraître

Dalhousie French Studies

revue d'études littéraires du Canada atlantique

Dossier spécial
Léon-Gontran Damas

Sous la direction de **Kathleen Gyssels**

Kevin Meehan, Sandrine Bédouret-Larraburu, David Bédouret, Michael Reyes Salas
Alan Warhaftig, Dominique Achille, Daniel Maximin

Varia

Vincent Grégoire sur Camus et Mauriac
Mohamed Kamara on Kourouma and Bebey
Marianne Bessy sur Vassilis Alexakis
Sara Del Rossi sur Maximilien Laroche
Jeannette Gaudet sur Lydie Salvayre
Jean-Jacques Defert sur Boualem Sansal
Alessia Vignoli sur Dany Laferrière

Reviews

Volume One Hundred and Sixteen   **Summer 2020**

Dalhousie French Studies
Département d'études françaises
Université Dalhousie
Halifax, Nouvelle-Écosse B3H 4P9, Canada
Rédacteur en chef : Vittorio Frigerio

https://www.dal.ca/dfsjournal

Pour toute correspondance : dfs.editor@dal.ca.

Édition web : https://ojs.library.dal.ca/dfs/

Abonnement : 25 $ CDN/US par numéro ; 50 $ CDN/US par année papier
seulement ; 70 $ CDN/US par année papier + web ; 40 $ CDN/US par
année web seulement. Frais de port internationaux en supplément.